Given to Brande and
Perry as a guide
into the halls of
united togetherness.

Love,
Mom and Dad
6-5-76

The Bride's Guide for Young Marrieds

The Bride's Guide for Young Marrieds

By Betty Rolston and The Editors of The Bride's Magazine

Illustrations by Mel Klapholz

GROSSET & DUNLAP
A NATIONAL GENERAL COMPANY

Publishers   New York

Copyright © 1972 by the Condé Nast Publications Inc.

Published Simultaneously in Canada

All Rights Reserved

Library of Congress Catalog Card Number: 70-149815

ISBN: 0-448-02029-7

Printed in the United States of America

Contents

Foreword

Dear Reader,

You're married . . . or about to be married. And you're happy; happier, you sometimes think, than you ever thought you could be. Yet in the midst of all the excitement that surrounds the wedding, you still take time to reflect upon that deepest of commitments—marriage itself. Because the style you create from now on as husband and wife will shape the future of your shared personalities, knowledge about how to live together from day to day is vitally important. True, knowledge—practiced, preached and perfected—soon becomes experience. But that takes time. And not having much of that right now, you need a short-cut. For you, then, this book was written. For between its covers is a treasury of basic, definitive, factual information on every facet of homemaking from money management and entertaining to cleaning, shopping and sewing. Betty Rolston's passionate attention to detail serves her reader well as she examines leases for a first apartment, contrasts good and poor quality in furniture and other household equipment, and determines the cost of borrowing money—whether for a single purchase or a whole new house. Never less than zealous, she also leads her reader through the intricacies of house and clothes-cleaning, dishwashing, supermarketing and, of course, cooking; all with the kind of deft direction that comes from never letting the subject overwhelm.

Leaf through this book the first time to see the abundance of reference material it contains. Then browse through, at leisure, lingering on the points that answer your most current questions. As time goes by, you'll find yourself referring to its pages over and over again. For this is the book for a lifetime of homemaking, and we at The BRIDE'S Magazine are proud to have it in *your* home.

Barbara Donovan
Editor-in-Chief
The BRIDE'S Magazine

Introduction

As a bride you have acquired both a husband and a new, exciting and challenging career—being a homemaker. If you prefer, a homebuilder. Whether your first residence is a one-room apartment or a twenty-room mansion it is still the establishment of your own home with your husband. What kind of a home it will be depends a great deal on you alone.

Advances in technology and science have provided improved equipment, more appliances and better household aids for the convenience of the modern bride. All of these are on the market to help you. But more is needed than just mechanical devices. Your own personal effort, both mental and physical, a strong sense of humor and a large dollop of common sense will help during the first, sometimes bewildering, months of homemaking. All-important is your own desire to set a firm foundation for your marriage.

Homemaking touches on a variety of occupations besides the obvious ones of cooking and cleaning. You may be called upon to act as a hostess, laundress, seamstress, chauffeur, handyman, engineer of sorts, banker, budget director, psychiatrist as well as general, all-around purchasing agent. Some of the skills in these fields will come easy to you, others will be harder to acquire. Although you may prefer that your husband handle the bigger expenditures of money such as rent, insurance and the purchase of a new car, you will spend a good portion of the family income on food, home furnishings and services, not to mention clothes and a myriad miscellaneous items. Obviously a sound knowledge of money management is going to help you live within your means.

A homemaking career should be rewarding and as much fun as your imagination will allow. Certain areas can and should satisfy artistic talents and needs. If you regard cooking as a creative art it seldom can be thought of as drudgery. Homemaking, like other professions, flourishes with experience, good organization and a flexible approach.

Problems will arise as you learn to share a life with your husband. Two individuals with two personalities and varying tastes are bound to conflict on occasion. How you deal with these problems depends on how good the communications are between you, how large the problems appear and the willingness on both your parts to reach an effective compromise.

In this book are guidelines to help you create the kind of home you want. The best ways and means of managing your income are discussed as well as when, where and how to use credit wisely. The various types of housing are listed, along with their merits, so you can intelligently decide which is the best for your needs. Shopping guides show how to select what you want and require in home furnishings, equipment, clothing and food. So that you can learn more about homemaking skills and how to master them, sections are devoted to household management, laundering, sewing, cooking and entertaining. And last, but certainly not least, you and your own personal challenges are considered. All of these are touchstones for the values which will help you attain the goal of a happy marriage and a successful homemaking career.

The
Bride's Guide
for Young
Marrieds

I

Your New Role as a "Mrs."

THIS NEW DIRECTION of your life—being a "Mrs."—can be viewed in several ways. First, as a wife, second a homemaker, and third, as a career woman.

AS A WIFE

This is first and foremost of the three roles. You have promised to love, honor and cherish your husband. Don't lose sight of these words because they will take you a long way toward success in your marriage. Almost every man likes to think of his home as his castle and himself as lord and master of this domain. Whether this attitude is on the surface or buried deep down, it's there. So accept it as such, even though you may think it's old-fashioned and even irritating at times. As a wife you are his romantic and sexual partner, sometimes just his companion. When situations are going well for him, cheer him on; when they are going badly, offer encouragement. In other words, let him know you love him and believe in him.

AS A HOMEMAKER

In this role you are laying the groundwork for a home that will bring happiness for both of you and reflect your values. Let us hope your husband will want to help plan for the household. Undoubtedly he has definite ideas on how he wants the home furnished, perhaps even how he wants to entertain. Encourage him and listen to him! He's indicating the kind of atmosphere which will make him comfortable, relaxed and happy. If there are differences of opinion, try to work out a compromise which will leave both of you satisfied. The actual management of the home is your responsibility, though.

AS A CAREER WOMAN

Many a bride will hold a job if for no other reason than to increase the family income. For some, you may be the only breadwinner if your husband is still in school working toward a degree. Some women have established careers and prefer to continue with them. Whatever your reason for working you need to be fairly well organized to cope with a full-time job and also run a home. Your time is necessarily limited so you don't want all of your spare time taken up with household duties. Plan to use outside services such as a commercial laundry. If you can afford it, hire a cleaning woman once a week. Enlist your husband's help. Let him dry the dishes, run errands to the cleaners and accompany you to the supermarket for a major shopping expedition. He won't be so shocked about how much you spend if he sees first-hand the cost of the purchases. More than one man has become interested in cooking through just such trips to the grocery store. Regard your leisure as a necessity and arrange for it accordingly. Since you are doing two jobs you need "time off" just to enjoy this newly married state.

Having become a "Mrs." you have changed your name legally. This change should be duly recorded in various places along with your new signature. This signature will consist of your given first name (or middle one if used), the initial of your maiden name and your new married last name. Thus, Jane Marie Smith who married John Doe now uses Jane S. Doe. Changes in some of these areas are required by law; others will save time and sometimes money. These changes should be made even though you might want to retain your maiden name for business or professional reasons.

1. INSURANCE

Your married name will now appear on all life, liability and property insurance policies. Contact the agent who sold you the policy or write directly to the insurance company. Usually you designate your husband as the new beneficiary and this can be done at the same time.

2. SOCIAL SECURITY

Apply for a new Social Security card through the payroll department where you work or directly to the district Social Security office. You will receive a new card with your new name on it but with the *same number*. Be sure the number has not changed so your Social Security includes all of your earnings.

3. BANK ACCOUNTS

Now is the time to decide if you want a joint or a single account for checking and savings. Fill out the necessary signature cards (both of your signatures are required for a joint account). Be sure new checks are printed, too. Determine now if you will have a special checking account (a small fee is paid for each check plus a monthly service charge) or a regular checking account where a required minimum balance must be maintained but checks are free and often there is no service charge.

4. PAYROLL RECORDS

Notify your payroll department about your new name and address and the correct number of tax exemptions you wish to claim. Sometimes a husband will take both of you as exemptions on his salary check.

3

5. HOSPITALIZATION

Convert your policy or your husband's into a family plan to include maternity benefits after a specified waiting period. Do not drop the old policies until the family plan goes into effect. One family plan policy is cheaper than two individual ones. Also take a good hard look at what kind of a surgical insurance plan you have. You may want to consider a "major medical" policy which takes over after a deductible amount and pays medical expenses upwards of $10,000 or more, depending on the plan.

6. CHARGE ACCOUNTS

Each firm where you have a charge account or a credit card should be notified either to close the account or reissue a card in your married name. Your husband may want to acquire duplicates of his cards for your use. If you both have accounts with the same firm consolidate them for convenience.

7. DRIVER'S LICENSE

Apply for a new one to be issued in your new name. This does not mean that you will have to be retested. Since a license is the most frequent form of identification used, be sure it is up-to-date.

8. CAR REGISTRATION

If you own a car the registration should conform with your new name. Automobile club membership and insurance should be extended to include both of you—rates are sometimes cheaper for married couples. In many states insurance rates will be higher for younger drivers. If your husband has a car he may want to keep the registration in his name only. He should, however, notify the insurance company of his married status so you will be included in the policy and so the policy is in effect when you drive. Your insurance agent will be able to advise you.

9. WILL

In some states an existing will becomes invalid after marriage. Check with your lawyer—have a new will drawn up if necessary. If you have not bothered to make a will or consult a lawyer, now is an excellent time to do both.

10. MAGAZINE SUBSCRIPTIONS

You won't want to miss issues of your favorite magazines so notify them of your change of name and address. Since this process can take as long as three months be sure to give them ample warning before the wedding. It's helpful to send in one of the mailing stickers that come on the magazine with your name and address. Publishers can use it as a reference point from which to make the change.

SOME AREAS OF FIRST PROBLEMS

Many couples regard marriage as a responsibility for each other's happiness and well-being. Other couples feel a sense of loss of freedom. Whatever your attitudes, almost everyone finds a certain amount of difficulty adjusting to all aspects of marriage.

"THE LITTLE THINGS"

Newlyweds often live in smaller quarters than they eventually hope to have, because of limited budgets. Being confined to a small space can make personal habits more apparent and differences much more jarring than if the living area were larger. The cause of the most constant source of irritation is sometimes a very small act such as failure to cap the toothpaste or to pick up soiled clothes. These "small things" can build into large disputes if they aren't aired for recognition. The offender might not even be aware he is offending. One or two annoying habits are sure to come up every day no matter how well you get along—so learn to live with them.

ADJUSTING TO MORE THAN ONE NEW SITUATION

Not only is a young couple adjusting to marriage but also many times to a new job. Frequently the husband has just started a new business undertaking or is working on an advanced degree in graduate school. The wife, chances are, is working to stretch the budget, at the same time trying to cope with her new household responsibilities. Adapting to two new situations can create tensions. Many husbands let off steam at home because they have to remain calm and collected in their job situations. This is a "safety valve" for the husband, but many a bride takes it as a personal

5

affront until she learns to place it in the proper perspective. On the positive side, being very busy is sometimes just what a new marriage needs. There's less time to brood over minor irritations.

FOOD

For some reason a prime area of argument can revolve around food. According to one psychiatrist, a man fears that the woman he marries will not take care of him—so, when she burns the toast she is only confirming his deep-down fears. On the other hand, the woman is on the defensive when she makes a mistake preparing food because she feels a little insecure about cooking, doesn't like to be criticized and reacts sharply. The solution: time! and a good cookbook, maybe.

PRIVACY

Newly marrieds sometimes feel they should share every interest. There are those who are afraid not to share every interest. But there is a definite limit on how much togetherness a union can stand. Everyone needs a little privacy now and then—to go out for a solitary walk or to sit quietly in a room alone reading or just thinking private thoughts. There are experts who believe that such a time of quiet is as necessary for well-being as sleep. If your husband is a sports addict he'll probably love you to play golf or tennis with him now and then. But if he likes an occasional game of sand-lot baseball he won't expect you to be on the team. He might want you to watch—he might prefer that you pursue an interest of your own. Privacy is one of the more essential ingredients for a good working marriage—it is a kind of mercy that allows love to live and breathe.

RELATIVES

What to call your mother-in-law can be a perplexing problem particularly if you see her often. Calling her "Mother" may be difficult for you because of your feeling for your own mother. You can call her Mother followed by her last name (i.e., Mother Adams) or perhaps a pet nickname or her first name. Why not ask her? She'll undoubtedly be flattered and may have suggestions to help solve your dilemma. Other problems dealing with relatives are bound to appear. Either they call too often (or not often enough) or advise too much (or not enough). Unless a really explosive situation is on hand, it's best to withhold petty criticisms of your mate's family in these first months when divided loyalties can surface all too easily. The best guidelines for getting along with in-laws are: be friendly, ask their advice if only on small matters and try to make them into allies, not enemies.

YOUR FRIENDS VS. HIS

During courtship you surely partied and double-dated with friends whose acquaintance you may have made together or whom one of you had known previously. Outside of this group you and your husband both probably have individual friends. For instance, his poker-playing buddies may not be your cup of tea, but there is no reason why he shouldn't see them once in a while. Your girl friend may bore your husband silly so have lunch with her or invite her over when he's out playing cards. There are always friends who won't fit into your idea of a social evening of mixed company . . . so see them separately. In your newly married social situation you may find it hard to incorporate single couples—it may be more difficult to keep up with their madcap pace because you have different responsibilities now and haven't the need to party until all hours. The best solution is to see less of such friends.

Even in this first stage of wedded bliss it may horrify you to think you are already in conflict in your marriage, but aggressive instincts are natural in humans and arguments are as inevitable as eating and sleeping. Many authorities believe quarreling improves communications between a couple in the first few years. Facing problems together helps to mature and strengthen your relationship. A successful marriage needs more than love—it needs mutual respect, consideration, sympathy and humility.

7

2

Manage Your Money Wisely

The key to many a successful marriage is good, sound money management. Newlyweds are often more romantic than practical on the subject of finances, and rarely is the management of money discussed during the courtship. Many of you have had your own income before marriage; many of you have been financially dependent on your parents and therefore have a rather vague concept of how to handle an income. To avoid unnecessary discord over money matters it is wise to draw up some sort of a financial plan as soon as possible after your marriage. Even if the first projection is something less than successful you've still taken a giant step toward understanding your money assets. In simple terms, a good, workable plan consists of knowing what you have to use, outlining what you want it to do for you and seeing that it does just that. Not only will planning help you make your funds go farther—it will also cause less preoccupation with money, less friction, and can lead to more trust in each other.

The first and most important step toward making a workable plan is to actually sit down and talk about what your income is and how you want it used. If both of you are earning money think of the combined income as "ours," not "yours and mine." Face money matters frankly, consider each other's wishes and attitudes towards money. These attitudes are often established early in life and are difficult to change without concerted effort. You may have been brought up in a very frugal manner with each expenditure viewed cautiously while your husband was raised to believe that money was meant for spending and let savings take care of themselves. Whatever your feelings, now is the time to let them surface and see what compromises have to be made. Write down what problems exist now. Does either of you owe money? Is your income a steady one or sporadic? Will you be getting cash gifts from parents?

The second step is to determine your goals, both immediate and long-term, in relation to earning and spending. Perhaps you or your husband have not finished your education, or the apartment you live in is too small. These are immediate goals that you want to achieve. Eventually you may want to own a house or a cooperative apartment—this would be considered a long-range goal since it's not in the immediate future. Do you plan to start a family soon? Will you continue with your job for several years? However the discussion of goals turns out, make sure that these goals are clear-cut and that you both agree about the most important ones. Compromise may be necessary to come up with a set of mutually acceptable values, but if you fail to communicate now, serious tiffs can arise later.

The third step is to decide who will handle the family finances. Is this to be a joint endeavor? Will one of you take over the reins almost entirely? Or will you have a split-manager system? It isn't necessary to be a financial genius to take over this role, but it does help to be accurate. Traditionally in the past the husband, as "head of the household," acted as financial disburser. With the changing status of women today, however, many wives have assumed this role since they handle so much of the household money. How you feel about it may come from your childhood memories. If your father always paid the bills and balanced the checkbook you may assume your husband will do the same. He, on the other hand, may feel that since his mother kept the books in his family, it's your responsibility. Some couples have found a split-manager system works the best, particularly if both are working. The husband may use his income for rent, utility bills, car expenses, insurance, entertainment and his own clothes. The wife may buy food, her clothing and use the rest of her income for savings. Decide which system you think will work best for you— and if it doesn't work be flexible and try another system.

Step four is to determine your actual income and specify where the money is going. This plan is called a budget. You may cringe at the mention of the word "budget," but there's really no need to if you are realistic and allow for a certain amount of flexibility. It's merely a guide to show you where a large part of your income goes on set expenses and how much you have left over for the more flexible items. A set percentage cannot be allotted strictly to each category because it depends upon where you live, how you live and what your income is. There are national statistics which show approximately what you can allot so you know how much of your income you can afford to spend on housing, food, clothing, health, transportation, household expenses, recreation, taxes, personal spending and savings.

MAKING THE BUDGET

ESTIMATE YOUR INCOME

This is the next logical step in your planning session. Cover any convenient period you wish, but most couples prefer to make it a one-year period. You may find it easier to deal with a three-month period to see how it works. *List the gross income.* Include in this salary or wages, profits from business or farms, interest on savings, dividends, rents from properties, commissions, pensions, annuity or insurance income, any money you have coming in regularly and any expected cash gifts. *Do not use this figure as a basis for your budget.* Next, *subtract all payroll deductions* including income tax (federal, state and sometimes city), social security, union dues, withholding for pensions, retirement or insurance payments (which may include life and health insurance). If you are self-employed, subtract the estimated income tax, Social Security and other items if they apply. You now have your *net income* or your spendable income.

ESTIMATE EXPENSES

It's admittedly hard for newlyweds to do this because you have no previous experience. The best way is to keep a record of expenditures for one month to get a fair idea of what you spend where. The next best way to calculate expenses is to consult another friendly couple about your age who are in the same circumstances, financially, but have been married for a year or so. Your parents also may have some constructive ideas on how to make estimates. At this stage of the game your best bet is to set up a trial spending program. First, *list fixed expenses* you need to consider monthly such as rent or mortgage payments and any payments due on installment debts or loans. Now list periodical fixed expenses such as property taxes, car license fees, insurance premiums that you pay directly and vacations. Money must be put aside monthly to take care of these expenses when they come due. Consider saving a certain amount each month (whether large or small) as a fixed expense so it will become a habit. If at all possible set aside an amount of money for an emergency fund. Unplanned-for extras have a nasty way of turning up just before payday. Second, *enter flexible expenses.* These are the expenses that can vary from time to time. Include in this listing food, clothing, health, transportation and utility bills. If you are starting your plan in the summer allow for seasonal changes that come with winter such as higher utility bills (for electricity and heating), costlier winter clothing and even winter maintenance of the car. Under flexible expenses allow for a personal spending allowance for both of you. It will give you a sense of freedom, no matter how small the allowance, and make the whole process of budgeting much more palatable.

SURPLUS FOR FUN

Subtract the fixed and flexible expenses from the net income and, hopefully, you will have some left. This is for future vacations (the costlier ones), gifts, entertaining and home furnishings above the bare essentials.

ALLOTMENTS FOR BASIC CATEGORIES

HOUSING 20-27%

Undoubtedly it will be your major expense. The range is wide because so much depends on where you live, how you live and how large your income is. Probably you'll be renting a small apartment for the first few years and saving for larger quarters in the future. If entertaining is important to your way of life you may need more space right now. Or perhaps you have already bought a house and have to allow for major improvements. Housing costs usually run higher in and around large cities unless you are very lucky and just happen to get a great place for little rent.

FOOD 15-20%

The second largest expenditure should not go over 20% of your income unless there are extra people around frequently. A bride tends to underestimate what it costs to feed two people. Your husband may like a whopping big breakfast while you've been used to fruit juice and coffee. If the food bills run too high it's time to carefully plan menus, write out a grocery list to curb impulse buying and learn to prepare dishes from less expensive cuts of meat (see Chapter 9). Be realistic in food shopping not only for the cost but also for a well-balanced diet which will appeal to both your tastes. And if your meals have been simple and cheap, splurge once in a while. It's good for your sense of well-being. Records of food purchases for several months will show where you've done well and where you've wandered too far from the budget. By this time your shopping habits will be more or less automatic and it won't be as essential to keep track of every food purchase. Probably, too, you've discovered the stores that give you value for your money and frequent them more often.

CLOTHING 10-12%

This is a very flexible category, particularly in the first year of marriage. If you were lucky enough to have a fair-sized trousseau you have little to buy for a while. It may come as a surprise to you how much your husband's clothes can cost, especially if he is required to wear a business suit to work. If both of you are employed your clothing allowance will necessarily have to be greater, but your combined income will be greater also. The type of position you have can well determine the type of clothing needed. Common sense tells you to set aside a certain amount each month so an occasional large purchase such as a winter coat won't send your budget calculations into a tailspin. Cleaning and pressing bills go in this section, too, so some judicial clothes' care can cut this expense. To keep within the 12% limit, buy good quality clothing for your basic wardrobe and learn to care for it properly (see Chapter 6). If you can sew enough to turn hems or make other easy alterations you've saved a good bit of cash. Shop for end-of-season specials when prices are lower, mainly for such basics as underwear, socks and shirts. Use layaway plans for items not immediately needed. Take advantage of do-it-yourself dry cleaning establishments for garments that need little or no pressing. Best of all, try making your own clothes, especially the simpler, easy-to-do ones.

HEALTH 5%

Included here are dental and doctor bills, required medicines, drugs, and special medical care such as X rays and laboratory tests, hospitalization insurance (with surgical and medical benefits) and accident insurance. Even if you are the very picture of health have periodical checkups—preventive medicine is by far the cheapest. Read your health insurance contract carefully and know exactly what it includes (see pages 28–30).

HOUSEHOLD EXPENSES 7–10%

Consider this section as being what it costs to run the home (excluding rent and food). Include here utility bills (electricity, gas, water and heating bills) that you are responsible for, telephone charges, home furnishings, appliances, repairs and general upkeep of your home. Any cleaning materials purchased as well as garden supplies come under this heading, and also a cleaning woman's salary, if you have one. It stands to reason if you live in a house the repair and upkeep are probably going to be higher than if you live in an apartment where the building owner is responsible for this expense. Most brides glean a fair amount of table and bed linens, blankets and many kitchen gadgets from bridal showers. Some are fortunate enough to have a completely furnished home. Most of you newlyweds, however, will still be furnishing so the cost in this section is liable to be high. The best way to cut costs in this area is to look for sales and close-outs. Nothing will be as satisfactory as good, new furniture or appliances, but in a pinch you might watch newspaper want ads for second-hand buys; people moving sometimes don't want to take some nearly new items with them.

TRANSPORTATION 6–12%

Allot money to this category whether you own a car, use a commuter train, take a bus or subway. It's quite easy to calculate the cost of public transportation, but figuring the expense of operating a car is much harder. The average car owner has to allow up to 12% of income for gas, oil, insurance, servicing and repairs along with car payments (if a loan was used to buy it) and depreciation. In some states if you are under a certain age a higher insurance rate is in effect. Don't forget also to calculate how much will be spent on tolls, parking meters and, in some communities, parking stickers.

SAVINGS 5–10%

A certain amount should be earmarked for saving from the very first. If you leave savings to the end of the budget there is often nothing left to save. One wise authority claims saving should be done as regularly as paying rent. Money you put into life or term insurance, annuities, investments of stocks or bonds or even real estate is considered as much in the savings category as putting it into a bank savings account. You will want an account where money is readily available, in case of emergency, and also earning for you. For short-range goals regular savings accounts are the best, but for long-range planning you would do well to seek the advice of a professional in the investment field.

RECREATION 5–7%

Certainly your budget should allow money for relaxation. Place your leisure expenditures here—movies, theater, books, hobbies, party supplies, occasional weekend trips, gifts and vacation costs.

PERSONAL SPENDING 5%

Everyone needs pocket money that doesn't have to be strictly tabulated. Both you and your husband need cash for lunches, newspapers, magazines, cigarettes, contributions, haircuts, cosmetics, trips to the hairdresser and many other small costs.

TAXES

Although federal and state taxes as well as Social Security may be withheld from your paycheck (if you are not self-employed), there may be other taxes which are not. Property taxes must be paid separately as well as some city income taxes. If your state, county or city has a sales tax this is on a pay-as-you-go basis. When income tax time rolls around don't forget that earnings from savings accounts, investments and sale or rental of property are all taxable. Because a sizable proportion of your taxes is taken care of through withholding you may not have to be too concerned about setting aside a percentage of your budget for this section. If the taxes amount to much more than was withheld, the emergency savings account can come to your rescue.

CASH VERSUS CREDIT

CASH

Cash is certainly the most common method of paying for many household items, the groceries, minor services and all the sundries of personal spending. Providing you have enough in your checking or savings account you might prefer to make a large purchase such as a refrigerator or a new sofa with cash. There are definite advantages in this way of buying: you have paid for it outright, therefore no worry about periodic payments; you have spent the cash on hand, therefore no overspending; you can shop in any store you wish, not just in a store offering credit; you may be able to buy at a reduction because of ready cash and you have kept your credit reserve for other items, therefore making it easier to get in emergencies. If cash is used, take care to keep the receipts in case there is an exchange involved; do not send money through the mails, send a personal check, bank check or money order; do not carry large sums of money with you and, finally, handle money with care.

CREDIT

This can be a sound way of financing, used correctly. It's used primarily to improve the standard of living since items can be acquired early in the life history of a family and be used as you pay for them. Consumer credit is really a way of pledging future income for current needs. Three ways in which credit is used most frequently are: to buy a house or apartment, to buy consumer goods like appliances, furniture or cars and to acquire cash for your own specific purpose. There are quite a few advantages to buying on credit; you don't have to carry cash with you; if you have a charge account you are on a mailing list and are notified of sales in advance; exchanges and returns are easier; you can order by telephone; you have the use of purchases while paying for them; you can take advantage of lower prices without having the cash on hand; and by making regular payments when due you are establishing a sound credit rating. Keep in mind that it usually costs more to buy on credit—you are not only buying the merchandise but also the money to pay for it. Credit wisely used can help you realize some of your goals immediately. Used improperly it can create serious financial problems.

How much credit can you afford on your budget? Experts say total monthly installment payments should not exceed 15 to 20% of your net monthly income. Do not regard credit as extra income— the payments must be made out of your own net income. If you are going to use credit, plan for it in your overall budget. Use only as much as you can pay for without straining. Make sure of the total cost of credit used—shop around for your credit, compare cost, terms and convenience. If you use it make your payments promptly and correctly so there will be no penalties for tardy payments.

THE KINDS OF CREDIT

1. CASH LOANS

Sources for this form of credit are: banks, consumer finance companies, insurance companies (policies with cash value can be borrowed against) and credit unions (for members). Cash loans are made for a stipulated rate of interest with the interest and principal repaid by the end of a specified time. Usually these loans demand collateral for security. Installment loans are repaid in equal monthly payments over a given period while single payment loans are repaid in one payment at an agreed date.

2. RETAIL CREDIT

You are permitted to buy goods and services either by charge account or on a time basis. Contracts for retail credit may be offered by the same merchant who sells the goods or services. Sources for retail credit are retail stores and credit card plans offered by banks or by such organizations as American Express. Three types of retail credit are:

A. The charge account. You are promising to pay in full within a period of time after being billed (usually 30 days). There is no additional cost for this convenient type of credit if paid on time. It is offered by stores, professional services and utilities.

B. The revolving charge account or credit plan. You are allowed a stipulated amount of credit each month, but you are required to pay only a certain percentage of the total each month. For this credit privilege they charge you 1½% on the previous month's balance. Added up, the charge comes to 18% a year. A written agreement is customarily required.

C. Time payment or installment plan. A written agreement is made with each purchase stating the amount of each payment, when and where it is to be made. As a rule you are required to make a down payment or a trade-in with the balance of the purchase price to be paid in equal installments over a specified period. In most cases, the seller holds title to the goods until the final installment is paid. Service charges for this form of credit vary—be certain you know the actual dollar cost before signing the agreement. This agreement or contract can be sold to a bank or finance company, but it does not alter the contract. You will just have to send your payments elsewhere. Time payment is used mostly for buying cars or major appliances.

A WORD OF CAUTION

If you use credit cards and charge plates make sure you keep track of them. If you lose one notify the store or company at once. If you carry them with you in a wallet or purse make sure you have a list of the cards at home in case your purse is lost or stolen. If you decide to discontinue the use of a card or have an address change, destroy the old one by tearing it in two. Petty thieves prey on credit cards—don't be one of their victims by being careless.

BEFORE YOU SIGN

Sign your name with care. Read carefully, including the fine print, the document you are about to sign. If you don't understand it fully have someone explain it and only sign when the explanation has been made to your satisfaction. Do not sign a contract which an eager salesman offers to "hold" while you make up your mind. Don't sign a blank contract. Have all oral agreements written into the contract. Some states have a law prohibiting the transport of unpaid-for goods across the state line without the specific consent of the seller. If you are planning to move before a major purchase can be paid for, check on this law before you sign.

Look for the following information on a credit agreement before signing it: 1. all blanks are filled in and description of the merchandise; 2. the price of the merchandise or exact amount of money you are to receive; 3. a list of charges for credit and other costs such as insurance; 4. the total amount to be paid; 5. the number of payments, the amount of each, dates and place due; 6. security pledged as a guaranty of payment; 7. penalties for late payment; 8. basis of refund if loan is paid ahead of time; 9. down payment or trade-in allowance; 10. seller's guarantee, if any, about maintenance, servicing or replacement of the merchandise or its parts; 11. in case of repossession how it affects indebtedness; 12. check with your local Better Business Bureau or Consumer Affairs Department.

SIMPLE WAYS TO SAVE MONEY

Every couple has money problems, particularly the first year of marriage when you both are still learning so much about each other's attitudes and emotions about money. If more cash seems to be going out than is coming in take a good, hard look at your flexible expenses. Can you trim them? Here are some suggestions that may help.

1. Avoid impulsive buying. Shop with a list so you aren't tempted to buy what you "want" rather than what you "need."
2. Cut down on some of the personal spending. Go to a less expensive hairdresser or wash and set your own hair. Try to give up smoking.
3. Use your own skills. Make simple curtains. Avoid alteration costs by doing them yourself. Use a laundromat instead of a commercial laundry. Wash your own car.
4. Whittle down utility bills by making long distance phone calls in the evening when rates are lower. Turn off unneeded lights. Replace worn washers in faucets to avoid water leaks. In winter, lower the thermostat by 10 degrees (no more) at bedtime to save fuel.
5. Use free community services for recreation and education such as museums and art shows, concerts, lectures, libraries and park facilities.
6. Shop for vacation buys or weekend specials. Travel rates and accommodations are much cheaper off season. Look around for a room or cottage with cooking facilities to make one or two meals a day.
7. Take in an auction or two and see what fun it is to shop this way.
8. Watch for seasonal sales on clothes, household linens, fabrics, food and even cars.
9. Get estimates on servicing costs of such items as television sets, washing machines and cars. You will find quite a variation, and the most expensive is not always the best.
10. For anything you hope will last a long time look for quality and compare prices.
11. At the end of the day both of you empty loose change from your purse or pockets and put it in a container. At the end of the week deposit it in your savings account.

You are indeed lucky if your first financial plan was moderately successful. If it wasn't, ask yourself whether both of you really tried to make it work. Perhaps your plan was too rigid or maybe it was so flexible that it allowed for too many leaks. The most successful plan has to be reevaluated from time to time as your circumstances change and as you both get the knack of handling your income.

HANDLING YOUR MONEY

The financial plan shows more or less where your income will be spent. The future goals you listed before making the plan can serve as a valuable guide for balanced spending now and later. Of course you want to put your money where it will be safe and also grow. To pay current expenses you will need to have some of your income someplace accessible such as in a bank checking account. For long-term growth you probably will want to consider stock or bond investments, some type of personal insurance or simply a savings account in a bank.

CHECKING ACCOUNT

This is one of the most common forms of handling money—it's safe, convenient and acts as a record of proof of payment. When you open an account in the bank you deposit money and the bank furnishes you with a checkbook containing blank checks. By filling out one of these checks you are directing the bank to pay from your funds a stated amount of money to a designated person. No interest or dividends are earned from checking accounts and there may be a small service charge depending on what type of account you have. Each month the bank sends you a statement showing all of your transactions, deposits and checks drawn along with the cancelled checks.

To write a check, enter the date, the number of the check (for your own records), to whom the money is to be paid, the amount in figures, the amount in writing and sign your name, exactly as you recorded it when opening the account. Do not sign it Mrs. John J. Jones, but rather Jane R. Jones. Record the transaction accurately and legibly on your check stub, subtracting the amount of this check from the funds you have in your account.

TYPES OF CHECKING ACCOUNTS

1. Special checking. When the bank issues you a checkbook you are actually paying for each check. The bank will deduct from your account a small fee for the checks used. In addition you will be charged a monthly service fee. Both of these charges are quite small. With a special checking account a minimum balance of funds usually is not required. Remember, though, even if you haven't written a check in a month, the monthly service charge will still be subtracted from your account.

2. Regular checking. The bank does not charge you for the checks used but does require that you keep a minimum balance in your account. If this account falls below a specified balance or if you write more than an average number of checks in a given period a service charge will be levied.

Should you and your husband have a joint checking account? The advantages are that both of you can write checks against a mutual account and there is only one checkbook or desk checkbook ledger so that an accurate picture of the bank account is always on hand. It also helps build up a trust in your marriage relationship because you are sharing. But if one partner is careless about recording checks written it may be easier to have separate accounts. Some couples have found the easiest way is to have one account for household expenses only, with the wife handling the money.

Balancing a checkbook. Reconciling the checkbook (records you have kept on the stubs) with the monthly bank statement is often viewed as one of those disagreeable chores couples hate. It needn't be. Assuming that you can add and subtract and you have kept accurate records, this task should be simple. Here's how:

1. Check off the canceled checks returned by the bank against the amounts shown on the statement.

2. Check the deposits shown on the statement against those entered in your check stubs.

3. Add up the deposits shown in your check stubs which are not shown on the bank statement.

4. Arrange canceled checks by date or number and check them off against the stubs in your checkbook.

5. Add up all outstanding checks from the checkbook stubs

that have not been returned with the statement. If you have a special checking account remember to add the charge for each check.

6. Write down the final balance in your monthly statement.

7. To this, add the total from Step 3.

8. From this amount (Step 3 plus Step 6) subtract total of Step 5. This is your correct current balance.

9. Subtract from your last checkbook balance the monthly maintenance charge (if there is one) and any other charge originated by the bank.

10. This figure should agree with the final total of Step 8.

SAVINGS ACCOUNTS

You can open a savings account jointly or individually with a small deposit. Subsequent deposits can be made any time later and in any amounts. Withdrawals can be made at any time although banks can legally require you to give them 30 days' notice. You may not get a monthly statement. Your record is your passbook which duplicates the record kept by the bank. Your passbook shows deposits, withdrawals and earnings which your money has accrued over a specified period. Savings banks call these earnings dividends; commercial banks call them interest. The earnings are credited and compounded either daily, quarterly (once every 3 months,), semiannually or annually. How often your earnings are compounded can make a difference. For example: you have $100 in the bank that earns 5% interest; after a year the money will have earned $5.00 if it is compounded yearly (5% of $100). If your bank compounded quarterly, the earnings would have been $6.14. (1¼% of $100 each quarter added to the quarter before).

SAVINGS CERTIFICATES

Sometimes these are called certificates of deposit. These earn a higher rate of interest than money in your savings account, but you have to deposit and leave a certain amount of money in the account for a specified time to earn this rate of interest.

22

UNITED STATES SAVINGS BONDS

Bonds sold by the federal government to individuals. There are two types—Series E and Series H. They differ in cost, rate of return and time of maturity. Series E defers interest payment until the bond either has matured or has been cashed in. Series H pays interest periodically.

TYPES OF FINANCIAL INSTITUTIONS

Commercial bank A corporation with a charter issued by the state in which it does business or by the federal government. It is owned and operated by the stockholders and has a board of directors, officers and a staff. It is examined regularly by federal or state officials to see that it complies with the laws. Both checking and savings accounts are offered by a commercial bank. Other services available are safe deposit boxes, cashiers investment counseling, personal and mortgage loans, sale of government savings bonds and their redemption, travelers' checks and trust facilities. A commercial bank is set up to take care of all your banking needs. Deposits are insured up to a certain amount by FDIC (Federal Deposit Insurance Corp.).

Mutual savings bank This type of bank is chartered in only 18 states. It is owned by the depositors and its prime purpose is to accept savings deposits. State laws under which it is chartered regulate the type of investments the bank can make—mostly mortgages on owner-occupied homes, commercial property, municipal and government securities and corporate stocks. Since there are no stockholders there are no dividends to be paid to them, and so the money is passed on directly to the depositors (after operating expenses have been deducted). Hence, the interest rate of a mutual savings bank is often higher than in a commercial bank. Here, too, deposits are insured up to a specified amount by FDIC.

Savings and loan association This financial institution operates like a mutual savings bank but is chartered both by state and federal governments. It is the only nationwide mutual association that is owned by members. By opening an account you become a member. The money in your account earns dividends that can

23

vary depending on the conditions within the association. This type of association is strictly regulated by law and has two purposes: 1. to provide a safe place for savings and 2. to lend money to families for building or buying homes. A board of directors is responsible for the operation. Four different types of accounts may be available: passbook accounts, bonus accounts, investment accounts and certificate savings accounts. Deposits are insured by FSLIC (Federal Savings and Loan Insurance Corp.).

Credit Union A cooperative association whose members are all from a common group with similar interests either by occupation or a community. They save their money together and make loans to each other, thus encouraging saving and also extending credit. Because the group is well defined the risk of the loans is limited. Like a bank, a credit union is chartered by state or federal government and examined regularly. Credit unions vary in size as do their assets, depending on the size of the group. All members are shareholders and have a voice in running the union. There is a board of directors and sometimes paid clerical help. On becoming a member you purchase shares—dividends are paid annually. Withdrawals can be made at will but, legally, 60 days' notice may be required. Because of all of these factors a credit union can often offer its members higher rates of interest. Shareholdings, however, are not always insured so investigate carefully how well a credit union is run before joining it.

Consumer finance company A financial institution that lends money rather than accepting savings from the public. The money comes from funds invested by the owners of the company or from borrowed funds. A finance company is regulated and supervised by state laws. State legislatures determine the "loan ceiling" or how large a loan one person can be given. The company's function is to make personal loans for such purposes as the purchase of household goods, medical expenses, education, auto payments, etc. to consumer considered credit-worthy. A higher rate of interest is charged for these loans because the company takes a greater credit risk.

LIFE INSURANCE

The primary concern of life insurance is protection—a way of providing income in case the family breadwinner dies. It can be considered a means of saving, also, since many policies build up a cash value. Some policies provide a way of setting aside income for education of children or for retirement. Life insurance is sold as ordinary, group or industrial. Consult a qualified, responsible agent with a good reliable company to find out what kind of policy is best for you and your needs.

Ordinary life Since this is sold on an individual basis it is possible to have provisions suitable for your needs. Premiums are due periodically. There are several types of ordinary life insurance.

1. TERM INSURANCE-This provides protection for only a specified period such as 5 or 10 years or up to a specified age such as 65. It can be purchased so the policy can be continued after the period is over without another medical examination but at a higher premium at the older age. This is called a *renewable clause.* A *conversion privilege* will allow you to change the policy to another form of life insurance whenever you want without another medical examination. Term insurance is considered cheaper than other forms because the premiums are less, but the policies do not build up cash values. Advantages are if your husband dies before the term expires, money is provided for raising a family, paying off the mortgage or whatever—a maximum financial protection for a minimum of cash outlay.

2. STRAIGHT LIFE-Lifetime protection with specified premium payments made until the policyholder's death, at which time a specified amount is paid the beneficiary he has named. The premium, considered low, is determined by age and remains on the same level always. A reserve is built up as premiums are made so the policy has a cash value. If you drop the policy this amount of cash value will be returned to you *or* if you stop paying premiums and don't cash in the policy the reserve will be there for a given time. It's called *extended-term* value. Your policy also has loan value, an amount stated in the policy, which can be borrowed from the company. Interest is paid on the loan at the rate indicated on the policy. The value of your policy is reduced by the amount of the loan until it is repaid.

25

3. LIMITED PAYMENT LIFE-This provides protection for life except that you pay premiums within a certain number of years or to a certain age. Full protection, however, remains in force for life. Since the premiums are paid over a limited period of time they are higher than straight life, but the policy also builds higher cash and loan value over a shorter period of time.

4. ENDOWMENT-A combination of life insurance with a "forced savings" device. Premiums are paid over a stated number of years or up to a certain age, say 65. If the policyholder dies during this period the beneficiary gets the full amount. If the policyholder lives to the maturity of the policy he may take the sum all at once or in installments. Premiums are higher than straight life because of the added advantage.

Special combinations of life insurance

FAMILY INCOME-combining term with straight life insurance. The term part is for a specified period—if the policyholder dies during this term the family gets a monthly amount until the end of the term at which time the beneficiary gets the rest of the face value of the policy. If the holder survives the term the family is then protected by the straight life part of the policy. A premium is paid for the life part in addition to an extra premium during the family income period.

FAMILY POLICY-is also a combination of term and straight life insurance with the straight life on the breadwinner and the term on the mother and children. It can be converted when the children grow older.

MODIFIED LIFE-is the same combination of term and straight life insurance, but for a shorter specified period of years (say 5 years). When the term is over the policy automatically converts to a straight life policy. The premium is lower while the term is in effect (lower than if it were straight life) and rises when the term is converted. Modified life gives the family lifetime protection of permanent insurance before you are earning enough to pay for it.

RETIREMENT INCOME-offers a combination of life insurance and annuity provisions. If the policyholder dies before the policy matures, the beneficiary is protected by the life insurance part. When the policy has matured, the policyholder, if alive, or his beneficiary receives a set monthly income to continue for life or for the time set forth on the policy.

MORTGAGE INSURANCE-is a form of term insurance with the payable amount shrinking each year as the unpaid balance of the mortgage shrinks. The premium stays the same, an average of the whole term. If death occurs before the term is up, the policy-holder's mortgage is paid. Sometimes this type of insurance is sold with a life or long-term policy, sometimes separately.

GROUP LIFE INSURANCE-One policy is sold to a business organization, such as a labor union, industry, professional group or other common interest group, which covers the whole group. No medical examination is ordinarily required, and each member of the group receives a policy stating the amount of insurance, benefits and rights and the name of his beneficiary. Sometimes the policyholder (the company) pays the whole premium, sometimes only a part. This insurance usually has a renewable clause for one year and no cash value. Insurance bought in a group manner has a low premium compared with individually purchased insurance. If you leave the group you often have the opportunity to convert the insurance within 30 days to another form of life insurance at a higher premium but without medical examination.

INDUSTRIAL LIFE-This is ordinary life insurance but in small amounts such as $1,000 with premiums paid weekly to a company agent who calls at your home. The premiums are higher than ordinary life because of the expenses of collecting. Not so much of this type is being sold today.

Annuities Buying an annuity is a direct way of saving your money for a future guaranteed income. It is sold by life insurance companies but is not really life insurance. It is designed to provide the purchaser with a retirement income, and the amount of this income depends on how much you have put into your annuity. There are two kinds: straight life and refund annuities. The straight life annuity stops when the owner dies. It costs less but pays a larger income since it is only on the life of the policyholder. The refund annuity pays to the beneficiary if the owner dies before receiving the amount paid into the annuity.

Social Security Our federal government administers a social insurance plan which provides funds for the elderly, survivors (widows and minor children) and disability insurance for those unable to work any longer. Contributions are compulsory for those working in occupations covered by the program, and most occupations are included. You are issued a social security card with a number when you start earning money and make your first contribution. This is your number for the rest of your life, even though your name may change. You pay as long as you earn money in a covered occupation. Social Security contributions are determined by law—if you are employed you and your employer contribute equal amounts, your share being deducted automatically from your wages. This money, plus your employer's share, is paid to the federal government and is invested in interest-bearing federal securities as well as paying benefits to those eligible to receive them. If you are self-employed you pay a set percentage of your yearly earned income due with your April 15th income taxes and paid to the Director of Internal Revenue.

Health Insurance Since accident and illness are unpredictable and very often costly, you will surely want to have health insurance of some nature as part of your financial plan. It will protect you against hospital and medical costs or loss of income due to accident or sickness. Many organizations provide this type of insurance: insurance companies, hospital and medical service organizations (such as Blue Cross and Blue Shield) and independent groups that are sponsored by unions or other consumer associations. Health insurance can provide cash or service benefits. Insurance companies pay cash benefits direct to the insured or, if you instruct them, pay to the doctor or hospital. If your policy is one with service benefits, the payments are made directly to the physician or hospital. As in all types of insurance, the policies vary with the extent of coverage, benefits and length of time these benefits will be paid. Health insurance can cover a multitude of costs such as prescribed medicines and drugs, physician's fees, hospitalization, laboratory costs, surgery, nursing care and loss of income due to a disability.

If you are buying health insurance individually, be sure the company and its agent are reliable and licensed in your state. Know exactly what kind of coverage you have. Be sure the

benefits will adequately take care of your family needs. If you are
in a group insurance plan, find out what happens if you leave the
group. Is the policy terminated or is there some provision for
converting the insurance into individual coverage?

The following are types of voluntary health insurance:

DISABILITY OR LOSS OF INCOME-The form can also be called
accident and sickness indemnity in which you are paid cash
benefits if you are unable to work for these reasons. Sometimes
there is a waiting period, depending on your policy. Cash
benefits, the number of payments and the waiting period before
payments are determined by your policy. If your company pays
for a certain amount of sick leave, it would benefit you to have
a less expensive loss-of-income policy with a waiting period to
coincide with the period before the sick leave runs out. Check
with your company before purchasing this policy.

HOSPITAL EXPENSES-A specific amount is allowed per day for
room and board in the hospital along with routine nursing care
and minor medical supplies for a specific amount of days. In
addition, a lump sum is allowed for use of hospital facilities
such as operating rooms, anesthesia, laboratory uses, X rays
and physical therapy.

SURGICAL EXPENSES-All or part of the surgeon's fee for an
operation is paid according to a preset table of the insurance
plan which states the maximum payment for each type of
operation. Office visits dealing directly with the operation frequently are included in this payment. If the operation costs
more than the scheduled amount you have to make up the
difference.

PHYSICIAN'S EXPENSES-Payment is provided for non-surgical
treatment by a physician at the hospital. Your policy may also
cover visits to his office and your home—being limited sometimes to not more than 30 visits in one year. This type of health
insurance is included with a basic coverage, seldom as a separate policy.

MAJOR MEDICAL EXPENSES-Sometimes known as catastrophe
insurance because it helps pay bills for serious or prolonged
illness. This insurance takes up where the basic health policies

29

stop and is designed to financially help you if you are hospitalized for a long period of time, if your surgical bills drastically exceed the maximum amounts in surgical policies or if you require extensive medical attention. Major medical has a high maximum limit, from $5,000 to $20,000 or more, for one year. It also has a deductible provision anywhere from $50 to $500, which means that you pay this amount—anything over this and up to the maximum in expenses is covered by your policy. There is a "co-insurance" clause which means you pay a percentage of the bill (20 to 25%) if stated in your policy. These three conditions are placed in the plan so you are able to purchase this insurance at a moderate rate, so you do not use unreasonable or unnecessary medical service and so the plan is not burdened with small claims which are so costly to process.

DENTAL CARE EXPENSES-In some areas this kind of insurance is available, mostly through group plans or trade unions. The insurance can vary widely in cost as well as in benefits.

INVESTMENTS

The purpose of investing is to purchase certain income-producing assets which will yield profits in the form of dividends, interest, rent from real estate holdings or increase in value of some asset. If your immediate or future goals call for investments, seek the advice of a professional and let him help you make decisions before plunging into the stock market because of some "hot tip." The adviser may be a stockbroker, a banker, or Uncle Harry who has invested for years, knows the market trends and is knowledgeable about good growth securities at low risk. Before investing take careful stock of your income, start reading financial sections of your newspaper, follow the daily quotations of stocks and bonds, see if business magazines are on hand at your local public library. All of these sources can help you form a better idea of how you want to use the money earmarked for investment.

Securities These include stocks and bonds which are issued by companies, utilities or government (local, state or federal) to get funds for their operation, expansion and production. When you buy their stocks or bonds you get a return, either interest or dividends, and a possible increase in value of the security so you can also sell it at a profit. Sometimes there is a decrease in value, too, depending on the worth of the security at a given time.

STOCKS-Issued in units of shares they are certificates of owner-ship in corporations. Usually this ownership entitles you to vote on certain corporation policies such as the board of directors at the annual meeting. Your shares also entitle you to partake in the profits if there are any. When a corporation issues shares it is known as *going public* and these shares are traded on the open market. The value of each share will vary according to market conditions. Income is in the form of dividends paid at specified intervals on a per-share basis. A corporation may offer either common or preferred stock or both.

Preferred stock One which pays a fixed annual dividend. If the firm is liquidated this security has claim over a common stock. Not all corporations offer preferred stock.
Common stock The most popular investment and one which pays dividends as they are declared by the board of directors. The dividend can fluctuate with the financial fortunes of the corporation. When earnings are poor, the common stock value may decline along with the income it produces.

BONDS-Certificates that represent money lent to the government or corporation issuing them. In return they provide you with a fixed income, called interest, over a specified period of time and the face value (principal) at a definite date. Bonds are listed on the market at a per cent of their face value. Types of bonds are:

Government The federal government issues treasury bonds with maturity from 5 to 40 years; treasury notes, running to 5 years; treasury bills, from 91 to 192 days, and Certificates of Indebtedness for 1 year.
Municipal Bonds issued by state or local governments for buildings, highways or school construction. These are not subject to income tax as government bonds are.
Corporate Issued by private businesses. Since they are loans they lay claim to income and assets ahead of the stocks of the company.
Foreign Issued by foreign governments and corporations.

Mutual funds Investment companies who use the money of thousands of investors to buy stocks in a broad range of companies. Purchasing mutual fund shares gives you the advantage of professional management and diversification of your invested money. Sales charges, known as the *load*, run about 8% with little variation. Your cost can sometimes be higher than if you bought the stocks yourself, not through the fund. Shares in mutual funds can be sold for the asset value the same as stocks.

If you are going to invest in the stock market here are some common terms whose meanings you should know, if for no other reason than to be able to talk intelligently to your stockbroker.

Stock exchange A marketplace organized for buying and selling securities. Certain requirements must be met by companies to become members and be listed, meaning they can trade there.

Stock exchange trading floor A large area in the exchange where shares are traded in an auction market.

Brokerage House A firm that handles buying and selling of securities for investors and usually belongs to several exchanges. A standard fee is charged for services ranging anywhere from 1 to 6% depending on the size of the order.

Stockbroker An employee of the brokerage house who handles customers' accounts.

Trading An agreement between buyer and seller on a price for exchanging shares.

Account Like a store charge account. Your broker buys shares for you, enters the cost plus his commission fee and submits the bill to you for payment.

Ticker tape An electronic device which instantly and continuously transmits current prices of securities to brokers' offices throughout the world. These transmissions are recorded on tape.

Securities All types of stocks and bonds.

Portfolio Whatever securities you own at a given time.

Speculation Type of investment that offers greater potential gain at a greater risk.

Diversification Having stocks in a variety of industries for protection against any one failure.

New issues Stock being offered to the public for the first time. The price is set by the one offering the stock, not by supply and demand.

Over-the-counter Individual negotiations between dealers, not on the floor of the exchange. New issues of stock or companies not qualifying for the exchange are usually traded this way along with most government and municipal bonds.

Quote The price your broker can give you of a certain security at that particular minute. If the sale is not executed immediately, the price may change in the course of the day as the stocks are traded in the market.

Bull market When security prices are going up.

Bear market When security prices are going down.

Capital gains The profit made when selling a security or other capital asset.

Margin The amount of money an investor has to give the brokerage house to buy securities on credit. This practice is regulated by the Federal Reserve Board and requires the investor to have a certain percentage of the market value.

Market value The price at which a security can be bought or sold at any given time. Since this has to do with supply and demand, the value can fluctuate daily.

Asset value The net or book value which is the stated value of the stock if the company is dissolved. If the company is a mutual fund this value is based on the market value of all the stocks owned by the fund.

Par value Full face value of a bond returned to the owner on maturity. This value may be above or below the market value.

Yield The percentage of the market price of the yearly dividend or interest. For example, if your stock is worth $100 and the annual dividend is $4.00 a share, the yield on your investment is 4%. Very often growth stocks have low yields.

Growth stock One which has shown a healthy increase in the selling price of the stock. It must also have good prospects of continuing on this upward trend.

33

Blue chip A stock of very high quality, usually that of a large industry with a consistently good record for paying dividends.

Debentures Bonds which are only a promise to pay, not backed or secured by assets.

Convertibles Preferred stock or debentures which may be converted into common stock at a specified price with a set period (frequently in the same company).

Warrants Options to buy securities, mostly common stocks, at a specified price. These options are valid for long periods.

Equity As a stockholder, your ownership interest in the company.

Annual report The yearly report you receive as a stockholder from the corporation in which you own the stocks. The report shows the company's general condition and its earnings for the previous year.

Selling short Speculative practice of selling unowned stocks, hoping for a price decline so you may buy back at a lower price. The difference between the two prices is your profit or loss. The risk is high and not recommended practice for novices in the market.

Load The fee you pay for buying shares in a mutual fund, divided between the broker and directors of the fund.

Open end Investment companies which issue new shares of stock each time an investor buys shares. Most mutual funds are all open end investment companies.

Closed end Investment companies issuing a limited amount of stock, then traded on the open market the same as other securities.

Front end loading The policy of mutual funds to offer contractual plans so most of the sales charges are deducted within the first year or two even though the contract probably runs about 10 years. If an investor cannot complete the contract he is paying a very high load.

No load funds Mutual funds sold without load charges. Rarely are these available from a broker and they must be purchased directly from the sponsor or underwriter of the fund.

Real estate Investing in real estate is yet another way to build funds for the future. If you buy a house in a well-chosen location in a desirable spot, you may well expect this property to increase in value as the years go by, and this piece of real estate would be considered an excellent investment. (See Chapter 3 for more details.)

Property for real estate investment can be commercial, residential or rural. Land with buildings is considered *improved* while land which is vacant is called *unimproved.* The latter is more in the way of a long-term investment, the idea being that the land is bought to be held in the hopes it will increase in value and then be sold at a profit. Local property taxes are almost always less on unimproved land.

Land value can fluctuate with general economic conditions. But it is generally thought that real estate investment is protection against inflation.

Before buying a piece of property a thorough investigation should be made into various conditions which may influence the future value of your land. Find a good, reliable real estate agency with a realtor who understands what kind of property you want. If there is a doubt about land values, seek the advice of a professional appraiser. In purchasing any real estate here are some questions you should ask. What are the local conditions (zoning laws, building codes, type of community)? In addition to the initial investment how much will have to be paid out periodically to maintain the property? What are the taxes and is there reason to believe they will escalate rapidly in the future? Above all, have your attorney check all of the legal aspects of buying the property before giving even a deposit. And before you actually purchase the property outright he will have the title "searched" to make sure it is clear, and he will probably insist on title insurance to protect you.

MAKING A WILL

Just as you and your husband are planning to meet future goals through savings and investments so should you plan to draw up a will to guard these assets and see that they are distributed according to your wishes in case of death. You may pooh-pooh the whole idea and think it's ridiculous at this time of your life. Not so at all! Married couples very often have the misconception that the surviving spouse automatically inherits the entire estate from the other. If you or your husband die without a will (die *intestate*) your assets and property are distributed by a court-appointed administrator according to the laws of the state. The court may rule that part of the estate goes to other relatives as well as the surviving spouse. It's very possible that your assets, no matter how little, would not go to whom you wished. Settling an estate in this manner without benefit of a will is much more expensive because of court costs, and your heirs are at the mercy of the courts.

Making a will need not be complicated and can be written to stand for years, but you should seek professional legal advice. A good lawyer will be familiar with the state laws and therefore be able to advise you how best to bequeath your assets and personal effects as you wish, whom to name as executor or trustee, whether to stipulate if he must post bond and how to protect your heir or heirs from undue expenses. Having a will is almost more important when there is little money to leave than when there is a great deal. It may be necessary to update your will in the future as you have a family and your financial circumstances change, but this is easy to do when the change in the will is needed.

THE IMPORTANT PAPERS IN YOUR LIFE

There are certain documents which are permanently important to you—others which are temporarily important. Some records must be kept for a time at least, and yet they must be readily accessible. Make room in a nook, cranny or desk drawer for filing the sales slips you need to keep, records of installment payments, warranties on appliances, maintenance instructions, bankbooks, income tax records, canceled checks, social security records, some insurance policies (such as car), checkbook and credit cards. For those documents which are very hard to replace it is worthwhile to have a safe deposit box which is fireproof and burglarproof. Here you can store your marriage and birth certificates, military records, educational diplomas, U.S. Savings bonds, stock certificates, deeds, life insurance policies, passports, wills and pension plan records. Whatever you do, make a list of what you have and where it is filed whether it's in the bank, at home, at your lawyer's office or even in your stockbroker's safe. Not only will it give you a clear idea of where all those bits and pieces of your financial life are, but will also help your husband if he needs to find a record in a hurry and you aren't at home.

3
Your First and Future Home

STATISTICS SHOW that, during the first year of marriage, the majority of newlyweds rent housing, whether it's an apartment or a house. There is a good possibility that the first residence will be temporary, and you will move on to larger, more permanent quarters as you can afford to spend more on housing or as a new living pattern emerges for you. Home ownership may certainly be one of your future goals.

The first home, be it temporary or not, is where you are going to learn much about what kind of furniture and decor pleases both of you, what it costs to run a house and what you ultimately want in the way of future housing. A small rented place probably is just right for now—maybe about all you can manage at first without feeling overwhelmed by all of your new homemaking responsibilities. Here you have the opportunity to perfect your skills in home management, rectify at least some of the silly mistakes and accumulate home furnishings while saving for future requirements and goals.

Whatever your concept of housing is you will be spending from one-fifth to one-quarter of yearly income on it whether you rent or own it. If you live in or near a large city housing may cost you even more. In case you are planning to relocate in the near future include moving costs in the housing budget—these expenses can run high.

Since there is such a vast difference in what people want in housing it's very necessary for you as a couple to decide what kind of home you want. Be realistic about how much you can spend now and later. Get as nearly the kind of home you want as is within your income possibilities. How much space will you require? How large a family do you want? Is location a big consideration? Do you want the responsibility of home ownership, or would you prefer a rented apartment where you are relieved of a great deal of basic upkeep and maintenance? Do you want to build, or do you want to remodel a house or apartment? Will you look for old or new housing? All of these questions, and many more, should be answered by both of you with complete honesty if you are to arrive at a sound concept of what you want for future living quarters. To help determine what kind of a roof you'd prefer over your head here are some suggestions on what to look for and how to go about finding it.

If You Rent

The decision to rent offers some very distinct advantages:

MOBILITY

If you expect to relocate frequently or if you cannot foresee what future housing needs might be, the ability to pull up stakes (depending on your lease) and move is great.

NO OWNERSHIP RESPONSIBILITIES

No worries about the heat, outside upkeep, general maintenance and repair of the property. You can lock your door and go on vacation with not a worry about whether the pipes are going to freeze.

A TIME FOR SAVINGS

If you lack ready cash for down payment on buying a house, save now for future shelter goals. You might just find better housing for less money by renting rather than buying.

UNDECIDED FUTURE

Perhaps you cannot make up your mind where you want to live in the future. Renting will give you a breathing spell and time to make a decision.

LOCATION

Renting is a good way to find out if you like a neighborhood well enough to buy housing there. Renting gives you the opportunity to judge the type of community best suited to your way of life.

NO CASH OUTLAY

You have no capital invested, therefore, no risk. Housing expenses can be calculated with a high degree of accuracy.

APPLIANCES PROVIDED

The landlord almost always furnishes the major appliances and sometimes laundry facilities. It's also his responsibility to maintain these appliances.

As in everything there are disadvantages to renting, too.

NO EQUITY IN THE PROPERTY

Although there is no capital invested, the money you are paying each month shows no return. Rent is not tax deductible either, unless some portion of the property is used for business purposes.

LIMITED FREEDOM FOR IMPROVEMENTS

You may or may not be able to install certain fixtures or make improvements on your rented property. Sometimes there is an extra charge for the installation of such items as a washing machine or air conditioner.

GARAGE FACILITIES

They can be lacking entirely, or you might have to pay a monthly rent for the space (this applies to apartments more than to houses).

MAJOR APPLIANCES

These can leave much to be desired, depending on how old they are and how well the last tenant took care of them. The landlord may be a little slow in maintaining them properly, too.

LACK OF GENERAL MAINTENANCE AND REPAIR

Some landlords pride themselves on keeping up their property and seeing that necessary repairs are done promptly. Others—all too many—will do only the minimum, and that only after a considerable time lapse.

There is quite a difference between renting an apartment and renting a house. By taking an apartment you have to share a common hall with other tenants on your floor, and noise can be a consideration for both you and your neighbors. Unless you live in a garden apartment there's little chance to have any private lawn space to call your own. Living in a good-sized apartment building can be an impersonal experience—you may never know your next door neighbor. Many couples like this kind of privacy—they would live no other way.

If you rent a house, you will probably get more indoor space and some kind of lawn area, and maybe even a garage. You also assume some of the responsibilities of ownership when renting a house, because you are expected to keep up the yard and maintain the house, by installing storm windows and screens, shoveling sidewalks, etc. Usually the tenant is responsible for utility costs (water, gas, heating, garbage and trash disposal) and for minor repairs. Quite often houses are rented with major appliances, but this can depend upon the area in which you are renting. The landlord is expected to take care of major repairs and decoration, but be sure his responsibilities are explicitly stated in the lease. Houses which have been rented for years can show the wear and tear of former tenants, just as apartments can.

Where do you look for a place to rent? Any number of places, beginning with the classified ads in the newspapers under "Apartments to Let" and "Houses to Let." If the ones listed are not for you, insert a classified ad of your own and specify what you want. List your name and needs for housing with a good real estate agency. There's no charge unless the agent finds you a place. Ask friends and acquaintances if they know of places. Look for signs saying "vacancy" or "for rent" when you are out for a walk or drive. Talk to superintendents of apartment houses and see if anyone is moving out shortly. If you work for a large company see if it has a real estate division that looks after the needs of its personnel. This is especially likely if the firm has branch offices in other parts of the country and has to transfer its people periodically.

When you have found a suitable place to rent there are definite points of information you should have before entering into any formal agreement with the landlord. Know who owns or manages the building, your obligations to him as well as his to you. Are there any restrictions you should know about? Will you have a lease and if so for how long? Can you sublet? What services does the management provide? How are garbage and trash disposed of? Is the place furnished or unfurnished? The best way to find out about how an apartment building is run is to talk to other tenants, if it is possible.

THE LEASE

This is a final agreement between the landlord (or person authorized to rent the property) and tenant. As a written agreement it is a legal document which clearly states the responsibilities and obligations of both landlord and tenant. Verbal agreements are valid but offer less protection to both parties because there is nothing in writing. Many times sublets are rented by verbal agreements. When you rent by sublease you are actually renting from the tenant who holds the lease. Before signing a lease read it carefully and understand the provisions set forth in it. If there are verbal agreements, too, it is wise for your own protection to have

41

them written into the lease as well. Here are some points you should check before signing the lease.

1. How long does the lease run?

2. What is the rent, paid when and to whom? What is included in the rent (utilities, garage or parking space, maintenance services such as window washing)? Can the rent be increased before the lease expires?

3. Are you required to give one or more months' rent as security to the landlord? What happens to the security if you move before the lease expires?

4. What are the provisions for periodic decorating? Must you pay extra for any specific decorating?

5. Are there extra charges you must pay? Are you penalized for late payment of rent?

6. If you must move before the lease expires can you sublet? Is there a fee for subletting? Can you choose your own tenant? (Some landlords will write in an agreement releasing you from responsibility if you are transferred before the end of the lease.)

7. How long a notice must be given before moving when your lease expires? (In some areas if you do not move and do not sign a new lease and if the landlord accepts your rent, it means your old lease is still in effect.)

8. Can your lease be canceled under certain conditions? Can your rent be raised without a new lease?

9. When may the landlord and/or his representative enter your home? (He can inspect his property, but you have the right to set up conditions to protect your privacy. Unless there is an emergency he should not enter without your permission.)

10. What rules and restrictions does the building have? Can you keep pets, install extra equipment such as a washing machine? Can you install wall-to-wall carpeting?

11. Is the landlord responsible for any damage to your personal property? (Some leases hold the landlord unaccountable to any claims whether or not it is his fault. If this clause is in your lease be sure your insurance is adequate to cover your property.)

12. Are all the agreements in writing? (If the landlord promises to make certain allowances or adjustments such as repairs

and redecorating, have them written down, initialed by both parties and attached to the lease.)

If You Buy

There are several choices open to you providing you want and can afford to buy a home. You can buy a house, either new or old, a cooperative apartment, a condominium or a townhouse. Some venturesome couples have purchased houseboats, powerboats or sailboats with sleeping and eating quarters to be used as year-round homes. Other traveling couples make their homes in trailers. It all depends on your taste in housing, your needs, your location and, last but not least, what you can find that's available. Whatever your preference, buying a home is an important step representing a sizable investment of money and this step should not be taken lightly. Just like any other investment the resale value of your home is a consideration. Here are factors to consider in buying whichever type of home suits your requirements, your taste and your budget.

NEW HOUSE

There's something extremely appealing about moving into a brand-new, never-lived-in house. Everything is new and should be in the best of condition. Any appliances included with the house are new and spic and span. Since most new houses must be constructed by the latest building codes you will have the advantage of having the latest heating and cooling systems, adequate electrical wiring to take care of your appliances and many modern conveniences in the kitchen and bathrooms. Very likely the house has been designed to utilize space in the best possible way. You may even be able to have a choice of colors for decoration.

Don't be blinded, however, by the shiny newness of the house—look for such important features as good workmanship and materials. If there are new houses in the area, inspect them and compare for value. Find out something about the builder, if you can. Local realtors and bankers may give you a clue about his past performance, but the best source would be someone who lives in a house he has built. Ask him if he gives a guarantee with the house. Often a year is allowed in which the builder or contractor will see to adjustments and minor repairs. A new house normally takes about one year to shake down. You may find tiny diagonal lines from the door jams radiating to the ceiling—these are normal settling marks. Large cracks are abnormal, of course. During the first year hardwood floors may develop creaks, and they also may develop spaces between the boards. New floors left bare or partially covered by rugs will absorb more wax or whatever finish you apply during the first year, but as the wood becomes more seasoned it will absorb less. Grouting around bathroom fixtures and tiles may need to be redone as it withstands daily use. Calking around the shower or bathtub may prove insufficient. Flashing around a chimney can cause fireplace leaks when heavy rains come if the flashing has not been installed correctly. The first year your heating bill will undoubtedly be higher, assuming you live in a temperate-to-cold climate, because the house is actually drying out. Plasterboard walls can reveal nailheads and tape where the sections are joined, if the workmanship was not precise.

Any landscaping will need tender, loving care the first year unless the builder was very conscientious about watering the shrubs and grass. If you are fortunate enough to have old trees on your property, they may look great the first year, then slowly die. This happens if they were "smothered" by excess earth around the trunk for too long while bulldozers were grading the land for your house. Trees can be carefully protected to prevent this condition, but often they are not.

OLDER HOUSE

Many prospective homeowners will want an older house in an established neighborhood with its charm, individuality and mellowness. An older house can be anywhere from five years old to pre-Revolutionary and comes in as many assorted designs and shapes. Even with a newer-older house the landscaping is now established and much of it is perennial. Most of the first-year headaches have been thrashed out by the former owner and frequently he has also remodeled to suit his fancy. All of this can be advantageous to you if his additions add to the beauty and function of the house and have been done carefully.

You can expect to do a certain amount of repair work, redecorating and maybe some modernization when buying a house over ten years of age. In this case, consider the cost of the repairs along with the initial cost of the house. If extensive work has to be done, have a contractor give you an estimate on the work. Let him go over the house carefully to see if the beams are sound, the plumbing is in good shape, the furnace works and the electric wiring is safe and adequate. By all means have the house inspected for termites before buying it—exterminating companies very often inspect free of charge.

The down payment required on an older house is frequently more than that required on a new house. Banks are reluctant to give out extensive mortgages on old houses, the theory being that old houses will deteriorate faster than new houses. The appraised value will probably be less, though, making your property taxes less. Construction materials can very well be of better quality in the old house although less modern. You can find some beautiful paneling in old houses along with expensive marble for door sills and other treasures that would be too expensive in this day and age for a builder to install. You can also find plumbing pipes that have to be replaced with copper ones and a heating system which has been converted from one fuel to another. The walls are likely to be of plaster in pre-World War II housing, giving more sound-proofing between rooms. The doors are paneled solid doors, in many cases, as opposed to the hollow flush doors of modern housing. Beware of wallpaper—it might be hiding some disagreeably bad cracks that signify a leaky roof or severe settling cracks. There is no guarantee on an older house so keep your eyes peeled and look beyond the "darling sun porch" or the lovely stained glass window to a possible sagging floor which could mean an expensive and extensive repair bill.

TOWNHOUSE

This is a row house found more commonly in metropolitan areas. It has a front and back but shares side walls with the house on either side. Customarily, there is a back yard with a wall or fence for privacy, and there may be a very small yard in front as well. Very often a house of this nature has three or four floors and is narrow in width. In cities a townhouse is considered quite a luxury for the added space it gives by comparison with an apartment. Before purchasing a row house it would be wise to find out what kind of people live on either side of you. You are going to be very close neighbors and also share a common wall of your house.

45

This house can be an economy because it does share walls with other buildings and the land is at a minimum in area. Some of the points you should check on are: the soundproofing of the shared walls; the parking facilities; the usable living space considering how much is taken up by stairways and halls; any restrictions on altering interiors or exteriors, and the general condition of the backyard.

COOPERATIVE APARTMENT

This can be an ordinary apartment as far as appearances are concerned, but instead of renting, you acquire an equity in property if you buy. To purchase a cooperative apartment you make a down payment and receive stock in the corporation that owns the building along with a lease which entitles you to occupy a specific apartment unit. This makes you a tenant-owner, and monthly you pay a carrying charge which is a proportionate share of the taxes, mortgage and maintenance costs of the entire property. Part of this monthly charge can be deducted from your income tax because you are paying property taxes. The tenant-owners, or shareholders, elect a board of directors who guide policies and supervise management according to the bylaws of the corporation. Professional management is hired to see to the maintenance and general operation of the building. The board of directors screens all prospective tenants. A proprietary lease, granted by many cooperatives, contains clauses adapted to the specific conditions of a tenant-owner. If these clauses are flagrantly violated, the board of directors can force out the tenant-owner. A proprietary lease often runs from 15 to 25 years and is renewable.

Since buying into a cooperative is an investment of money, check carefully to see how the building is run, who manages it, the appraisal of the property and whether the value of the property is likely to increase. Improvements in the apartments have to be approved by the corporation. If you want to move from the cooperative you can sell your stock back to the corporation. You are subject to a tax on capital gains in the same manner as though you were selling a private house.

CONDOMINIUM

When buying a unit in a condominum, you actually purchase the apartment outright, gain joint ownership of the common areas and facilities of the building and receive a recordable deed. You even own a proportionate share of the land on which the building stands and lawns, if there are any. To finance the purchase of the condominium you arrange for your own mortgage—FHA insures mortgages if the city or municipality agrees to assess each unit individually. You pay property taxes individually on your unit, the fractional interest in the common areas, and you pay separately for building maintenance and service. Condominium owners have to agree among themselves how to manage the building and share maintenance costs. Usually a board of managers is selected to supervise the property and see that it is run according to the bylaws in the description of the property.

Since you arrange for your individual mortgage you can retire it earlier than you had planned without being concerned about the financial actions of your fellow unit owners. You cannot lose equity in your unit if the mortgage payments are kept up; in a cooperative, theoretically, you could lose your apartment if the corporation went bankrupt. Real estate taxes can be deducted from your taxable income.

A great advantage to owning a condominium unit is the right to make improvements without consulting a board of directors since you actually own all the space to the middle of the outside-unit walls. A disadvantage looms if you happen to get an unpleasant neighbor. Unlike the cooperatives, there is no owner board to screen prospective buyers.

Because of the many legal complications that can crop up, condominiums are only constructed in certain states that have passed laws which define the rights and possibilities of condominiums.

CHECKPOINTS TO CONSIDER IF YOU BUY

Many of these areas can be considered if you are renting, but they are primarily for the buyer because of the sizable cash investment. After all, you do want your property to serve your needs and remain as valuable in the future as it is now.

1. Neighborhood Is it well kept, attractive and orderly? Do people take pride in the appearance of their homes? Is rubbish and garbage in containers and out of sight? Is there a great deal of noise and traffic? Do you like the character of the community and

47

would you be comfortable living in it—be able to fit into the social life of the neighborhood?

2. Location of the property In the community are you near a shopping center, recreation facilities, churches, schools, libraries and parks? Where is the real estate located on the street? Do you have a corner lot which can give the illusion of spaciousness or are you more in the center with the possibility of more outdoor privacy?

3. Zoning restrictions What do these regulations stipulate for the community and particularly for the section you are considering? Are changes due soon? How strictly are these ordinances enforced? Does the community regulate air and water pollution? (The clerk in the local municipal hall can answer many of these questions. If plans for building a paper mill or superhighway are in the town's future plans, it might just influence your decision to buy.)

4. Transportation What types are available, where do they stop, and do they have a regular schedule? What about commuting if either of you has to consider this—what does it cost and is there local transportation to the train?

5. Taxes Are property assessments considered high, medium or low by comparison with surrounding communities? How often is property reassessed? What is your property tax per $1,000? What is your school tax per $1,000? Is there much tax-free land in the community? (Some communities have so many churches and schools along with other institutions affiliated with these groups that the percentage of tax-free land places a greater burden on the individual homeowner.)

6. Design of the house Is it pleasing to you with the design effectively used? Is it in keeping with the neighborhood? Did the builder know how to use his site well? Does the design fit in with your concept of furnishings? (Avoid faddish motifs that can tend to pall in a few years.)

7. Exterior of property What are its exact boundaries? Are there any easements (the right of someone else to use portions of your property for specified purposes)? Is the yard landscaped and in good condition? Is there room for privacy and space for outdoor living? Is the property graded slightly away from the house for better drainage?

8. Utilities Is the house connected to a public water system or does it have a well? If so, how deep? Is the water considered hard or soft? Is there a natural gas connection? Does the sewage drain into a municipal drain or does the property depend on a septic tank or cesspool? (The local or county health department can give you information on septic tanks and cesspools, how large they should be, how effective they are and when they should be cleaned.) If you will be heating with oil where is the tank located and what is its capacity? What provisions are made for storm sewage?

9. Exterior of the house Is the house siding durable and in good condition? (Streaking and blistering of paint is a sign of moisture in the walls.) Is the masonry in good condition? Do the gutters and downspouts appear to be in good condition or do they show signs of deterioration? (Downspouts should empty so they drain away from the house or into a catch basin.) Does the roof seem to be in good condition and does the chimney look sound? Does the foundation show deterioration? (Check the earth around the foundation to see if there is any moss growing there or if it is soft and spongy—a sign of moisture.)

10. House interior—general condition Does the overall appearance of the house suggest it has been maintained well? Are the floors level, and do they have a minimum amount of squeak? (Gently bounce on them to see if they are solid.) Do the walls and ceilings show large cracks that might indicate bad settling signs? Are the walls plaster or plasterboard? Is immediate redecorating necessary or merely a matter of taste? If there is wallpaper, what is underneath, more than one layer, or paint? (Some plasterboard has to be especially treated before it can be painted, so if there is wallpaper on plasterboard make sure you can remove it and can apply the primer coat of paint.) Is the general carpentry good, with moldings joined neatly and baseboards meeting precisely at corners? Where there is tile, is it cracked or loose? Are windows well placed for privacy but allowing for a maximum of light and air? Are storm windows and screens available with the house?

49

(Raise the windows to see if they work well. Where there are casements, open them to see that the hinges work well.)

11. Room layout Is the utilization of space good or is much taken up by hallways and stairwells? Is the traffic pattern convenient or must you, for example, walk through the living room to get to the kitchen? Are bedrooms placed for maximum privacy and minimum noise? Is there adequate wall space in the rooms for the proportion of your furniture and floor coverings? (Get the exact floor dimensions—don't ever be fooled by the way someone else's furniture makes a room appear.) Are closets and shelves ample and well placed for now as well as for future requirements? (You can accumulate lots of necessary equipment once you start a family.) Are the bathroom facilities situated well for the other areas of the house? Is there a basement or must you rely on storage space in the main part of the house?

12. Kitchen Is it well arranged, light and airy? Does it have an exhaust system to help get rid of cooking odors and excess heat? If major appliances are being sold with the house, is their condition acceptable? (Since the stove is sold with the house in most states, examine it well. It can be your best friend or worst enemy.) Are the cabinets in good condition, and do they allow for adequate storage? Are the countertops made of durable material and easily cleaned? Is there room for the kind of refrigerator you have or want to buy? Are there enough electric wall plugs for your smaller appliances? Is there a broom closet? Can you get to the kitchen from the outside easily?

13. Bathroom Is it adequate in size? Are the fixtures in good repair? Do the faucets leak? Is there a water cut-off on the toilet? Is the calking around the bathtub and shower and grouting between the tiles in good shape? Is the water pressure good? (Check this by flushing the toilet and turning on the water faucet at the same time. If there is no noticeable drop in pressure, it is good.) Is there a powder room for guests?

14. Basement Does it appear to be dry? Is it above grade or below? Does the foundation show cracks from inside? Are there several windows so it is fairly light and allows for circulation of air? Is there a floor drain? Is there space for laundry facilities, workshop and future recreational room? Is there an entrance

50

directly to the outside? (If the ceiling is not finished and covered, check to see what the beams are like and how close together they are.)

15. Garage Is it attached or separate? If it is attached is there a fire door leading into the house? Is the garage accessible and well lighted with an easy working door? Is there room for storage in the garage? Is it wide enough for your car? (Beware of some of the old garages.) If you have a carport is it located away from the severest winter winds and weather? What is the condition of the driveway?

16. Attic In case there is one, is it accessible and finished enough for storage space?

17. Electrical wiring Are there enough outlets in all the rooms and are there enough circuits with adequate service? (The fuse box or circuit breaker box can give you a rough idea how many circuits there are. There should be no fewer than eight circuits with several of these located in the kitchen for individual appliances. Newer houses have 100-ampere service with both 120- and 240-volt circuits as a minimum requirement for electrical needs of today. Old houses may have as little as 60-ampere service.) Are switches convenient and lighting fixtures well placed? (If you are buying an older house, it would be prudent to have an electrical contractor advise you on the adequacy of the service and wiring. With so much modern equipment using more current, such as color television sets, automatic washing machines and all kitchen appliances requiring heat, it might be a wise investment to have some of the suspect wiring replaced.)

18. Heating What kind of fuel is used and how old is the furnace? How do you start and control the heating unit? Are the controls accurate and automatic? (Test by raising the thermostat and listen for undue noise and how long it takes the unit to respond to the control.) Does the unit have a large enough capacity to heat the house adequately and evenly? Is the house insulated well enough for effective heating? Are the windows tight fitting to prevent drafts? (In a not brand-new house ask the owners to see the previous year's heating bill. As noted before, the heating will be more costly the first year after a house is built.) Are there provisions for cooling as well as heating? If the house is

51

old with radiators do they show signs of "spitting" or "thumping"? (If so, they may need new vents or valves or both.) How is hot water heated? How old is the heater, what is its capacity and is it a "quick recovery" type? (The best ones are glass-lined and have a warranty that runs from 15 to 20 years. Open the door at the base of the heater and look for any signs of rust or leakage.)

19. Plumbing What are the pipes made of, copper, galvanized steel, iron, wrought iron or brass? (Although iron and steel are good, copper or brass cost more but will last longer. In some areas copper piping is mandatory in new housing.) Is the material of the pipes suitable for the type of water? (Very hard water can leave a mineral deposit on certain pipes, thus eventually cutting down the water pressure.) Can you run both hot and cold water without noticing an appreciable drop in pressure? (Low water pressure can be partially solved if you live on a good size hill by having the water company install a slightly larger meter which lets in a larger stream of water.)

It is almost impossible for a layman to judge the condition of a house in such areas as electrical wiring, plumbing and heating, along with construction details that may not be apparent to you. Particularly in purchasing an older house, it may be economical for you to hire a general contractor to go over the house and inform you what needs to be done. Ask your realtor to recommend one who is reliable and competent. For a modest fee you could save future headaches and repair bills.

If You Build

Building your own could very well be the answer to your housing problems. Certainly it can be an exciting and rewarding experience, if you have a fairly clear idea of what you want, what you need and the money to buy the land. Be advised, though, that building your own can be more expensive than you may realize. It takes time and energy to select the proper building site, to decide on the exact house plans and specifications, to arrange the financing for building and to get the best professional help you can find and afford.

BUILDING SITE

The land you buy can influence the kind of house you build. To find this land check the local newspapers for ads under "land for sale," "acreage for sale" or "lots for sale." Register with a reliable real estate agency who might have listings of undeveloped land. Other suggestions: note all undeveloped land or lots in the area that particularly interest you and find the owner by going to the county courthouse where records of deeds are kept. Contact him to see if he wants to sell to you. Or, inquire at the courthouse about upcoming tax sales where land is sold for back taxes.

Assuming now that you have found the property you wish to buy, in a neighborhood that suits you, what should you know about this property?

1. The zoning and building restrictions of the area.
2. Whether there is a lien on the property for any reason.
3. Whether a building permit can be obtained.
4. If the property has adequate street frontage.
5. If the property is accessible to sewers, municipal water and utility lines, and how much it will cost to connect with them.
6. If there are improvements required such as street, sidewalks and driveway.
7. The actual boundary of the land and its shape.
8. The soil content, whether there is adequate topsoil and subsoil. The presence of clay can mean poor drainage, while the presence of springs can mean a marshy condition that might need drainage tiles.
9. The rock formation of the land, if any. Drilling or blasting through rock can be very expensive.
10. Whether there are easements on the land. A utility company may have a pipeline ten feet below the surface and has the right to use that portion of your property if the pipeline breaks and needs repair.

Your architect can advise you about the suitability of the property you have in mind. In lieu of an architect, ask a good contractor if the land will make a good building site.

53

HOUSE PLANS

Even though you know exactly the kind of dream house you want, there's a need for definite blueprints and specifications. There are several ways you can go about getting them.

1. Hire an architect. He will design the type of house you request and probably will be able to skillfully guide you so you get what you want the way you want it. He may or may not hire the contractor who supervises the actual building, but he will certainly act as adviser as the building progresses. Along with the design he will give you estimates of cost, usually quite accurate. The costs cannot be determined, though, until the plans are submitted to a contractor for bids. If difficulties arise during construction, costs may mount above the original estimate. The architect's fee is based on the cost of the house and the services he renders.

2. Buy a prefabricated house. This is a factory-built house which comes with sections of wall, floors, ceilings and roofs manufactured at a plant, partially assembled and then shipped to your building site for final assembly. A contractor must be hired to lay the foundation, do the masonry work, then assemble and finish the house. A "prefab" may be sold under the name of the manufacturer, the architect or even the home builder. The house can come in various states of completion. Some designs are excellent and allow for many individual variations on both exterior and interior. There is a fair price range along with a variety of designs. A word of caution: make sure your "prefab" meets with the local building code and the design is adaptable to the land site. Often "prefabs" are used by builders of large development tracts.

3. Buy a stock house plan. National magazines and dealers in building materials sell stock house plans, usually architect-designed. These plans include a set of blueprints showing the floor plan and construction details along with suggested building materials and specifications. Your architect or contractor should look over the plans to see how complete they are, whether they meet with local building codes, whether they can be adapted to your building site and whether the specifications are accurate in cost and quality of materials.

4. Select from one of several plans offered by a contractor or home builder. Choosing from several model homes that a builder has constructed, you select your lot preference and let him proceed. In most cases the plans, lot and cost of the house are included in one price. There can be a certain amount of flexibility for variation inside the house. Along with a few minor changes you might want to make, such as closet space and extra bathrooms, you will undoubtedly have the opportunity to select decorating colors, linoleum, tile and counter tops. In some housing developments these houses come "as is," but all of these details should be spelled out in your contract with the builder. Building this way means savings for you in land, plans and construction. It is most important that you find out if your builder has a good reputation in his profession, is experienced, demands good workmanship, uses acceptable materials and is solvent financially.

5. Buy a house shell. In some sections of the country an unfinished house or shell is available. Of course this type of new house is lower in cost, and if you and your husband have the skills to finish what is necessary, you can effect even further savings. Otherwise a contractor will have to be hired to complete the job. Before buying, determine what materials have been used in the shell construction, what still has to be done for completion, how long the shell has been standing and if you have the time, energy and know-how to complete it. Financing may be harder to get on a shell.

PROFESSIONAL SERVICES AVAILABLE TO HELP YOU

Since buying or building a home can be a major financial transaction, most couples seek the services of one or more specialists to help them solve their problems of housing. Probably the most important of these professionals will be the architect, the contractor or builder, the realtor and the lawyer.

Architect A person trained to design a house which fills the specific needs of his client and to see that the house is built well with quality materials. Besides drawing up the house plans he may help select the lot and choose the contractor. Obviously you and the architect must have a mutual understanding so he can give you the kind of house you want and know approx-

55

imately how much you can spend. Select your architect by consulting several—ask to see other houses they have designed, discuss what they charge and what services they are willing to give.

Contractor A builder who is responsible for constructing your house with quality materials and workmanship. He makes sure the house is built according to specifications and plans. He buys the materials, has them delivered as he needs them and hires sub-contractors who do parts of the construction, such as plumbing and electrical wiring. In most cases you pay the contractor a lump sum based on his original bid or some other cost-plus amount which is arranged in your contract with him. Depending upon your arrangement with the architect (if you have one) he may or may not work directly with the sub-contractors. Look for the same qualities of skill and reliability in the contractor as you look for in the architect. Your agreement with the architect or contractor should include a waiver of lien so a sub-contractor cannot file claims against your property if the architect or contractor fails to pay them.

Realtor An agent for a real estate agency whose primary function is to get buyer and seller together to bring about a sale. For this he receives a commission which is a percentage of the sale price. Because he is familiar with sale listings in his area, their relative value and features, plus the existing local condition, he can save you time and money by showing you property you want and can afford. The realtor represents the seller in almost all cases so you must look to your own interests at the time of the final transaction.

Lawyer A specialist you can ill afford to do without whether you buy or build because of his knowledge of the legal aspects and technicalities of contracts. Your lawyer knows the real estate laws of your state, and it's his business to make sure certain provisions in any agreement protect your interests whether the agreement is drawn by another source or by himself. He should advise you before you make a deposit to bind a sale. Ask him to explain any legal phrases you do not understand, along with your rights and obligations, before you sign an agreement. Before taking title to property he checks provisions: the title is clear and insured (you have clear ownership of a surveyed property with definite boundaries); there are no liens on the property; the description of the property in the deed is correct; nearby zoning is such that it will have no adverse effect on the property; mortgage terms are satisfactory to you; any possible deed restrictions; all verbal agreements or guarantees are written and the closing date and costs of closing, other than his fee. If you do not have a lawyer, several sources such as realtors, local bar associations, banks or even your own employer can refer you to qualified attorneys.

Financing a Home

Not too many people, particularly just marrieds, have enough cash to pay for a home all at once. The conventional manner of financing the purchase of a home is by getting a mortgage. In this way a percentage of the total cost is made by you as a down payment, and the rest of the property cost is lent by the holder of the mortgage. A mortgage is a conditional title to the property held as security until the loan is repaid. This is arranged by making periodic payments (monthly or quarterly) to the mortgage holder over a specified period of years. The interest paid on this loan is calculated at the beginning and does not vary for the life of the mortgage. The periodic payments are equal, but you will be paying more in interest at first than on the principal of the loan. Gradually, as the loan is repaid, the interest is paid up until you are finally paying only on the principal. Lending institutions that deal in mortgages have schedules available showing how much of each payment goes toward interest and principal.

The institutions that hold mortgages are quite realistic about giving you a mortgage and the size of it. Your age, income, credit rating and the type of property you buy will be considered in granting you the loan. The amount required for the down payment will depend on the type of mortgage you are given. For instance, the purchase of an older house will require more of a down payment and a shorter mortgage period than if you are buying a newer house. Whatever the down payment is, it should not deplete you of all your savings. Leave some for the emergencies. If your chances of increasing your income are slim for the near future, it might be financially sounder to seek a mortgage over a longer period of time, thus making the monthly charges less. Mortgage payments can include property insurance, property taxes and special assessments. If these expenses are included, the payments may have to be adjusted to allow for change in these areas. Some mortgage holders require that you place a certain amount of money with them to cover these expenses.

When you build, the mortgage is handled a bit differently. There is no down payment, but most lending institutions require that you own the land free and clear. The lender advances the money as the building proceeds. A certain amount is allocated for each stage, and usually the building is inspected by an expert from the lending institution. Often a building loan note is signed by the lender and you. The exact amount of the loan appears on the face of the note. As each payment is made to the contractor by the lender, with each stage of the construction, it is duly noted on the note. After the house is built you pay off the mortgage very much the same as you would on any other house. There can be an extra fee for a building loan because of the periodical inspections and added paper work.

MORTGAGES AVAILABLE

There are three kinds: conventional, FHA and VA.

1. Conventional: The down payment is about 25%, leaving the mortgage loan to cover 75% of the property's total cost. This type of mortgage usually runs 15 to 20 years, once in a while to 30 years. Rates of interest vary depending on the money market (more demand for money means higher interest), the lender, the state laws and the locality.

2. FHA: A mortgage granted by a lending agency is insured by the Federal Housing Administration against loss. The FHA only insures mortgages up to a certain amount and has definite standards of building which must be met along with an appraisal of the property for estimated value. An FHA insured loan quite frequently demands a lower down payment and a longer mortgage period. The interest rate is established by FHA with ½% going to FHA insurance. There are now programs for low-income families.

3. VA: In the same way the FHA insures mortgages so does the Veterans' Administration. It, too, insures up to a certain amount with an established interest rate. It does not, however, require a down payment, but the lending institution very often asks for a small one. A mortgage may be insured by both the FHA and the VA. Qualified veterans of the armed forces are eligible for this kind of long-term mortgage.

Another way of financing a house purchase is to take out a *second mortgage*. If you lack money, this is a means of covering the difference between the first mortgage and the seller's price. Not all holders of first mortgages will allow a second mortgage. You do gain title to the property and the holder of the second mortgage receives secondary claim on the property after the first lender is satisfied. Meeting the payments on both mortgages may be too much for your income and the cost of the second mortgage can be high because of the risk involved to the lender.

THOSE WHO GRANT MORTGAGES

Mortgage loans for homes are available through many lending institutions. Customarily it is the realtor who obtains the mortgage for you on the best terms possible. Consult several prospective lenders yourself to get an idea of what is to be had at what interest.

1. Commercial banks grant conventional, FHA and VA insured mortgages. They are apt to have strict practices with conventional mortgages, asking a good-size down payment and short repayment period.

2. Mutual savings banks invest most of their depositors' savings in mortgages on homes. These banks, too, give conventional, FHA and VA insured loans and are apt to be more lenient regarding conventional mortgages. (Mutual savings banks operate in only 18 states.)

3. Savings and loan associations also invest most of their depositors' money in mortgages, then pay dividends to the depositors. They grant mainly conventional mortgages with lower down payment and longer repayment period. FHA and VA insured loans are given less often.

4. Insurance companies give conventional, FHA and VA loans with conventional ones requiring high down payments but long repayment periods. Often these mortgages are handled by brokers or agents for the company.

59

5. Mortgage companies arrange for conventional, FHA and VA mortgages, then sell them to insurance companies. They frequently continue to service the mortgages.

6. Private individuals grant mortgage loans occasionally of the conventional nature. When a second mortgage is granted it is generally held by an individual.

INSURANCE

For homeowners there are several kinds to consider. Rates will vary according to where you live and the value of your property.

1. Fire insurance If you have a mortgage on your home, the bank or lending institution will require you to carry enough fire insurance to equal the amount due on the mortgage loan. Insurance protection against fire and lightning should be calculated on the replacement cost of the house for your own protection as well as for the requirements of the mortgage holder. Ask your agent about water-damage coverage, also.

2. Comprehensive personal liability A policy of this nature protects you against damages if someone or their property should be injured on your property. It also covers any personal or property damage your family should have anywhere, exclusive of auto liability.

3. Homeowners' policy Here is an "all-in-one" policy which offers protection against a number of risks at one premium. It includes both property and liability coverages. In some areas it offers coverage against wind damage and vandalism. The cost and amount of coverage depends upon the stated limits of the policy.

4. Life insurance There are policies written that pay up the remainder of your mortgage should you die before paying it off in full. (See page 27 on Money Management.)

There are many terms used by amateurs and professionals alike in the field of real estate. In your quest for housing, whether you are renting or buying, you should be acquainted with these terms and their meanings. Here is a glossary of the more commonly used terms.

EARNEST MONEY-Cash put forth by a prospective buyer of real estate as a deposit to show evidence of good faith.

ESCROW-Property or money held by a third party in trust for the first and second parties until conditions of a written agreement are fulfilled by the first two parties.

CONTRACT OR AGREEMENT-In real estate a written document in which the purchaser agrees to buy a property and the seller agrees to sell it on conditions set forth.

LEASE-An agreement, almost always written, between landlord and tenant in which the tenant acquires the use of property for a period of time for a stipulated amount of rent.

SUBLEASE-An agreement between a tenant holding a lease, and another tenant who wishes to hold the property *under* the first tenant.

LESSOR-The landlord or one who rents the property to another.

LESSEE-The tenant who rents the property from the landlord.

VENDOR-The one who sells real estate to another.

VENDEE-The one who buys real estate from the vendor.

DEED-A written agreement by which title to a specifically described property is transferred from seller to buyer. Upon being signed and delivered it supersedes the contract for purchase and sale of the real estate.

DEED RESTRICTION or RESTRICTION COVENANT-A clause in the deed limiting the use of the property described either perpetually or for a limited time.

EASEMENT-The right of someone else to use a portion of your property for a specified purpose.

RIGHT OF WAY-Almost the same as an easement but usually refers to someone having the use of a strip of land on your property such as a railroad track bed or a utility company's pipes underneath the land.

BUILDING CODE-The ordinances regulating building construction within a municipality.

ZONING-Municipal ordinances which regulate the character and use of property. They very often specify the minimum amount of land required to build a home in a specified section or zone.

CAVEAT EMPTOR-A Latin phrase meaning "Let the purchaser beware." It is up to the buyer to examine and know what he is buying.

SUBDIVISION-A tract of land which is divided into plots suitable for building houses.

EQUITY-The interest or value of your property over and above the mortgage against it.

AMORTIZATION-The gradual liquidation of mortgage loans through equal periodic payments.

PRINCIPAL-The actual amount of money borrowed by mortgage loan to make up the difference between the down payment and the cost of the real estate.

DOWN PAYMENT-The amount of money you actually give to the seller for property.

INTEREST-Cash paid for the use of money which has been lent. On a mortgage this rate is determined when the mortgage is granted and remains the same for the life of the mortgage.

APPRAISAL-An estimate of the value, quality and quantity of the property.

SURVEY-A precise way in which land is measured to find out its exact boundaries.

TITLE-Clear evidence of ownership of property.

TITLE INSURANCE-A policy of insurance which guarantees the title is clear and reimburses the owner if there are any defects in the title.

ASSESSMENT-A demand made against a property owner by a municipality, county or state for a part of the cost of some improvement such as a new sewer or street.

ASSESSED VALUE-An appraisal made of property by a unit of government for the levy of taxes.

MARKET VALUE-The price for which your property could be sold on the open market at a given time.

LIEN-A claim which someone has upon property of another as a pledge for a debt, taxes or a mortgage.

MECHANICS LIEN-Specifically a claim against a property by those who actually performed work or sold materials when the building was constructed or renovated.

VARIANCE-A special permit by a municipal board to allow a building (usually under construction) not to conform to some part of the zoning or building ordinances.

SETBACK-A specified distance from the curb or street edge in which a building cannot be erected.

OPEN END MORTGAGE-A clause in the mortgage allowing you to borrow additional money for remodeling or making other home improvements on the house.

CLOSING DATE-A time when the buyer and seller and their representatives come together for the purpose of transferring title of the property, reading the deed, taking over the mortgage, if there is one, and receiving title insurance.

4

A Shopping Guide for Home Furnishing

THE FIRST HOME you have may be small or large, furnished or unfurnished, rented or owned. Whatever it is, it's your nest to do with as you will. Here is the place that will reflect the personalities of both you and your husband. In a variety of ways it will show what you really like, what you think, who you are and what makes you comfortable. Your husband may or may not have definite ideas about decor, but include him in all major planning sessions and even shopping tours. Take into consideration what colors and textures he likes, his interests, his tastes and his hobbies. How will you find out his likes and dislikes, his idea of a really comfortable chair, unless you ask him?

Approach the problem of furnishing by first deciding what basics you need now! Which of the essentials do you have on hand—from previous living quarters, from parents' homes, from wedding presents? Basics include a good bed, a chest of drawers, easy chairs, essential lamps, dining table and chairs and kitchen appliances. After deciding on the basics, take the second step and list some of the non-essentials, the accessories which give accent to your home, such as end tables, area rugs, pictures, a television and a record player.

While making the list of essential furnishings, ask yourselves whether the furniture you require now can be used in the future. Is your apartment a large single room where your bed has to serve a dual purpose as a sofa? Is your home so small that you have to buy a smaller scale of furniture to fit in than you would for the house you eventually hope to have? Perhaps you must think of some of the basics as temporary. In this case, less sturdy and cheaper items could be a better buy for you right now. If the basics are to be regarded as permanent, shop with care for quality and workmanship. If money is a problem at present, think about using credit for purchasing the more expensive basics. (See Chapter 2.) The use of credit can be a practical solution to allow you to buy good quality furniture which will last for years instead of inferior merchandise with a much shorter life span.

Many young couples prefer to furnish and decorate their homes themselves. Rigid rules of the past have been abandoned—quite often a mixture of brand-new along with "early-attic" from mother or a secondhand store can produce some surprisingly good results. And you can always be proud that they are your very own. There are those of you who will have an excellent eye for what goes well, a certain flair for creating exactly the atmosphere you want in your home. There are those of you who haven't the knack. Don't despair—most department and furniture stores have decorating services (usually free) to assist you in making selections, and to offer sound advice. There are also many excellent magazines devoted to decorating the home. And there are professional decorators who can help you with the furnishings alone or with the whole decor of the home. Just as an architect builds your home to suit your taste and needs, so the decorator functions to furnish the inside of it. Of course, calling in a professional is likely to be more expensive, but it may be a saving for you to get exactly what you want.

However you plan to approach the problem of furnishing, here are some basic principles to keep in mind for best results.

SCALE

Really look at a room—get out a tape measure and find out the exact dimensions. Bare rooms can give the illusion of being larger than they actually are. Notice how the windows and doors are placed, how much blank wall space there is, how high the ceilings are and whether the rooms are light or dark. The size of the furniture you choose should be directly proportionate to the size of the room. For instance, if you have a relatively small living room, a large upholstered chair is going to take up too much space and may be outsized for the room. The best way to be sure furniture will fit is to draw the exact dimensions of the room to scale on graph paper; for example, let ½ inch on paper equal 1 foot of room dimension. Take the graph paper with you when you shop and ask the salesman for the exact measurements of the furniture. By translating these dimensions to the scale of your room on the graph paper, you can quickly tell if the piece of furniture will fit in the space you've allotted. Careful grouping of furniture can achieve desired results: a favorite occasional table which is too small to be placed next to a bulky couch can stand importantly when placed between two small side chairs. Much the same technique can be used with small pictures by grouping them in an interesting arrangement.

SPACE

Here are some basic rules to follow to make the best use of *space:*

FOR SMALL ROOMS

Select furniture that is slim with simple lines; avoid massive pieces. Walls should be in light tones; wallpaper with a small, uncomplicated design. (Dark walls and flamboyant wallpaper will only make the room appear tinier.) Designs in rugs or upholstery should be simple and small. Wall-to-wall carpeting can make a room appear larger. Wall-hanging lamps and storage pieces such as a desk will do away with unnecessary clutter. The use of a mirror on one wall can give the illusion of double space. Glass-topped coffee tables do their duty without taking up visual space.

FOR LARGE ROOMS

Choose furniture larger in size with a more massive appearance. Vibrant colors can be used along with bolder and more dramatic patterns and textures. Space can be broken up by grouping furniture into defined areas used for conversation, for music, for desk work. An area rug will make the room seem smaller, and a wall in a different color from the rest can make it seem closer. A large, important piece of furniture placed at the far end opposite the main entrance will give the illusion of less depth.

FOR CEILINGS

To make high ceilings appear lower, use a darker shade than the wall color and concentrate on the use of horizontal lines in the room. To make low ceilings seem higher, apply a lighter shade of paint than the wall color and accent the vertical lines in decorating, especially in the treatment of windows.

FOR WINDOWS

Narrow windows can be made to seem wider by extending the curtain rod beyond the window frame so the folds of the curtain do not cover the glass, only the wall. For windows that are too wide, do the opposite: let the folds of the curtains hang over part of the glass. If there is a series of narrow windows, consider draping them as one unit. If your room has several unbalanced and unmatched windows, be sure the color of the draperies is not too overwhelming in contrast to the walls.

BALANCE

Balance results from the order in which objects or effects are placed around a certain point. These effects can be gained in several ways—by color, texture, grouping, size or shape. *Symmet-*

rical or formal balance is achieved when identical objects are placed equally distant from a center point; for example, placing two matching lamps on either side of a couch. *Asymmetrical or informal balance* can be established by placing dissimilar objects unequally in relation to a center point. An example of this would be two candlesticks on one side of a mantel with an ornamental vase on the other side. Symmetrical balance is easier to produce successfully but can become monotonous if carried too far. While informal balance is more difficult to form and control, it can create a warm, friendly atmosphere in the room. To achieve asymmetrical balance remember certain factors: dark colors seem to outweigh light colors; vibrant colors outweigh hazy, muted tones; splashing designs are more dominant than dainty all-over designs; rough textures seem heavier than smooth ones and, of course, overstuffed chairs will appear more massive than lighter, though larger, pieces of furniture. One of the easiest ways to experiment with informal balance is to group pictures of all sizes and shapes on one wall. Here you will be able to see how readily color values and shapes influence the balance of the total group.

COLOR

One of the most effective elements in decorating is color—an important tool in unifying seemingly unrelated elements and objects. It can give the impression of a larger room, it can bring intimacy to the room, it can brighten a dark room and tone down a glaringly bright room. Most of all, it can reflect your personality. Every good color combination must have variety, interest and harmony—dark and light, dull and bright. The best approach is to visualize what the room demands in the way of color. Bear in mind how you are going to cover the walls and floors and what colors have been predetermined for you. Consider the mood you want to establish, the colors you can live with. In developing a color theme think in terms of color families: blues, greens, yellows, reds and neutrals. Professional decorators find there is enough variation in tone and difference in intensity in one family to let it predominate. Take the blue family—you have a range from navy to pastel blue, from aqua to purple and all the shades in between. Complementary colors can then be used for accent.

The neutrals—black, white, gray and beige—can play a very important role in sharpening or muting your color theme, however you wish to use them. For the very daring with a discerning eye, the sky's the limit on what you can do with color. Below is a color guide showing where the colors fall on the spectrum along with terminology used when referring to color relations.

Primary colors—yellow, red and blue—mixing these yield all other colors.

Secondary colors—colors produced by mixing two of the primaries: orange (from yellow and red), green (from blue and yellow) and purple (from red and blue).

Triad colors—three colors equidistant on the wheel, such as red, yellow and blue.

Complementary colors—colors directly opposite each other on the color wheel, such as orange to blue and green to red.

Analogous colors—colors either next to each other on the wheel or similar, such as yellow and orange, blue and green.

Monochromatic color—consisting of one color.

LIGHTING

Another powerful factor in decorating is lighting, which goes hand in hand with color. Light, either natural or artificial, can brighten or soften a room. A color can differ in shade with the use of various types of lighting. Once considered a stepchild, lighting is recognized today as a very influential element in decorating. Manufacturers give you a selection of so many kinds of lamps and bulbs that there is no longer an excuse for anyone to have insufficient illumination. Lights should be planned with a specific purpose in mind and for a definite area. Quite naturally your kitchen is going to need a different light from that in your bedroom. More than one type will be needed for the living room because there is probably more than one area of activity in that room. Some lighting will be used to create atmosphere and some for more functional purposes. Slim fluorescent tubes are now easily installed invisibly under shelves, behind moldings or over counters to give bright, shadowless light for work areas. There are rheostat controls to brighten or dim lights for dining or entertaining. One of the most romantic ways to light is with the warmth and softness of candlelight. Candles come in a great number of sizes, shapes and colors, and with a vast range of holders. Young moderns are well aware of the advantages of recessed spotlights to beam on an isolated area or to light the whole room. A recent system of illumination utilizes small spotlamps clipped to a ceiling track; the spotlamps slide wherever you want them. This system helps do away with unnecessary clutter of floor lamps in a small room. There are all sorts of bulbs on the market today—some simulate candlelight, some twinkle, some shimmer and some light up in crystal ball fashion. All kinds of effects can be created from lights hidden behind panels in the ceiling. In some homes, lighting is almost an art in itself.

CENTER OF INTEREST

In a well-planned room there is always a focal point, some feature to which the eye is drawn as a center of interest. Quite often, in a living room, it will be a fireplace. Lacking this, you can always draw attention to a beautiful piece of furniture, a wall of books, a work of art, a colorful rug, an unusual screen, a window treatment or an outstanding display of house plants. Make sure, however, that what you wish to emphasize is worth being made prominent and has enough beauty and charm to withstand constant scrutiny. Although the focal point should be the main feature in the room, it should also be an integral part of the total decoration in character, style and color. It should not be so overpowering that the rest of the room fades by comparison; rather, it should serve to enhance the lesser articles in the room.

USE OF WEDDING GIFTS

Take a careful inventory of wedding presents. Is there enough storage space in your new quarters for the silver, china, linens and small appliances that you've received? There's a good chance you'll have to buy some sort of modular unit for storage. If this is a problem, investigate dual-purpose furniture, such as a hollow ottoman with a hinged top and loads of storage space inside, or an occasional table that opens to a small cupboard for glasses. Instead of storing away some of the presents that seem to have little use in your home now, reexamine them to see if any can be pressed into another use for the present time. A large sturdy tray could be put on a collapsible base and used as a small coffee table. A cocktail shaker or pitcher makes a good vase for flowers or leaves. Spare sheets have been known to be very dramatic full-length draperies or may be cut off for shorter curtains. When a gift cannot be exchanged and does not harmonize with your home, ask yourself if it can be altered—by paint, by dye or by colorful decorator tapes. There are some gifts which defy use and will never fit or enhance your home. In that case, tuck them away and try to remember to bring them out for display when the giver visits you.

BUYING GUIDE

This is a guide designed to help you select the best value and quality in furnishings for your home. How to care for them will be discussed in Chapter 5.

FURNITURE

Start with a definite plan: what you consider basic and permanent and what you consider basic and temporary. It will make a difference in how much you spend and how you spend it. Do you know what furniture style you want? Will this period of furniture adapt itself to another home if you move? There are five major furnishing styles: Early American, formal traditional (French, Italian and English antiques), Mediterranean, contemporary and eclectic (a mixture of several styles). Many department and furniture stores have model rooms set up to help you decide on the style you want. See which one makes you feel comfortable and "at home." Whatever your preference, go to a reputable retailer and buy intelligently—read labels, ask questions about the materials and construction, the manufacturer and the guarantees. A good furniture salesman will be able to answer many questions, so discuss your decorating problems with him. After making a decision on what to buy and how to buy it, check on the delivery date.

71

Although most furniture and department stores deliver free of charge, make sure you are not paying extra for cartage. And do be certain someone is at your home to accept the delivery when it comes.

WOOD FURNITURE

Know what kind of wood you are getting, how it has been finished and what you can expect from it. A wood has to be properly seasoned and finished, otherwise it can warp and crack with variations in humidity and heat. There are eight hardwoods most commonly used in furniture today.

Birch A light, cream-colored wood with a slight reddish tinge. It is strong, hard, satiny smooth and fine-grained. It's used in modern furniture as well as in the Colonial style, where it is stained brown.

Cherry A fruitwood that is strong, red-brown with a straight satiny grain, sometimes with a ripple in its depths. It resists warping and takes a fine polish. It was used in Colonial furniture and is found in some contemporary.

Mahogany A very versatile, light, mellow-brown wood, somewhat softer than other hardwoods. Because of its firm texture, deep, rich grain and ability to take a variety of finishes, it is considered the aristocrat of the cabinet woods. It grows only in the West Indies, Central America, South America and Nigeria. Philippine mahogany is not true mahogany but a wood resembling it.

Maple A smooth, strong wood with even texture and very fine grain, it was used extensively by Colonials. The many varieties of maple run from very hard to soft and the colors from light gray-brown to dark brown. Sugar maple is the variety used most in furniture. The grain can contain bird's eye figures, can be wavy or curly. Although maple is not easily glued, modern production methods have overcome this problem. No fill is needed in maple so paint adheres well. The best maple takes a high polish.

Oak A very strong, hard, durable and open-grained wood which ranges in color from light yellow and gray to dark brown and takes distinctive finishes. Used for centuries, it is resistant to climate changes, takes abuse well and needs less care than most woods.

Rosewood An exotic wood from Brazil or India which varies in color from light tan (in younger trees) to deep red-purple (in mature trees), streaked with dark pigment. Once used for pianos, this heavy, oily wood, which takes a high luster finish, is used in much Scandinavian furniture. It is suitable for cabinet-work and for variegated inlay.

Teak Another exotic wood from Burma or Siam, extraordinarily heavy with colors ranging from honey to warm brown, sometimes with near-black stripes. Long a favorite with Scandinavian and oriental designers, it's now used in contemporary furniture. Some teak has a rich cross-grain. It is also used in veneer form.

Walnut A wood used in fine cabinetwork for centuries, it varies in color from light to rich warm brown. It is very strong, workable, shrinks less than most woods so it can withstand almost any climate and takes to oil finishes very well. The American variety, known as "black walnut," is actually medium brown. Burls in walnut are sometimes so beautiful that they are made into wall hangings. Walnut is used in solid as well as veneer form.

Softwoods, such as pine, redwood, cedar and cypress, are most often used in outdoor or unpainted pieces. These woods are less expensive, less durable and not as beautiful as the hardwoods. Pine can be used for the basic construction in cheaper upholstered furniture.

TRADE TERMS IN WOOD

Solid wood If the label says "solid," you know all exposed surfaces of the furniture consist of the solid wood named.

Veneered wood Not a poor second to "solid" but usually stronger and less apt to warp. It's made up of several layers of wood held together with an adhesive. Finally, a front veneer of fine cabinet wood is applied along with a back veneer and the whole

73

piece is laminated together permanently in a high-pressure press.

Genuine The furniture is made in the wood named, but it can be of both solid and veneered lumber.

Combination Several different woods have been used in making the furniture. Try to find out the specific woods used.

Finish A term that can be misleading; sometimes it means simply that a stain was applied on a piece of wood to make it resemble another wood, such as a "walnut stain" on a piece of oak. Finish can also mean that the wood has been bleached or given a finish to accent the grain. A damage-resistant film can also be called a finish. Ask the salesman exactly what the finish is on the specific article you want.

CONSTRUCTION DETAIL

Flaws in construction are apt to be spotted more easily in cabinet pieces than in upholstered furniture where so many of the basics to the life of the chair are hidden. Included here are things to make sure of when buying tables, chairs, chests and other furniture made of wood.

1. The furniture stands evenly and solidly, with no wobbles.

2. Undersides of tables and backs of desks and chests are smooth and attractive. High quality pieces have backs and undersides stained and sanded while lower-priced furniture often has a plywood back nailed on. If you are planning to use the cabinet with the back showing, be sure it matches the front and sides.

3. Cabinet doors open and shut easily, fitting smoothly into the frame.

4. All knobs, pulls and other hardware are firmly attached, well placed, strong and well chosen for the design of the furniture.

5. Drawers glide in and out easily, have side and center rails and stops to prevent them from being accidentally pulled completely out. Corners of the drawers should be dovetailed and a dust panel attached to the frame under each drawer to prevent dust slipping through.

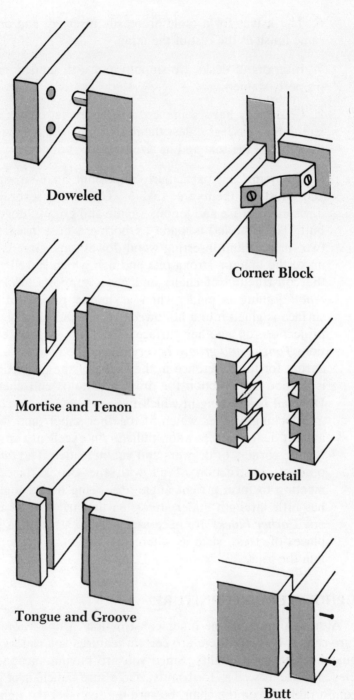

Doweled

Corner Block

Mortise and Tenon

Dovetail

Tongue and Groove

Butt

6. The leaves for a table are easily inserted, and are in the same finish as the rest of the table.

7. Interiors of desks are smooth and well sanded as well as properly stained.

8. Chair legs have some cross support (stretcher) to add strength to the legs unless the design specifically bars it. Note the pitch of the seat and its size to insure comfort.

9. The joints are particularly important for a strong frame, and most of them are visible. There are several kinds: doweled; mortise and tenon; tongue and groove; dovetail and butt. The *doweled* is made by boring a hole in each of the two surfaces and inserting wood dowel pins. Glue is used to make the union a strong one and one which is well suited to the construction of chairs and chest supports. *Mortise and tenon* joining is made when a shaped projection on one surface is glued into a hollowed groove, the same size as the projection, on another surface. This, too, is good construction. *Tongue and groove* is very much like mortise and tenon except for the difference in the shape of the projection. This is a good construction for drawer bottoms and chest sides. Dovetail is a joining in which two surfaces are notched with interlocking wedges which fit together snugly and withstand a great deal of stress when pulled. An excellent construction for the corners of drawers and cabinet sides. The *butt* is the poorest construction of all with the two surfaces simply meeting to form a right angle and being nailed together. It has little strength under stress, particularly if used in drawers. *Corner blocks* are necessary to help strengthen joints in places of stress, such as where the legs of chairs and tables join the tops.

UPHOLSTERED FURNITURE

Although much of the inner construction in upholstered furniture cannot be seen, there are certain features you can look for as guidelines to good quality. Since you are buying an upholstered piece for use as well as for beauty, make sure the chair or couch is comfortable. Sit on the chair, be sure the seat is at the right height and depth so you can lean back restfully and get up easily. Think of your husband's comfort also, particularly the proportion of a chair he may want to call his own.

Covering fabrics for furniture can vary widely in types and quality. Furniture can sometimes be purchased covered only with muslin so that you may use slipcovers exclusively. The cost of an upholstered piece is determined not only by its workmanship and construction but also by the price of the covering fabric. The covering you select, and you usually can choose unless it is sale merchandise, depends entirely on your taste, how much you want to spend and how the finished piece will fit in your home. Fabrics and coverings break down into the following groups:

Jacquard weaves Damasks, brocades and matelassés, all patterns with a satin weave.

Flowered prints Chintzes, toiles.

Pile weaves Velvets, velveteens, moquettes, furs, fake furs and plushes.

Tweeds and wool plaids Textured fabrics, some handwoven ones.

Leathers and suedes

Vinyl plastics Simulates the look of leather, fabric or straw.

Whichever kind of covering you select should be treated so that it is resistant to soil, wrinkling, fading, shrinkage and general wear. A woven fabric must have a good firm weave to be snag-resistant. If the covering is not treated a protective finish can be added. Vinyls are durable and easy to clean. Leather is easy to care for but is more expensive.

Unattached seat cushions are available with a variety of fillings. The label must tell you what they contain—sometimes you can order a specific filling content.

Fillings:
LATEX FOAM RUBBER OR POLYURETHANE FOAM for a firm seat which remains in shape.
POLYESTER FIBER-FILL for a softer seat which remains in shape.
COMBINATION OF POLYESTER AND POLYURETHANE FOAM for a soft seat which remains in shape.

77

DOWN AND/OR FEATHERS for a very soft seat, very luxurious and more expensive, but needs plumping after sitting.

Construction:

1. The frame is made of good, well-seasoned wood (beware of soft pine) with joints well constructed and braced with corner blocks.

2. Webbing under the springs is strong, closely interlaced and firmly attached to the frame. Webbing can be of jute, plastic or steel.

3. Springs are closely fitted together, tied securely to the frame and padded so they are not felt through the upholstery. Flat wire is used in place of coil springs where bulk is undesirable.

4. A good protective padding of horsehair or similar material is used over the springs.

5. Platform seats (forming the complete top) have sturdy, durable filling. Medium to expensive furniture has rubberized hair, latex foam or polyurethane foam. Less expensive furniture has rubberized sisal, flax or cotton.

6. Legs are good and sturdy, in keeping with the general design of the furniture. See that legs on couches are strong and well braced. If the couch or chair has a skirt on it, check to make sure the legs are of good design in case you want to reupholster without a skirt some time in the future.

7. Extra-long sofas have an extra leg in the middle of the front for additional support.

8. Lift unattached cushions to be sure the fabric underneath is good, durable and either blends with or matches the upholstery color.

9. Upholstering fits well with straight, unpuckered seams and smooth welts. Skirts hang straight and pleats are even. Zippers are concealed. The grain is straight (in pile fabrics it must run all one way) and if there is a pattern, it matches at the seams and is centered in front and back.

METAL FURNITURE

Though it was formerly regarded as outdoor furniture only, metal furniture is being seen more and more indoors. Materials can be wrought iron, aluminum, cast aluminum, enameled steel and chrome-plated steel. Contemporary designers are now combining metal frames with leather or fabrics to make very exciting furniture. Many dinette sets have a metal base or at least metal legs. Wrought iron has come back in style with use of the old "ice cream parlor" chairs and tables. Now you can buy dining sets which are excellent copies of them. In buying metal furniture the important points to watch for are : rust-proof finish, smooth edges, legs tipped so they won't mark the floor, good weight and strength of metal and sturdy joinings.

PLASTIC FURNITURE

Giant steps have been made in plastics for furniture. Some of the designs are delightful whimsey and some are extremely functional. Because of its ability to be molded, plastic lends itself very well to the contemporary style. Molded plastic can produce furniture which is strong, lightweight, comfortable, easy-to-care-for, and practically unbreakable. Guidelines to help you buy : check the thickness (too thin and it might crack), see that all surfaces are smoothly polished, make sure there are no bubbles and see how the joinings are made—some are by adhesives, some by plastic-capped bolts. Because acrylic plastic does scratch, such tables are often topped with glass.

UNFINISHED FURNITURE

Many occasional pieces can be purchased already built, but in raw wood for you to finish, either by staining to a wood finish or by painting. These pieces are quite often in softwoods such as pine. Occasionally you will find some made of poplar or birch. Although unfinished furniture is considered less expensive, remember to count how much it will cost for the finish you will have to add. If you paint it, you will need a primer coat before the finish coat. Some mail order houses have furniture kits you can send for and assemble yourself. These can prove expensive but the woods are good and the designs can be replicas of antiques. If you're handy and inclined toward period furniture, this can be a lot of fun.

BEDS

The purchase of a bed can be the most important decision you make in furnishing the home. Comfort is the key word! This is not the item to buy cheap, unless you just happen to come across a genuine sale. Before approaching the bedding department, know what you want. Are you going to buy twin beds or a double one? Does your husband like a soft or a firm mattress? One with a quilted or plain surface? Is he too tall to be comfortable in a standard bed? (The mattress should be 6 inches longer than the tallest sleeper.) If you can't agree on the degree of softness for a double bed, the salesman may suggest one partner use a bedboard under his side of the mattress for added firmness.

Standard mattresses come in these sizes:

Twin	39" x 75"	California King	72" x 84"
Double	54" x 75"	King	78" x 80"
Double Extra Long	54" x 80"	King, Extra Long	78" x 84"
Queen	60" x 80"		

The filling of the mattress is vital to its durability, life and comfort. There are two basic types: foam and innerspring.

Foam If you want firmness, consider a foam mattress. There are two varieties: *latex foam* which is a natural product made from the milk of rubber trees and *urethane foam,* a synthetic substance. A mattress of foam is very durable, pliable and conforms well to the body. A pincore type, with tiny air vents, helps to dispel body heat, thus letting you sleep comfortably. The mattress is from 4½ to 6 inches thick, non-allergic, odorless and mildew-proof. It is bendable, probably easier to turn if you are considering an outsized bed, and will not sag. Be certain, however, that the mattress is heavy enough so that sheets and blankets will stay tucked in under it.

Innerspring Made up of wire coil springs, this type of mattress improves in quality with the number of springs (500 to 800 in a standard double mattress). Three kinds of coil constructions are made: *open coil, cloth-pocketed coil* and *free-end coil.* The *open coil* and *free-end coil* are joined together with steel spring wire. All have commendable points if they are manufactured by a reputable firm. The *cloth-pocketed coil,* in which each spring acts independently, is thought to be better for double beds—his heavy weight won't cause you to slide all night. Over the coils, top and bottom, is an insulation made of either wire mesh or sisal pad.

(Sisal padding doesn't wear as well.) This, in turn, is topped with a layer of cotton felt or foam and covered by ticking. The ticking is finished either smooth, quilted or tufted with buttons. Since you cannot dry-clean or launder your mattress, a zippered cover is an excellent way to keep the dust and blanket fuzz from the mattress. You'll want a mattress pad between the sheets and mattress to act as a blotter.

The bed springs are a vital support to the mattress. Bedding experts usually recommend that you buy the mattress and springs as a matching set so they will function as one unit. Several kinds of springs are to be found: box springs, metal coil and flat.

Box springs Made of steel spring, wire coils mounted on a wooden base. The top is padded with cotton felt, then covered with ticking to match the mattress. This is the most expensive type of springs but it doesn't leave rust on the mattress nor cause damage from protruding coils. Manufacturers often discourage fitting legs to the box springs base; they feel all-around support is better and recommend a metal frame which adjusts to the mattress and has provision for attaching a headboard.

Metal coil Cheaper than the box springs, this type of springs is not covered nor padded but does give adequate support. Double-deck coils are preferable to single-deck coils because they have greater resilience and durability. Metal coils require cleaning and can get rusty.

Flat springs The cheapest base you can buy consisting of metal strips of woven wire attached to a frame by springs. Sagging can be a problem.

FLOOR COVERINGS

A wealth of designs and ideas is waiting for you in the field of floor coverings to help you furnish with warmth and unity. The best part is that many of the innovations can be done inexpensively—some floor coverings are designed as do-it-yourself projects. When making plans for your floors, be concerned about the needs of the various areas. In a place directly accessible to the outdoors as well as the kitchen you will require a floor covering that will withstand hard wear and resist stains and moisture. For the living room and bedroom you will want something with a feeling of warmth and softness. If you are fortunate enough to have beautiful hardwood floors, you may want to leave them bare or cover them only partially with an area rug.

Floor coverings can be classified in four categories: resilient flooring, rugs and carpeting, wood flooring and masonry flooring.

Resilient floorings The most popular of these types are: vinyl tiles, asbestos vinyl, asphalt, linoleum, vinyl-sealed cork and rubber tile. Certain floors, especially in solid colors, tend to look alike but feel differently underfoot. Ask to walk on a floor sample before buying. Quality depends on the color, design, ease of installation, durability and ease of care. If flooring is already installed in your new home, try to find out the identity of your inherited floor so you'll know what to expect of it and how to care for it.

LINOLEUM—comes in 6-foot-wide sheets, is relatively inexpensive, durable and needs little care except washing and waxing. It lacks the high luster of vinyl. By far the best and most durable is inlaid linoleum, which is installed by professionals and should be 3/32" in thickness. There are many patterns, some simulating brick or tile, some in chip designs. Embossed patterns will help conceal dents.

SHEET VINYL—comes in 6-foot-wide sheets and is more costly than linoleum. Some types are inlaid, offering a longer life; some have printed patterns coated with clear vinyl. Standard thickness is .0652" to .090".

PRINTED VINYL OR ROTOVINYL—a rotogravure-printed design on felt or asbestos backing, then protected by a clear film of vinyl. Comes in 6-foot widths with great decorative patterns but when the vinyl wears, so does the design. Relatively low in cost. Not good for heavy traffic areas.

ASBESTOS VINYL TILE—available in 9- or 12-inch square tiles with a thickness of 1/16". It's used a great deal below grade (in basements), wears well and is easily installed, especially with the new adhesive-back variety. It resists grease, is economical, but dents fairly easily. The design should penetrate 20% of the tile.

CUSHIONED VINYL—backing of a thick layer of foam on a heavy-duty surface, this type is very durable, quiet, easy to walk on and can be installed over an existing floor with a new fast-setting adhesive. It comes in 12-foot widths, thereby virtually eliminating seams.

POURED VINYL—a layer of polyurethane is poured over the existing floor and while it is still tacky, a layer of thin vinyl acetate chips is scattered over it. Coats of clear polyurethane top it until a satisfactory surface has been built up. Another type of poured vinyl starts with a base coat, then designs are made by pouring on another color. Both floorings are durable, stain-resistant once they are dry, and without seams. Professionals are needed for the pouring.

ASPHALT TILES—inexpensive tiles in 9-inch or 12-inch squares. They come in many designs, and you can install them yourself, but they are noisy.

RUBBER TILES—not seen very much, come in several tile sizes, are very quiet and comfortable to walk on.

Wood flooring Most wood floors are called "hardwood" because the woods used for them are almost always of that variety. Oak is used more than other woods, followed by walnut, maple, birch, cherry and even teak. The floors can be laid in several ways: in strips, in a parquet design or in planks (some with hand pegs in them). Light wood floors are sometimes stained to a dark walnut. If treated properly, wood floors become more beautiful over the years, much like antique furniture. They have to be sealed in some manner before waxing. For less care, many people prefer to finish their floors with a polyurethane coating which gives a high gloss without wax and withstands heavy traffic.

Masonry flooring These floors are a joy to maintain. They include: ceramic tile, mosaic tile, quarry tile, marble, terrazzo, slate and brick. Floors of this nature are expensive and are installed when the house is built. Since most of them are heavy, the sub-floor of the structure has to be unusually strong if they are to cover a wide area. Most of these floors will be noisy and may stain but they are long-lasting.

RUGS AND CARPETING

These soft floor coverings bring warmth to a room, reduce noise, cushion falls and unify through color, design and texture. In making the decision about what kind of carpeting or rug to get, you must consider quality, size, color, design, texture, fibers, construction and underpadding.

Quality Construction is the prime factor in judging the durability of the carpet. The density of the pile is the clue; the denser it is, the longer the wear because each fiber is bearing less weight. Judge the density by bending a corner of the carpet over your fingers—very little backing should be visible. Next, look at the depth of pile, combined with the density. A shag rug can have deep pile but if there isn't much of it, it won't wear well. Fiber will also determine durability (some are stronger than others). A high quality rug has a good strong backing, one that resists stretching, shrinking and buckling. Carpeting is classified for light, medium or heavy use by manufacturers: before making your selection, take into account where you are going to use it. It is best to get a better quality for wall-to-wall carpeting.

Size There are three sizes: wall-to-wall, room-size, and area or accent rugs. *Wall-to-wall* carpeting covers the whole room and is more or less permanently installed. It comes in broadloom widths (9, 12, 15 or 18 ft.), has to be cleaned on the floor and is often used in smaller or cut-up rooms to pull together a space. You can have it cut to the exact dimensions of the room and bound, instead of being tacked down, thus giving the same effect. This allows you to turn the carpet for even wear, but you can only do this if your room is regularly shaped. A *room-size* rug can be cut from broadloom carpeting or be a rug with a self-contained design. Several inches of floor are left to show around the edge of the rug. An *area* rug is designed to cover only a part of the floor to give accent. There is a wide range of colors and designs as well as cost. Beware of using too many in one room.

Color, pattern and texture All three can influence the design of carpeting. Color must be planned with the whole room taken into consideration. Light colors make a room appear larger and lighter but also show dirt more easily. Dark colors have the opposite result, but can give a warm effect to a cold-looking room. Although dark colors do not show dirt as much, they will show lint and threads. Ask about color fastness. *Texture,* the surface appearance of the pile, can create interesting effects with plush, tweed, shag, high-low loop, cut and uncut twist. Tight loops and dense-twist textures are best for heavy traffic areas. *Pattern* is the design created by color or texture. If the rug is to be the center of interest, you will want to choose a bold pattern.

Fibers Your selection of fiber content should depend on its appearance, the cost and how you want to use the rug. There are natural fibers (wool and cotton), there are synthetic fibers (nylon, acrylics and polyesters) and there are blends. Each has its advantages:

WOOL—still the classic; less expensive than 15 years ago but not cheap. It's mothproofed, resilient, wears well, resists soil, gives good coverage, can be woven or tufted and takes colors beautifully.

COTTON—wears well and takes colors well, but soils and crushes easily. It's used almost exclusively now for area rugs. Low to medium price range.

NYLON—the most widely used synthetic and fairly inexpensive, depending on quality and style. It comes in every kind of construction, woven and unwoven, takes hard wear, is easily cleaned and gives good coverage. Its one drawback is the production of static electricity. Some makers are now adding anti-static agents.

ACRYLIC—resembles wool with a thick appearance, is resilient, cleans well and resists soil. Medium to high in cost.

POLYESTER—resembles wool, cleans well, resists soil and is resilient. It's gaining popularity and looks well in long, tufted shag rugs and high pile carpets. It tends to flatten in heavy traffic areas. Medium to high in cost.

POLYPROPYLENE—also known as olefin or polyolefin—used as indoor-outdoor carpeting. Non-absorbent and stain-resistant, it resists abrasion and stands up under extreme heat and cold, sunlight, rain and snow. Low to medium in price.

RAYON AND ACETATE—tend to crush and soil easily. Like cotton, both are used more as area rugs.

OTHER FIBERS—hemp, rush and sisal are also used in rugs. They are low in cost and come in a variety of colors. Durability depends on closeness of the weave. Some rush and hemp rugs are left in their natural colors.

Construction Different carpet construction can alter the appearance of the rug, but good quality and durability can be produced in any of five methods: weaving, tufting, knitting, needlepunching and flocking.

WEAVING—the oldest method with pile yarns and backing interwoven in one operation. The weaves are Wilton, Axminster and velvet.

TUFTING—a more economical method in which a multiple-needle machine attaches tufts into a prefabricated backing. To hold the tufts in place a heavy latex coating is applied to the backing.

KNITTING—made on a knitting machine with pile yarns interlooped with backing yarns. The backing is coated with latex to secure the yarns.

NEEDLEPUNCHING—for indoor-outdoor carpets. Felting needles interlock fibers. The back is then coated with latex and other weather-resistant material. Indoor carpeting can have a foam backing.

FLOCKING—for indoor-outdoor carpeting. Chopped fibers are electrostatically charged, then embedded into an adhesive-coated backing.

Padding Some experts claim proper padding can reduce the wear and prolong the life of a carpet by 50 to 75%. The padding should be firm, but soft enough to act as a shock absorber. If it is too soft the carpet backing will stretch and break under the weight of furniture. Firm support and long wear can be expected from padding made of all-hair or a hair and jute blend. (A layer of foam is sometimes added.) This type of padding is better for wall-to-wall carpeting than for area rugs because it has a tendency to shed. Latex and foam rubber are widely used, giving firm support and long wear. Special area carpeting such as the kind sold for kitchen and bathroom use is cushion-backed and does not require a pad. Manufacturers predict that soon all carpeting will be sold with its own cushion backing.

WALL COVERINGS

Since walls serve as backdrops for the whole room, the way you treat them can influence the success of your decorating plan. Again, color, design and texture all play equally important parts in the treatment of walls. Points to check are: the condition of your walls, the ease with which the wall covering can be applied, and the cost. Paint and wallpaper head the list of most-used wall coverings, with paneling a close contender. Walls tiles are becoming more desirable as manufacturers develop better designs and easier ways to mount them. Some people even use lightweight rugs as wall coverings.

Paint A relatively inexpensive wall covering you can apply yourself in almost any color and one of three finishes: flat, semi-gloss and gloss. Ceilings and walls are painted in flat; semi-gloss and gloss are used for woodwork, kitchens and bathrooms because they wash clean readily. For unusual decorating effects, a high gloss paint is used. Before painting, mend cracks in the wall and see that the wall is dry and free of dust. Different types of paint include:

LATEX—a rubber-based paint (also known as water-based) that is used extensively because it is easy to apply, thins with water and is fast-drying to a rather flat finish. It's durable and washable after it is "cured" or set. Rollers and brushes can be cleaned with water.

CASEIN & RESIN—also know as whitewash. It comes in liquid or powder form to which water is added, covers well and is fast-drying but tends to chalk off easily and washes poorly.

ALKYD—an oil-based paint which is durable and washable but may take two coats to cover. It's difficult to remove stains and dirt from the surface. This comes in all three finishes.

GLOSS PAINT OR ENAMEL—is very durable and washable with a high gloss finish but difficult to apply smoothly without running.

87

Wallpaper For walls that have defects or for sheer design, wallpaper is an excellent solution to decorating problems. New vinyl wallpaper has been manufactured which is truly imaginative, washable, durable, and you can actually hang it yourself. The cost of wallpaper depends on the type, quality, design and finish that you buy. Just be sure your walls are prepared according to manufacturers' instructions before hanging. Wallpapers available are:

PAPER-BACK VINYL—wallpaper with a coating of vinyl plastic; washable but fragile.

CLOTH VINYL—vinyl laminated to lightweight cloth with the design printed right on the fabric. This is scrubbable.

HEAVY-DUTY VINYL—design is printed on fabric also, but this type is thicker than cloth vinyl and designed for concentrated-wear places.

PREPASTED WALLPAPER—can have a coating (but not always) to act as a "wipe off" finish. To hang, dip in water to activate the chemical paste on the back.

SELF-ADHESIVE PLASTIC—paper must be peeled from back to reveal adhesive backing. There are excellent designs but this can be expensive.

Tiles There are many squares and tiles designed for walls, both for limited areas as well as for an all-over effect. The method by which they are installed varies with the product.

METAL TILES—come in tones of copper, gold, stainless steel and aluminum. Special adhesive tabs are used to mount them. These may be difficult to take off.

MIRROR SQUARES—used often as decorating accents in bathrooms, powder rooms or foyers. They come in plain glass or antiqued with gold veins or flecks crossing their surface. They can have self-sticking backs or require adhesive tapes to press the tiles against.

CORK SQUARES—used extensively although steam and grease may harm them. A knife or razor blade will cut them to fit.

88

Some squares have an adhesive back; others require linoleum paste for mounting.

SELF-ADHESIVE PLASTIC PANELS OR SQUARES—sections in 12-inch squares made of styrene or vinyl which are self-sticking and can be cut with scissors. Some unstick where there is much moisture in the air (bathrooms and kitchens). These panels are made to simulate woods, marble, 3-dimensional wood carving, brick, stone, mosaic and ceramic tiles.

Wood paneling New paneling materials have lowered the cost of a once expensive wall covering. Your husband can even install some types himself. Woods traditionally used for paneling are walnut, pine, mahogany, ash, cypress, maple, redwood, gum, oak and birch. Besides the solid wood there is also plywood and hardboard or chipboard.

SOLID WOOD PANELING—is made of solid pieces of wood 6 to 12 inches wide. It can be unfinished or stained, oiled or waxed. Price depends on the kind of wood you buy.

PLYWOOD PANELING—is made of several layers of wood with a top layer of veneer laminated together by adhesives. Finishes can be varnished or lacquered and also made flame-resistant. The surface comes plain or rough, V-grooved or striated. The cost depends on the type of wood you get. Panels run about 4 feet in width.

HARDBOARD PANELING—known also as chipboard, in which fibers made from wood chips are pressed together into panels about ¼ inch thick and 4 to 5 feet in width. The paneling can be plain or finished with the characteristic markings of the wood.

WINDOWS

As you know, the primary function of a window is to let in light and air when required; its secondary function is to be harmonious with the room and offer privacy from the outside world. Windows can be fun to work with in decorating—they can also present problems unique only to them. One room may possess several windows of unequal width, placed so they give no balance whatsoever. Another room may feature a whole row of windows overlooking an undesirable area. There are, however, a host of fabrics and many types of shades and hardware to treat your windows well and help you to overcome difficult problems. You can even buy modular arches made of fiberglass with telescoping columns to unify several windows. Before buying any window dressings know the exact measurements, from rod to sill, from side to side. Decide how long you want curtains or draperies—to the window sill, to the apron or to the floor. The kind of window treatment you give to a room depends on its furnishing and flavor—whether you decide on draperies, curtains, shades or a combination of several of them.

Curtains Usually these are regarded as window hangings which are transparent or translucent, giving some privacy and at the same time letting in light. Window curtains can be ruffled and crisscrossed with tie-backs or hung straight to form "glass" curtains. "Café" curtains are another type, affording more privacy because they hang with rings or clips from a rod extended across the center of the window. They are made from translucent or opaque fabric and can be single or double-decked.

Fibers found most often in curtains are:

POLYESTER—as a fiber this synthetic has excellent strength, high resistance to heat and sunlight and good abrasion resistance. The fiber is often blended with cotton, rayon, silk or acetate for a variety of textures in such fabric types as batiste, ninon, marquisette and organdy. For a shimmery appearance, polyester is combined with antron nylon.

FIBER GLASS—a fiber that does not deteriorate from sunlight or heat, keeps its shape, does not shrink and does not wrinkle. It does, however, have low resistance to abrasion. All fiber glass curtains must be hand-washed or washed by machine on a delicate cycle setting and drip dried. Kinds of fabrics made of this fiber are knits, sheer bouclés, textured weaves, batiste, marquisette, prints and flocked patterns. Fiber glass can be irritating and abrasive to your hands with excessive handling. Think twice about making your own curtains from fabric made of this fiber.

COTTON—in curtains it's best used in shady windows since prolonged exposure to sunlight and heat can weaken the fabric.

The advantages are: it has good strength, resists abrasion, can be either machine or hand-washable. Most fabric made from cotton is treated for shrinkage control (see label) along with crease resistance. Popular types include organdy, batiste and lace along with any opaque printed cotton used for café curtains. Daring brides, with an eye for economy and a flair for decorating, use sheets as curtains, either draping a room with them from floor to ceiling or cutting them short.

Draperies Nearly always, draperies are considered heavier than curtains and are quite often lined. Some are even insulated to keep out extreme temperatures. Their main functions are to shade for privacy and to enhance the beauty of the room either by color, line or design. Draperies can hang to any length and can cover a whole wall or only one window. Some are designed to remain stationary on either side of a window with perhaps a valance unifying them across the top. Others are hung from ceiling traverse rods and can be closed by means of a cord on one side. As a rule, draperies are more expensive than curtains, but it depends on the fabric used and whether they are custom-made, ready-made or homemade. Read the label for fiber content; be sure of a firm weave for the least amount of sagging and check color-fastness. Fabrics suitable for draperies include brocades, burlap, chintz, crewel embroidery, cretonne, faille, damask, gabardine, glass fabrics, glosheen, piqué, pongee, poplin, rep, taffeta, tapestry, grosgrain, velvet and corduroy.

Shades, shutters and blinds Professional decorators use shades and shutters with or without curtains to give windows unique and attractive effects. With such a variety available, they may help you solve a knotty window problem. A sampling of what you can find in this category includes:

VENETIAN BLINDS—long-time favorites made of horizontal wooden or metal slats held together with tapes. They adjust for light control by means of cords, hang from a headbox. Marco Polo is said to have brought them back to Venice from China.

BAMBOO BLINDS—made of bamboo slats held together by periodic rows of stitching. The horizontally installed blinds roll up to a headbox by means of a cord. Vertical slats can be hung from rods as draperies.

91

ROLLER SHADES—can come in light or opaque materials. Fabric can be laminated to the shades so that they can take the place of curtains. Some designs are treated with vinyl for easy cleaning. Decorative tapes are occasionally sewed to the edges of plain shades for effect.

AUSTRIAN SHADES—usually made of a treated fabric, they fall from the top of the window, gather in swags when raised by means of vertical tapes placed at intervals.

ROMAN SHADES—similar to Austrian shades but they gather up in straight folds when raised rather than in swags. Tapes can have a design, making a striped effect.

LOUVERED SHUTTERS—also called French shutters, they are attached to the inside of the window with hinges. Louvered sections are tiltable either up or down as in Venetian blinds. Some are made in sections which also fold back on themselves so you can open them only partially, if desired. These can be bought unfinished so you can stain or paint them yourself.

LOUVERED SHADES—wide metal slats which run vertically and adjust in the same way as Venetian blinds.

Just as there are many treatments for windows so there are many types of windows:

Casement—hinged windows that open outward from the center.

Cathedral—high, long windows having slanting frames.

Clerestory—small windows high up, often found in living rooms with vaulted ceilings.

Dormer—windows that jut out from the roof.

Jalousie—made up of glass slats which tilt open in unison by means of a crank.

French—full-length windows which open as doors (which they are also called).

Picture—wide windows, sometimes floor to ceiling and sometimes with side sections, found in contemporary or remodeled homes.

Ranch—wide windows, shorter and higher than usual, used in contemporary houses to allow light and wall space but give privacy. These often slide sideways to open.

Sash—windows which open from bottom or top.

SILVER AND RELATIONS

Gleaming silverware is considered by many to be the epitome of elegance and gracious living. Eating and serving utensils such as knives, forks and spoons are called "flatware." The term "hollow ware" refers to pieces such as bowls, tea sets, pitchers, candlesticks and vases. While "sterling" is much in demand, silverplate is very close behind, with stainless steel winning a host of new devotees who like its practicality and contemporary look. Your preference depends on your taste and budget, but whatever it is, try to buy at least a table setting at a time when acquiring your flatware.

Sterling silver A solid metal which must consist of 92½ % silver that is alloyed with another metal (usually copper) for strength and wear. Good sterling will last for generations.

Silverplate A layer of pure silver is electroplated onto a base metal. The quality depends on how much silver is used on what base metal. A higher-priced product from a reputable manufacturer almost always signifies quality and long wear. If you've inherited a piece of hollow ware that looks "patchy" where the silver has come off, have it replated instead of throwing it out.

Goldplate A layer of gold is electroplated onto a base metal, very much the same way as silverplating. Goldplated flatware has gained in popularity recently.

Stainless steel Like sterling this is a solid metal made of an iron-chromium alloy which is almost completely stainproof, will not tarnish, wears well and is easily cleaned. In flatware, the weight is the key to quality. Lightweight is easily bendable and cheaper while heavyweight is more rigid, often highly buffed and scratch-resistant. Stainless steel serving dishes are much in demand, well designed, easy to care for and ovenproof.

CHINA

Since entertaining at home has become increasingly informal, especially for the newly wedded set, it is becoming less important to have a complete set of matching china. Indeed, many brides like the look of mixing colors, teaming plain with pattern or using glass or silver with china. If your budget is strained, buy the "good" dinnerware only as you can afford it. Make certain the pattern you choose is "open stock." This means the store can supply individual pieces rather than only in sets. The salesperson can probably tell you, too, if the pattern will be available for a period of time. The word "china" is often used to designate dinnerware in general—technically it is only part of the scene.

China or porcelain Made from fine clays and a glaze that fuse at high temperatures. This firing results in a fine translucent, delicate quality. *Bone china* is whiter and derives its name from the addition of ground animal bone to the clay. Fine china is nonporous and highly resistant to chipping and cracking. High quality china should have no pinholes, dark specks or splotches on the back. The glaze should be smooth with no waviness in it.

Earthenware Made of coarser clays, it is more porous than china and chips more easily. It can range from a fine, hard quality with a strong body to a soft-bodied, heavier and thicker product which is known as **pottery.**

Melamine A smooth, hard substance that makes very light-weight and almost break-proof dishes. Some of this dinnerware is very well designed, with the appearance of china. Avoid using sharp knives—they may score the plates.

GLASSWARE

Glassware of good quality should be clear and free of flaws. Some bubbles may be present but any more than a few denote poorer quality. The best way to examine glass is to hold a piece to the light, check its clarity and tap it to see if it rings. In buying stemware examine the base, stem and bowl to see that all are joined firmly. The stem should flare rather than indent at these junctions for less possibility of breakage. Be sure a decoration or engraving isn't used to camouflage a flaw. Glass types include:

Crystal and lead crystal Lead oxide is added to glass to give it brilliance and produce the "ring" when tapped.

Cut glass All-over designs are cut into the glass. The best is done by hand by holding the glass against small abrasive wheels.

Milk glass The opaque, milky appearance is achieved by adding tin oxide or fluorspar to the glass. Sometimes a tint is used.

94

Etched glass The glass is dipped in acid with the design area uncovered while the area to be left plain is covered with a wax coating.

Engraved glass Very much like cut glass but the design is more delicate and less deep. The best quality pieces are done by hand.

Crackled glass When the glass is hot it is plunged into cold water to give the cracked effect.

Heat-resistant glass The addition of a little boric oxide to glass makes it resistant to high temperatures. Used for ovenware.

HOUSEHOLD LINENS

Included in this section are: sheets, pillows, pillowcases, blankets, towels and table linens. Because so many of these items are used regularly and some laundered often, it is an economy to purchase a better grade for durability. The difference in price between a poor grade and a good grade can be small, but the difference in wearability can be large.

Sheets and pillowcases Once upon a time sheets were sheets—they were white and all you had to consider was the size and quality. Not anymore! They now abound in colors and designs, enough to make your head spin with decorating ideas. Curb the buying impulse, though, until you know what you are getting.

Types of sheets and pillowcases

PERCALE—fine combed cotton yarn is woven closely with a smooth soft feeling almost like firm silk. Combed yarn is smoother because short fibers have been eliminated leaving only the long, finer, more lustrous ones. The thread count can be 180 or 200 (meaning the number of threads woven per square inch). Percale is light in weight, easy to launder, strong and durable and more expensive than muslin.

MUSLIN—carded cotton yarn is woven more loosely than percale, heavier in weight with a coarser feeling. Carded yarn is coarser than combed yarn because the fibers have been straightened only and the short left in with the long ones. Muslin sheets are less expensive but are strong and long wearing. Three thread counts are available: 128, 134 and 140.

95

NO-IRON—in percales, combed cotton is blended with a polyester in either a 180- or 200-thread count. Muslins are a combination of carded cotton with polyester in a 128-thread count. The no-irons are more expensive than pure cotton but soft and smooth with quick-drying and no-ironing features.

Size of sheets and pillowcases

If you do not know the exact measurement of your mattress, get out the tape measure and record both the width and length. Size is particularly important in buying fitted sheets. Innerspring mattresses are 6 inches thick while foam mattresses measure 4 to 6 inches in thickness. To calculate the size of flat sheets you need: 10 inches to tuck under the foot; 8 inches to turn back for blanket protection and 13½ inches for overhang on either side. *Sheet sizes are given before hemming* so subtract 6 inches from the length. Note how much shrinkage is allowed for. Pillowcases also come in different sizes, and the length given is before hemming. To calculate the finished length, subtract 3 to 4 inches from the given length. Know the circumference of your pillows so you can buy the size of pillowcase which is 2 inches larger.

Bed size	Fitted sheet for innerspring mattress	Flat sheet in cotton	No-iron flat sheet
Twin	39″ x 75″	72″ x 108″	72″ x 104″
Twin Extra Long	39″ x 80″	72″ x 120″	72″ x 115″
Double	54″ x 76″	81″ x 108″	81″ x 104″
Double, Extra Long	54″ x 80″	81″ x 108″	81″ x 104″
Queen	60″ x 80″	90″ x 120″	90″ x 115″
California King	72″ x 84″	108″ x 120″	108″ x 115″
King	75″ x 80″	108″ x 120″	108″ x 115″
King, Extra Long	78″ x 84″	108″ x 120″	108″ x 115″

Pillows The quality, comfort and durability of a pillow depends on its filling. A good quality pillow is very often worth the extra cash—it will last longer. Check the pillow for weight, see if the filling shifts and note the filling contents on the label.

BATTING—polyester or acrylic fibers make up a non-allergenic, mothproof filling which is lightweight and resilient. It is better as one whole piece rather than in loose fibers or pieces which have a tendency to lump when used.

FEATHERS—goose feathers are excellent as a fill, and duck feathers are almost as good. Chicken and turkey feathers have to be artificially curled and tend to mat when crushed down.

DOWN—this is the most expensive and the best filling. Down is the soft, fluffy undercoating of a goose or duck. It is combined with soft feathers to give the pillow varying degrees of softness.

FOAM—made of latex rubber or a polyurethane, this filling is non-allergenic and very buoyant. Sometimes it is shredded, but the solid form is preferable.

The covering of a pillow must be closely woven ticking or twill so the feathers and/or down cannot penetrate through the weave. If an acetate or nylon covering is used it must be of a heavy weight.

Blankets Although blankets are now made from many different fibers and blends, the ones which are soft and fluffy are apt to give the most warmth. Those woven with high nap keep the cold air out, the body heat in. The bindings should be deep, and sewn so the stitches catch on either side, and of good quality silk, rayon or acetate.

ALL-WOOL BLANKETS—are very warm, stay resilient for years with proper care. They now have finishes to make them mothproof and machine-washable. Read the label.

RAYON BLANKETS—are less expensive but do not have the warmth of wool, tend to mat and shed when washed. For these reasons rayon is usually blended with another fiber.

ACRYLICS—blankets made from these synthetics are quite warm, light in weight, easy to care for and machine-washable. They are mothproof, non-allergenic and less expensive but do tend to pill (form small surface balls) unless specially treated. Often acrylic fibers are blended with wool for added warmth.

COTTON—lightweight blankets with little nap, usually considered summer coverings where not too much warmth is needed. They are easy to care for, washable and mothproof.

ELECTRIC—warmth is generated from the electric wires in the blankets. A thermostatic control can be set to the desired temperature (some double blankets have dual controls), and it will not vary, no matter how cold the room is. Read instructions on the care of these blankets very carefully and be sure they bear an Underwriters' Laboratory seal to confirm safe use.

THERMAL—lightweight blankets of any fiber but woven with air pockets which retain a great deal of warmth.

Towels No longer is terrycloth tame and subdued—colors are bold and authoritative with all sorts of designs. Bath towels even come in different sizes and shapes—some are called sheets. They are soft and velvety or firm and crisp. And they come in a wide range of prices and quality, too. Since towels must bear the strain of friction when you are using them and the twisting and rubbing of washing, they must be durable and absorbent at the same time. The *ground* or *underweave* is the towel's backbone, the part that really does the wearing. It is from this weave that a third yarn produces the loops on each side to make the surface pile. This underweave can be seen near the hem or on the side border and it should be closely woven and uniform. Loops contribute to absorbency and so the more loops the better. Terry with uncut loops is called *plain*. On some towels the loops are brushed and cut to create a velvet surface—called *sheared terry*. Towels with a woven design are known as *jacquard* since they are woven on that kind of a loom. When there is more underweave than loops, the rate of absorbency decreases. If the ends of the towel are fringed, they should be thick and even.

Although you and your husband will probably prefer face towels made of terry, you'll undoubtedly want a supply of fine lawn or linen guest towels, at least for entertaining. Excellent designs and manufacturing techniques are making paper towels very appealing as disposable fingertip towels.

Table linens To set a beautiful table with your best silver and china there is nothing to match a fine white linen tablecloth with linen napkins. Linen now comes blended with synthetics to give it added durability as well as easier care. You can also get wash-and-wear tablecloths which simulate the finest linen without the ironing problems. Place mats are made in a wide variety of materials, many in plastic which appears to be cloth. Even paper napkins are being made in dinner size with the look of linen. You can set a splendid table with color and design almost any way you want with all of the great table coverings available. Remember to protect your table properly from hot dishes—with tablecloths use a pad or a "silence cloth" (which can be just heavy cotton flannel). Make use of trivets or cork pads for hot casseroles if you are using place mats.

CHECK LISTS

Here are check lists of what you may require in the categories given. They serve only as guides to what you need for entertaining. As in all of home furnishings what you really find necessary is up to you, your budget and your style of living.

Silver Flatware

8 to 12 dinner knives   8 to 12 coffee spoons
8 to 12 dinner forks   8 to 12 butter spreaders
16 to 24 teaspoons   8 to 12 dessert spoons
8 to 12 soup spoons   8 to 12 salad forks

1 salad set (optional)
8 to 12 ice teaspoons
3 serving spoons
1 cold meat fork
1 gravy ladle
1 soup ladle
1 sugar spoon

China

8 to 12 soup plates   8 to 12 cups & saucers   1 gravy boat
8 to 12 salad plates   1 large meat platter   1 sugar & creamer
8 to 12 dinner plates   1 small meat platter   8 to 12 demi-tasses
8 to 12 butter plates   3 vegetable dishes
8 to 12 dessert plates

Glassware

8 to 12 water tumblers   8 to 12 cocktail glasses
8 to 12 water goblets   8 to 12 highball glasses
8 to 12 fruit juice glasses   8 to 12 old-fashioned glasses
8 to 12 sherbet glasses   8 to 12 all-purpose wine glasses
8 to 12 liqueur glasses

Bedding

6 sheets per bed   1 to 2 bedspreads per bed
3 pillow cases per pillow   2 mattress pads per bed
                At least 2 blankets per bed
                    or 1 electric blanket per bed
                1 comforter per bed
                1 summer weight blanket per bed

Bathroom Linens

1 doz. bath towels   2 bathroom rugs
1 doz. terry hand towels   1 shower curtain
1 doz. washcloths   1 doz. guest towels
2 bath mats   Paper fingertip towels

Table Linens

1 formal white tablecloth   2 to 3 sets cloth placemats
1 doz. formal white linen napkins   Plastic placemats
1 doz. luncheon napkins   Luncheon cloths
1 to 3 bridge sets   Hot pads for table

HOW TO BE INFORMED

There are many sources where you can obtain information to help you know to buy and what to buy. Here are but a few of them:

Service Articles

Magazines and newspapers have them in every issue, offering valuable information on new products and their performances, ideas on how to decorate and places to find specific articles.

Advertisements in Magazines and Newspapers

Manufacturers or distributors inform you about their products, their price, their merits and their guarantees. Individual stores advertise various items by brand names and inform you of upcoming sales.

Consumer Publications

Available by subscription or at your local library, these magazines often rate products which they have thoroughly tested according to their own standards.

Organizations

Many trade and civic associations, along with government agencies, are set up to help inform the consumer. For local ones, consult your telephone book. To name a few of them:

Chamber of Commerce	Extension Service
Board of Trade	Manufacturing associations
Better Business Bureau	Retail associations
Farm Bureau	U.S. Government agencies

Information Directly on the Product

Labels tell you a great deal. Read warranties and guarantees carefully. Some products bear *seals of approval* which mean that they have been tested and meet the requirements of the organization issuing the seal.

5
How to Keep House
with Ease

THE BASIS of running a home smoothly and efficiently is good planning. To establish an orderly atmosphere in the home so a marriage can flourish, it is necessary to see that both of you are well fed, properly clothed and comfortable. In order to create this desirable atmosphere the successful homemaker is consistent, uses a maximum of know-how with a minimum of wasted effort. You probably won't become a model housekeeper overnight—few brides do! But the right state of mind, the application of a few sound principles and practice will help to increase your skills.

Housekeeping may seem a little overwhelming at first. Until you get the hang of it, have a written schedule, listing the household tasks which must be done. A good plan will be geared to suit your temperament, your way of life, and will take into account other activities. Some brides set up unrealistic standards which are impossible to meet. What is the good of having the cleanest, shiniest apartment in the building if you are too tired to enjoy it? The well-organized homemaker explores possible shortcuts, takes advantage of labor-saving devices, tries out new products, treats housekeeping as a job to be done in the shortest possible time. Even with a career outside of the home, plus housekeeping duties, allow time for personal grooming and relaxation.

The schedule you devise is individually yours, designed to fit the demands of your household. How much you have to clean depends on what kind of furnishings you have. A white rug is going to demand much more attention than a gray one. Even if you have a so-called "maintenance-free" home there are certain inescapable tasks which must be done. Analyze what these jobs are—then divide them into daily, weekly and change-of-season routines. Try to stick with the schedule, but don't be inflexible. If the plan isn't working, change it. Experiment with other methods until you arrive at the routine which is right for you and your husband. After arriving at a workable plan, use it consistently. Stick to the plan—try not to neglect daily and weekly chores. The prudent housekeeper knows it's more difficult to clean anything that is overly soiled. When cleaning, don't be waylaid by a whole other set of chores you didn't plan to do. And when finished with the work, quit; don't overextend yourself.

Here is an example of how to set up a household schedule.

DAILY

Set your house in order before going to bed or before leaving in the morning. Waking up or coming home to a tidy house can help sweeten your disposition. Surface cleaning daily will speed the more thorough, weekly cleaning. Pick up every room, empty ashtrays and the garbage. Prepare, serve and clean up after meals. Make the beds. Sweep and dustmop at least every other day. Have pencil and paper handy to jot down market necessities as well as errands that must be done.

WEEKLY

Some of you will find it easier to do one weekly job per day so no one day becomes overburdened. Others will find it more practical or will prefer to devote only one day in a massive effort to perform all the weekly tasks. Clean the house thoroughly—pick up, dust,

103

carpet sweep or vacuum. Change sheets and towels. Sort laundry and dry cleaning and deliver. Wash and iron. Check for possible shoe repair. Plan weekly menus and do heavy supermarketing. (Lack of storage space may make midweek shopping for meat, vegetables and fresh fruits essential.) Store marketed supplies. Each week try to fit in a once-in-a-while job such as silver polishing or oven cleaning. Allow time for personal grooming.

PERIODICALLY

Once or twice a year you have to shift gears for seasonal changes. Put clothes and blankets in or take out of mothballs. Clean "in depth"—walls, woodwork, Venetian blinds, curtains and draperies. Shampoo rugs or have them cleaned professionally. If you have slipcovers, make seasonal changes. Clean and reorganize closets, reline shelves and drawers. Sort clothes and accessories for tossing out or donating to charity. If possible, switch curtains and turn rugs for more even wear. Try new furniture arrangements. Redecorate or have repair work done.

SPECIAL

These jobs may occur seasonally or weekly. Include here holiday and entertaining preparations and shopping; correspondence and record-keeping; sewing and/or mending; special cooking, perhaps for freezing; hobbies, and even gardening.

Housekeeping can be simplified for you by applying a few basic rules of neatness and order. Count your blessings if your husband has well-established and orderly habits. To ease housework:

1. Have a place for everything. This may take some experimenting and shifting until you arrive at the right place for each thing. If there isn't enough storage space, make room with the addition of shelves or modular units.
2. After using, put things away. When a book is finished, return it to the shelf. After reading the newspaper, fold it. Store the mending to be done, in one location, and after completing this task stow the mended articles where they belong.
3. Unless you are absolutely exhausted, hang up the clothes

after wearing. This will cut down on pressing bills and add life to the garment. Better yet, brush woolen garments, too.

4. Don't leave dirty dishes from one meal to the next unless they have been rinsed to remove the debris. Even if you have a dishwasher, rinse before loading if you aren't going to run it immediately.

5. Wipe your feet before entering the house. Leave the outdoor grime or moisture on the doormat, not on your rugs.

6. Arrange furniture so it doesn't have to be moved constantly from one area to another. See that an adequate reading light is placed beside a comfortable chair so it need not be moved. Group furniture in natural conversational units.

7. Leave the bathroom neat. Hang towels straight so they will dry quickly. Place the bathmat on the side of the tub or rack to dry. If water has escaped from around the shower curtain, blot up the excess on the floor so it can't be tracked. Do not comb your hair over the sink where loose hair can fall into it.

8. Avoid having excess bric-a-brac on display. Too many pieces give a cluttered look and serve as dust collectors.

9. Wear clothes appropriate to the job. If you are cleaning, wear an outfit that is washable or expendable. When cooking, protect a good dress with an apron.

THE RIGHT TOOLS

Good tools and cleaning agents are essential to good, efficient housekeeping. Every year products are being developed to lessen the drudgery of housecleaning. Many of the cleaners and waxes are excellent, and since they are relatively inexpensive they are worth a try. Browse around in your supermarket and hardware store and see what is available. Read the labels carefully for directions and contents. Heavier equipment, such as vacuum cleaners, electric brooms, floor polishers and rug shampooers, represent a bigger outlay of cash, and their merits are to be carefully considered before buying. Ask for a demonstration so you can evaluate the performance of a tool. Also keep in mind that many stores rent floor polishers and rug shampooers.

Check this list of essential tools and supplies you should have to clean even the smallest apartment:

TOOLS

broom	wet mop
dust mop	pail
whisk broom	toilet bowl brush
dustpan	sponge
lint-free dustcloth	

SUPPLIES

soap	toilet bowl cleaner
heavy-duty detergent	metal cleaner
ammonia	floor wax
scouring powder	furniture polish or wax
mothballs	disinfectant
silver polish	drain pipe cleaner

Tools and supplies you can use in addition to essentials if the budget allows:

TOOLS

vacuum cleaner and attachments	rubber gloves
electric broom	step stool or ladder
floor scrubber and polisher	brushes for Venetian blinds, walls
rug shampooer	squeegee for mirrors and windows
carpet sweeper	

SUPPLIES

rug cleaner	dishwashing detergent
spot remover	soap-filled scouring pads
oven cleaner	upholstery cleaner
wood paneling cleaner	saddle soap
aerosol dusting spray	glass cleaner
tile cleaner	counter-top cleaner

There are several types of vacuum cleaners and many reliable brands from which to choose. The type you select can be influenced by the furnishings you have chosen. A good vacuum cleaner, along with its attachments, can serve as broom, dust mop, upholstery brush and rug cleaner.

VACUUM CLEANER

UPRIGHT

Very effective for rugs and carpets. It's a heavy-duty machine which uses suction with a sweeping action from power-driven brushes. In some models agitation is also used. Usually attachments come with the upright, but they are not too effective (by comparison with other types) and can be clumsy to handle.

TANK-TYPE OR CANISTER

A straight suction vacuum cleaner with a powerful motor which is lightweight and moves easily on wheels. The attachments are excellent for cleaning floors, vacuuming rugs and upholstery as well as brushing walls and draperies.

HAND CLEANER

A small, lightweight vacuum either held by hand or hung from an over-the-shoulder strap. It's suitable for light cleaning of mattresses, stairs, upholstery, blinds and automobile interiors. It may or may not have attachments.

ELECTRIC BROOM

A lightweight upright designed to clean bare floors and light carpets. Some clean by suction while others have power-driven brushes. Attachments may be included. This easy-to-handle machine is excellent for quick daily cleaning and takes up little storage space.

BUILT-IN CENTRAL SYSTEM

A central motor and dirt container are permanently installed with plug-in hose connections located at various points about the house.

Another valuable tool for cleaning is the *floor polisher* which has more ability than its name implies. It has motor-driven revolving brushes with attachments to scrub floors, wax and polish them to a high shine. It can be also used as a buffer between waxings. A

107

dispenser holds the wax or cleaning agent with a shield to prevent splashing.

Tools must be cared for and kept clean. The head of a dust mop should be shaken free of dust and lint after using. Once in a while, remove the head and wash it. A wet mop, sponge or fiber, must be rinsed as clean as possible after mopping. See that the dirt container in your vacuum cleaner is not overloaded; it will reduce the efficiency of the cleaner. The belt that drives the brushes on an upright must be tight and in good condition. When the vacuum seems to have very little suction see if the hose is clogged. An obstruction can be readily removed by passing a broom handle through the hose. Avoid picking up sharp items such as pins and nails which can damage the working parts of the vacuum. Check the cords for possible fraying. Read the manufacturer's instructions carefully on care, lubrication and possible factory servicing.

HOW TO CLEAN A ROOM

DAILY

Air the room well—open draperies, push back curtains and open windows (unless you live in a centrally air-conditioned apartment). Avoid strong cross drafts, though.

Pick up the room, fold newspapers, shelve books and records, hang up any clothes, empty ashtrays and wastebaskets.

Dust surfaces at least twice a week.

Plump up pillows and cushions.

Change water for fresh flowers, remove faded ones.

Dustmop and carpet-sweep or use the vacuum lightly on the floors.

Close the windows, adjust draperies and curtains.

Check to see if the room is in order.

WEEKLY

Air the room as you do daily and pick up.

Have a tray to carry portable items to the kitchen for care— anything that needs polishing, washing, cleaning or watering. This will include ashtrays, small bric-a-brac that has become tarnished, vases of flowers and plants which must be groomed.

To clean thoroughly, start from the top and work down. With small brush attachment vacuum cornices or valances, draperies, tops of curtains, pictures, blinds and high moldings. Look for cobwebs in the corners. As you proceed downward with the brush, vacuum window frames, lampshades and lamp bowls where dead moths can accumulate.

Dust shelves, starting from the top. Books, records and bric-a-brac should be dusted by hand.

In lieu of a vacuum cleaner, use a brush or wrap a clean cloth around the broom, securing it with a pin, and gently brush to dust high places.

Brush or vacuum upholstery, being sure to remove any dust or lint under unattached cushions.

Dust the furniture with either a treated cloth or a clean lint-free one. A great aid to dusting is a spray used on your dustcloth to cut down the static electricity, thus removing all of the dust. Use furniture polish if necessary.

Dust baseboards.

Wash and polish mirrors, glass tops and pictures with glass.

Wipe switch plates and edges of doors for fingermarks.

Dust mop or vacuum the bare floor. Vacuum rugs.

Return items from kitchen after cleaning them.

Apply floor wax if necessary.

Check to see that the room is in order, the pictures are straight, the furniture is aligned and all is bright and shining.

Record on your shopping list any supplies running low.

HOW TO CLEAN A BEDROOM

DAILY

Air the room.

Throw back the sheets and blankets to the foot of the bed. (At night the bedspread is folded back to the foot or taken off completely.)

Pick up all clothes, shoes and other odds and ends. Hang clothes so the shoulder seams are parallel to the hanger, thus avoiding unnecessary sagging.

Put dirty clothes in the hamper.

After thorough airing, make the bed.

All drawers and closet doors should be closed.

Dustmop, especially under the bed where woolly bits of lint hide.

WEEKLY

Air the room.

Strip the bed of sheets and blankets.

Pick up. Examine clothes for possible dry cleaning and mending. (Check your husband's shirts for missing buttons.)

Remove mattress pad and vacuum or brush it to get rid of dust and lint. Turn the mattress once a month. Occasionally, wash the mattress pad.

Using clean sheets, make the bed. If you make "hospital corners" to tuck in the sheets and light blankets at the foot of the bed there is less chance of a restless sleeper pulling out the covers.

Replace bedspread.

Vacuum, dust and clean as you would any other room.

HOW TO CLEAN A BATHROOM

DAILY

Air the room.

Straighten towels.

Replace dirty towels with clean ones if needed. If soiled ones are wet, let them dry before putting them in the laundry hamper.

Blot up any excess water which may be on the floor. Put bath mat on side of the tub.

Wipe the mirror and the basin.

Empty the wastebasket.

Clean the tub with scouring powder.

Close the shower curtains and straighten so they can dry.

Check the soap dishes to see if new bars are needed.

WEEKLY

Replenish with a clean supply of towels.

Pour toilet bowl cleaner into toilet, following instructions on its use. Clean with a bowl brush. Clean the toilet seat on both sides.

Wash the bathtub thoroughly and, using tile cleaner or scouring powder and a brush, clean the tiles around the tub.

Make sure the shower head is not clogged if you have an old model.

Check the drain for hair and other debris that can be removed. If the drain seems slow, use a drain pipe cleaner to unplug it.

Check the medicine chest for supplies (toothpaste, aspirin and toothbrushes) which might need replenishing.

Clean the sink and soap dish. Polish the metal fixtures.

Vacuum or shake the rug.

Scrub the floor. If it is not tile, wax when necessary.

HOW TO CLEAN A KITCHEN

DAILY

Air and straighten the kitchen as you do any other room.

While preparing meals wash the utensils and mixing bowls as you go. Only the pots and pans emptied just before the meal should be dirty. They are easier to clean if they are left soaking while you are eating.

Wash the dishes and cooking equipment. For those with a dishwasher, rinse and stack in the machine if you are not going to run it immediately.

Once the oven has been used, wipe out the inside (when cool) with paper toweling. This prevents a grease buildup. If you have broiled food, drain away any grease and wash the rack and drip pan of the broiler.

Check the refrigerator for possible leftovers you may have forgotten, as well as stale or spoiled food to be discarded.

Wipe all counter and cabinet surfaces.

Clean the sink, checking the drain for debris that must be removed.

Empty the garbage.

Sweep the floor.

Empty the dishwasher and store the contents.

Change dish towels several times a week.

Consult your menu plan for the next day's meals.

111

WEEKLY

Clean the stove. (Daily care will help lighten this weekly chore.)

Clean the wall area around the stove with a solution of heavy-duty detergent and water to remove the grease.

Empty crumbs from the tray under the toaster.

Wash away the fingerprints from the woodwork and kitchen cabinets.

Use the counter-top cleaner to wax surfaces.

Defrost the refrigerator and clean the inside. If yours is frost-free, wash out the inside. Discard any spoiled or stale food.

Wash out and air the bread box and garbage pail.

Clean the sink and splashboard. If the drain is slow use a drain cleaner.

Dust or damp-wipe any pots, pans and utensils you may have hanging. Since heat rises, the normal greasy fumes from cooking can leave a deposit on hanging equipment.

Polish copper and brass cookware.

Clean the kitchen floor. Wax it as the condition of the floor covering demands.

SEASONAL CLEANING

Curtains, draperies, slipcovers, bedspreads and blankets should be washed or dry-cleaned. If you have two sets for seasonal changes, store one set after cleaning.

Change clothes with seasons, being sure everything is clean before storing. Moth-proof all articles containing wool during the summer months. Other out-of-season clothes should be stored in garment bags to shield them from dust. If storage space is at a premium in your home, ask the dry cleaner to store winter items for you. It's worth the small extra charge.

Wash all the windows, inside and outside, if you can reach. Clean blinds.

Empty and clean all closets—clothing, linen, utility and kitchen cupboards. Sort and discard all unwanted items. Repair damaged articles you want to keep.

Empty and clean all drawers, relining them with clean paper.

Rugs and carpeting should be washed, shampooed, dry-cleaned or professionally cleaned in your home. Shampoo or dry-clean upholstery, especially armrests.

Redecorate if it is required.

Wash all the woodwork and baseboards with a solution cf detergent, ammonia and water. The walls in the kitchen should be entirely washed.

Clean out the bathroom medicine cabinet. Discard old prescriptions no longer used or unidentifiable. If anything is dried up or shows signs of age, toss it out.

Wash the bathroom shower curtain. If the curtain is not washable, wash the liner.

Take inventory of supplies and small equipment—what you don't use, don't keep.

Wash dishes which are seldom used. Clean bric-a-brac.

Change accessories. Rearrange furniture, shift rugs and curtains—give your rooms a face-lift.

Clean the coils in a frost-free refrigerator at least four times a year according to directions.

EFFORT AND TIME SAVERS

Make lists. The most experienced homemaker has a pencil and paper on hand at all times to record what groceries and supplies are wanted. Make note of errands you intend to do—don't trust yourself to remember all of the miscellaneous stops when you're out on a major shopping expedition.

Get into a routine of doing housework. It may sound dull, but it works! There are always the exceptions, such as when you have guests. But if you keep abreast of the daily schedule, you can afford to skip a weekly routine now and then.

Plan menus for the week with an eye toward seasonal values as well as weekly prices.

Shop once a week, basically, unless your kitchen storage space is very small. Try to establish an emergency shelf of food supplies to fall back on, in case of unexpected guests or illness. You'll

113

probably have to make one or two other trips during the week for vegetables, fruit and delicatessen items to replenish the larder.

Keep your shelves organized so you can see what you have.

Keep a file which tells the fabric content of rugs, upholstery, blankets, curtains and draperies. Then you will know what can safely be washed and what must be dry-cleaned.

Mail in all warranties on time. Keep the instruction booklets on all equipment and read them.

Be careful about using plastic protectors on furniture. Sunlight filtering through plastic can change the color of the upholstery. It's better to have the upholstery guarded by a reliable finish.

If you live in a two-story house, have a duplication of essential cleaning supplies on each floor. This can save many steps.

Do not misuse your tools or equipment. A vacuum cleaner is more efficient when it is handled gently rather than being pressed into the surface. It functions better when the dust bag is partially empty, just as a refrigerator cools better when there is little frost on it.

STORAGE

A blessing to any homemaker is enough storage space. Having enough room to have a place for everything will make your job less difficult. Once you've established where something belongs, store it in the same place. By instituting this practice you, and your husband as well, will always know where to find a deck of cards or the spare light bulbs without turning the house inside out in search of misplaced objects.

Give serious thought to how and where you are going to store things. Temperature, light and moisture can play major roles in determining what is stored where. Allow enough room for each item, make it accessible, try to make it visible and avoid unnecessary stacking.

There are ways to combat a lack of storage. Designers and decorators have come up with all sorts of ways and means through the use of units, built-in or mobile. Decorating magazines show how you can construct a whole wall of storage, from floor to ceiling, with flush doors opening onto each section. The inside can be divided to include a variety of areas for built-in chests, shoe racks, linen and blanket sections, even a shelf to hold a small television set. Open storage units with shelves act as room dividers with or without the lower portions closed to hold small appliances or whatever. All sorts of modular units can be purchased and assembled to make an entertainment center. According to what sections you buy, they can hold books, records, accessories, a record player, a television—even a desk or a bar. Bed frames are built with storage drawers on the sides. Cabinets are designed to house anything from liquor to linens. Extra seating room and welcome drawer space can be gained by placing in tandem two low two-drawer chests with cushions on top in the living room. Some enterprising couples have beautiful old trunks which they use for the dual purpose of coffee tables and storage. Even a large sturdy wicker basket with a flat top can act as an occasional table and a blanket storer.

FOR CLOTHING AND ACCESSORIES

Because a man's clothes are usually bulkier, your husband is going to need more closet space than you do. If this is a serious problem and your clothes are going to be jammed together, think about buying an inexpensive wardrobe or a more expensive armoire. There are some tricks which can be employed to gain room in square closets. Utilize the sides to mount skirt, tie and pants racks, the kind that swing out to open up like a fan. Hooks can be screwed into a wooden strip to accommodate bathrobes and seldom-used clothing. The back of the closet door makes an ideal place for these racks, too.

Hang garmets straight on their hangers. Shaped, wooden hangers are a sound investment for heavy suits, coats and dresses. Never hang pants on a plain wire hanger. If it doesn't have a cardboard padding, make one by rolling newspaper around the wire. Seldom-used clothes stay fresh longer and gather less dust if they have shoulder covers or are put in garment bags. Skirts should be hung either from racks or on skirt hangers with clips. You can make up a very adequate one by using a wire hanger and two clip-type clothespins.

Shoes are stored on racks or in bags to keep them off the floor, away from dust and possible scuffing. When shoes are wet, stuff them with paper so they will dry to their original shape. Do not put shoe trees in them—shapes will be distorted.

Out-of-season clothing and blankets can be packed into storage boxes which you may buy in a closet shop or notions department of a store. The more expensive boxes are metal with hinged lids and peepholes so you can see what you've stored. Inexpensive ones, made of heavy cardboard, are just as effective and last, if they are treated gently. Don't forget to mothproof anything made of wool, and do not store any item which is damp. It's a good idea to stick a label on the outside of the box itemizing what is on the inside just in case you have to locate something in a hurry. For those of you who have a fur coat—put it in cold storage to extend its life. Department stores and cleaners offer facilities at a low cost.

FOR LINENS AND BATHROOM

Depending upon its size and location, the linen closet can accommodate only sheets, pillowcases, mattress pads and towels, or it can also hold many other things—extra blankets, pillows, table linens and even spare drugs and sundries too large for the bathroom medicine cabinet.

Arrange sheets in piles by size and in such a way that you will know, at a glance, the size and type you need. A good way to distinguish one type from another is to mark a corner of the sheet with a specific colored thread. An example would be to mark double bed-size sheets with blue thread, single bed-size sheets with green. Store out-of-season blankets in plastic see-through bags to keep them clean. Articles used less often are deposited on the upper shelves so the lower shelves can be reserved for articles regularly used.

One shelf of the linen closet is an excellent place to keep a reserve supply of toilet paper, facial tissues, toothpaste, shampoo, aspirin, hand soap, absorbent cotton and first aid supplies.

To have a good-sized linen closet next to the bathroom is a happy situation. Bath towels, washcloths, guest towels and all of the bathroom supplies are close at hand. You might even find a corner to stow the cleaning equipment. But if the location or size is not in your favor, you may have room in the bathroom for a slim, vertical cabinet to store at least a ready supply of towels and bathroom cleaners. A couple of shelves or even a hanging wall cabinet can solve the storage problem without taking up floor room.

FOR CLEANING SUPPLIES

The incentive to brush up and clean daily is much stronger if the supplies are readily accessible. To have everything in one place is even better. A large broom closet in the kitchen can hold a broom, carpet sweeper, dust mop, scrub brush, wet mop, whisk broom, toilet bowl brush, dustpan, sponges and brushes. The shelf above can hold all of the cleaning supplies—ammonia, waxes, cleaners for special surfaces and detergents. A tank-type or canister vacuum cleaner may fit into a large broom closet, but it is doubtful if an upright can be stored there. If the linen closet is of the walk-in type, store the upright and/or the electric broom in that space. Houses sometimes are designed to include utility closets that are large enough to concentrate all of the tools and supplies in one place.

Cleaning supplies for kitchen tasks (soap, scouring powder, scouring pads and sponges, along with rubber gloves) are more convenient placed under the sink. If you're really tight for space, buy a sturdy shoe bag, hang it on the inside of the kitchen or closet door and fill the pockets with reserve dust cloths, sponges, brushes and items for general household repair such as a tube of household cement, a box of nails, a card of thumbtacks and a can of light machine oil.

FOR EMERGENCY SUPPLIES

One place should be designated, preferably a cabinet, where everything for a household emergency can be kept. This includes: light bulbs, fuses, candles, a powerful flashlight, a fire extinguisher and even a kerosene lamp. Here is an excellent place to keep manufacturers' booklets on maintenance and care of appliances. A list of emergency telephone numbers from the furnace man to the fire department can be taped to the back of the door. For apartment dwellers, list the number of the superintendent or building manager.

THE CARE OF FURNITURE

WOOD FURNITURE

The finishes on new furniture today are remarkably durable; but simple, regular care is required to keep them at their peak. Occasional attention is needed even for the super-finishes that have been developed for table tops to resist stains and scratches. Too much care, however, improperly administered, can do as much harm as no care at all. Regular dusting with a dry, soft, lintless cloth, plus periodic waxing and polishing, are all that is necessary to keep furniture with a wood-tone finish in shape. Any carvings are dusted with a hand or vacuum brush. Although a great deal of furniture does need waxing, there are other finishes, oil, lacquer and paint, that demand a special kind of care.

WAXING WOOD-TONE FINISH

Several times a year furniture is given a treatment of wax. No one wax is good for all finishes—read the label to see which is suitable for your particular furniture. Test the wax on an inconspicuous part of the furniture piece. Avoid using too much wax—it can get gummy. Rub always with the grain of the wood, remembering that high-gloss finishes need more polishing than low-gloss finishes. Commercial waxes and polishes come in several forms:

Liquid One kind needs no polishing—simply saturate a cloth, wipe on, let dry to a haze and wipe off with a clean, dry cloth. Another kind is applied in the same way, but after drying is polished to a sheen with a dry cloth.

Spray No polishing is required. The surface is sprayed with the mist and wiped off immediately with a clean, dry cloth. Be careful not to use too much or allow the mist to settle on rugs or nearby upholstery. It might spot.

Paste It is usually preferred for antiques and fine wood furniture where the patina (sheen) is acquired by gentle rubbing. Apply the wax, let it stand, then buff to a gloss.

OIL FINISHES

Fine furniture, especially from Scandinavia, often comes with

118

this finish which is achieved by rubbing boiled linseed oil into the wood. To recoat, apply this oil, warmed, rubbing it into the surface with the grain of the wood. Let it stand for several hours before wiping off the excess and buffing. Or you can buy a commercially prepared oil which needs only to be rubbed into the surface to give a new finish.

PAINTED FINISH

The best care is probably the least for painted furniture. Polishes and waxes can lift off the color and decoration. Dust with a soft, lint-free cloth. If you must wax, use a harder paste wax only once a year.

LACQUER

Hard as this finish may seem, it can dent, craze or crack if treated roughly. Happily though, it needs little care. Fingermarks and smudges are removed by a damp cloth followed by a light buffing with a dry cloth. If the surface becomes dull, use one of the liquid non-polishing waxes to lift off the dirt and restore it to its natural luster.

SPECIAL CARE OF A PIANO

The wood should be cared for in the same manner as other furniture with the regular routine of dusting and waxing. The keys may be ivory or plastic—either one is wiped with a soft, dampened cloth which has been dipped into a solution of mild soap and water. Rinse and dry, washing only a few keys at a time. A grand piano should be carefully vacuumed to remove dust from the strings, using the soft brush attachment. This cleaning is harder to do on an upright model because it can't be opened in the same way to expose the strings. Since delicate felts have to do with the action of the keys, make sure moths don't destroy them by putting some mothproofing inside the piano. Ask your piano tuner the best way to mothproof. A piano is sensitive to heat, sudden changes of temperature and humidity; therefore, place it away from any radiator, fireplace and possible drafts. Too much heat can cause the wood of the sounding board to dry out. Too much moisture can cause warping and key-sticking. The strings are

119

affected by climate change—therefore, twice-a-year tuning is essential whether you play it or not. The piano should be played regularly, though, to enjoy good health.

FURNITURE MADE FROM OTHER MATERIALS

Wicker This flexible material comes from a small bush willow that is not very strong. It needs to be "wet down" to keep it from drying out and to float out the dust that gets trapped in the crevices. Apartment dwellers can use the bathtub for the drenching. Once a year scrub wicker with a stiff brush, mild soap and water; then rinse. If the furniture gets rough after washing, let it dry completely, sand the rough edges and apply a coat or two of shellac.

Rattan Made from a solid wood vine, this material is strong and flexible. It survives best indoors but can be used outdoors as long as it is protected by a roof. Excessive sunlight will make it brittle and discolored. Use a wax with a natural base if for outdoor pieces. The luster can be revived by spraying the surface with a clear varnish or plastic coating, having first removed any dust and wax. Wipe up spills with a wet cloth.

Bamboo Regular dusting and periodic light sponging will help keep this sturdy material looking fresh. Old bamboo pieces have lasted for years with little or no care. It's a good idea to protect the surface with a light wax occasionally.

Cane and rush Both are popular for chair seats because they are sturdy. Cane, the tough bark of rattan, is also used for backs and sides of chairs and sofas. Chair seats of cane will sag in time because of loosened fibers. When you notice this condition, wash the seat with a mild soap and water solution, using a brush. Rinse. Set in the sun to dry. This treatment will clean and tighten the seat.

Rush seats are thirsty, too, and need regular washing the same as cane. Neglected rush will become very seedy looking, crack and chip off. Any loose ends which develop can be anchored with a light coating of white shellac.

Leather Leather processing has changed in the last twenty-five years, and so has the care it demands. Make an effort to find

120

out the approximate age of anything made of leather if it is not new. Newer leather (since 1946) is washed with a well-wrung-out sponge using a solution of mild natural soap (not a detergent) and water. Rinse and dry the leather immediately, buffing it with a Turkish towel. Do not use oil or wax on new leather. To keep old leather (processed before 1946) from drying and cracking, apply a good paste wax just as you do on wood. Allow a light coat to dry thoroughly, then buff. Dust old leather daily, whether it's furniture or leather bindings. Steam heat and excessive dust tend to decrease the salts in the hide.

Plastic-laminate Wash with a solution of mild soap and water to remove the soil. Rinse thoroughly and wipe dry immediately to avoid streaking and filming. You can restore the luster by using a furniture wax or polish.

Marble and slate tops Both substances are very porous and quite vulnerable to stains and scratches. To minimize the inevitable, here are a few suggestions. On slate, apply lemon oil generously, let it stand for five minutes and wipe off with a clean cloth. By using the oil every three months the slate will acquire a patina to blend the scratches. New marble is very susceptible to stains. Use coasters under anything placed on a marble top, especially alcoholic beverages. Be careful about the edge of marble—it can chip very easily. Marble-cleaning kits that work fairly well can be purchased. The only solution to removing bad stains is to have the top reground and polished. Old marble with its dull finish seems to resist stains better. Old or new, clean it with a mild soap and water and rinse.

TO REMOVE SCRATCHES AND BLEMISHES

Although furniture may have the best of care, scratches and nicks are going to be inflicted. Given first aid treatment promptly, many of the minor scratches and burns can be erased. Those that can't, contribute to a mellowing of the furniture—the general aging which gives an article character and a certain grace. After all some very fine furniture which is brand-new is beaten with a chain to give it a "distressed finish" to simulate antiques.

Scratches Blend into the scratch, very much as you apply eye shadow, a soft grease pencil, an eyebrow pencil or hard shoe polish and let it dry. To create an antique effect, use a darker shade than the wood tone. You can buy pencils at the hardware store which match the wood finish. For deeper scratches clean with carbon tetrachloride, sand lightly with very fine paper, wipe clean, then apply a thin coat of varnish. When it has set, sand and varnish again until the scratch has been filled.

Burns Shallow ones can be treated by applying a paste made from lemon oil and powdered pumice. After smoothing the edges, polish. Deeper burns mean refinishing or considering them as interesting distress marks.

White rings They can be caused by heat or moisture. Hot dishes placed on an unprotected table top will cause them, so will sweating water glasses. Table pads, asbestos pads or coasters will prevent them. Some of the rings only have penetrated the wax, if the surface has a good protective coating. In this case, remove the old wax and rewax. Lighter rings can be eliminated by rubbing furniture polish or salad oil into them. Deeper marks may respond to camphorated oil or a paste of powdered pumice and lemon oil. If the varnish on the finish has been softened, the surface will have to be refinished.

Alcohol Blot up the excess promptly after a spill. Apply furniture polish and rub. A difficult stain might respond to the pumice and lemon oil paste.

Hazing The luster is dulled with a cloudy film caused by an overuse of wax. Apply a furniture-care product and buff to harden the wax. In time, the wax buildup will be removed. Sometimes this condition is caused by humidity rather than an excess of wax. When it occurs, furniture polish along with a drop in atmospheric humidity will probably bring back the luster.

Checking and crazing Hairline cracks in a crisscross pattern (also called alligator lines) take place in wood that has been exposed to too much sunlight or temperature extremes. It is often noticed on large expanses of wood surfaces such as tops of tables and grand pianos. Polishing can camouflage the condition, but the only real cure is refinishing.

UPHOLSTERED FURNITURE

The maintenance of upholstered furniture has been made simpler by the new man-made fibers, better weaving techniques and better fabric finishes. Regular care, in spite of technical advances, is still necessary. The fabric you have chosen for the upholstery will have a strong bearing on the amount of care it needs. Light, solid colors and napped surfaces will soil faster than patterned fabrics in darker colors.

Many upholstery fabrics come treated with protective finishes to help resist soil and stains. If the fabric is not already treated, ask the store if a finish can be applied before the furniture is delivered. There is a stain-repellent product packaged in an aerosol can to be found in the supermarket that you can apply yourself. This finish will not alter the appearance of the fabric and will not injure the wood trim or cushion materials. While any protective finish is a great stride forward, it makes fabric only resistant to soil and stain, not impervious. Spills, waterborne or oily, will "sit" or "bead" on the surface, allowing you to blot them. If the stain has been rubbed in, see if you can "float" the stain to the surface with water or cleaning fluid and then blot it. Not all fabric finishes are alike—some will resist only waterborne stains.

Upholstery thrives on regular care. Remove dust before it becomes deeply imbedded, with a whisk broom or vacuum brush attachment. Remove the cushions and brush out all the crevices where dust can settle. Do not vacuum cushions containing down unless you are sure there is a down-proof ticking cover under the upholstered cover. When the furniture has been thoroughly dusted, lift any spots. Follow directions for spot removal given by the manufacturer of the furniture or the store where you bought it. The padding under the upholstery can determine the kind of spot treatment you employ. Test the color-fastness of the fabric by applying a little of the cleaner to an inconspicuous part of the upholstered piece.

A guide to the removal of spots from fabrics with protective finishes follows:

Waterborne stains (blood, carbonated or alcoholic beverages, ink, iodine, catsup, coffee, tea, urine, vegetable and fruit juices)

Lift off solid or semisolid material with spoon or table knife. Soak up remaining stain with a soft cloth—don't rub into fabric. Blot lightly with a cloth.
Sponge with clear water.
If stain persists, sponge with detergent and water, then rinse.

Oilborne stains (butter, cold cream, oil, lipstick, mayonnaise, deodorant, etc.) Lift off solid or semisolid material with spoon or knife.
Soak up the fluid, not rubbing it in, blot remaining stain.
Sponge with spot remover or solvent with clean paper towel or cloth.
If stain persists, "float" it by sponging from the wrong side.

Waterborne and oilborne combination (chocolate, gravy, ice cream) Lift off solid or semisolid material with knife or spoon.
Soak up liquid, being careful not to rub, lightly blot remainder.
Sponge with clear water.
If stain persists, sponge with spot remover using paper towel under the fabric, if possible.
If stain still remains, use the floater method.

The basic methods for cleaning upholstery, which are easy and safe for most fabrics, are:

Dry-cleaning fluids that remove greasy soil. Read the directions carefully and use the cleaner only in a well-ventilated room. Furniture that is padded with foam rubber is cleaned only with a foamy cleaner that does not penetrate into the rubber. The fluids are absorbed more and soften the rubber, causing deterioration.

Absorbent powders (cornstarch, fuller's earth or French chalk) effectively remove fresh grease stains. Sprinkle on thickly, leave for several hours and brush off.

Detergent and water solutions will remove many food spills. Rinse with clear water and blot up the excess moisture with a sponge.

Despite regular care, your upholstery will last longer if you treat it to a professional cleaning now and then. It may not appear soiled, but after a while the overall soil can become ground into the fabric, especially on armrests, cushions and seat backs. Any color is bound to fade if an upholstered piece of furniture is placed in direct sunlight for hours. Rearrange the furniture occasionally or shade it from the intense sunlight.

THE CARE OF CARPETS AND RUGS

Today's carpets and rugs have a fair amount of soil resistance and texture retention engineered right into them. These features, along with new synthetics and blends, have made rug care easier. Synthetic carpets are mildew proof, mothproof and stain proof.

Regular care, daily and weekly, is the key to long life and satisfaction in carpeting. The area where the rug is placed (depending on the traffic) will have a lot to do with its maintenance requirements. If you live in a community where the air is laden with soot or smog, your rugs, along with the rest of the furnishings, will demand extra care.

There are two kinds of dirt to be reckoned with, loose dirt and hidden dirt or atmospheric soil. Loose dirt is tracked in, bothersome at the time but easy to control. A daily carpet sweeping or vacuuming can whisk it up in no time. The hidden dirt, that which is airborne, is the most harmful to carpeting. Almost invisible, it clings stubbornly to the soft surface of the rug where it builds up to dim the color and penetrate fibers. Before the airborne dirt gets ground into the pile too much, have your rug professionally cleaned. This is not an extravagance, but a good sound investment.

How much a rug should be vacuumed or carpet swept depends on where it is located, its color and the depth of its pile. A carpet is not worn out, though, by proper cleaning—the more it is vacuumed, the better it looks. To clean correctly, vacuum slowly with an even stroke, covering a small area at a time. You needn't press down as though you were pushing against the rug. The best type of vacuum cleaner for carpeting, especially with deep pile, is the upright model which has both suction and brush action to take up the surface as well as the ground-in soil.

To cope with spots and stains, have spot remover for rugs in your cleaning closet. When spills happen, take care of them immediately so they have no chance to "set" and become harder to

125

remove. Even if you have guests, don't be embarrassed about taking care of a spill. Scoop up any excess with a spoon or knife, working from the outside to the center to keep the spot confined. After lifting the excess, blot gently with absorbent cloths or paper towels. If the spot remains, apply a few drops of cleaning fluid and blot until the stain disappears. Don't use too much fluid or you may end up with a ring as well as damage to the rug backing. If the spot still does not respond, sponge with a small amount of cool water. Take care not to over-wet the carpet—you may leave a yellow or brown stain.

Rugs made of synthetic fibers, such as nylon, acrylic and polypropylene, do not retain stains because the fibers will not absorb them. It is wise, however, to lift up and blot spills promptly so they cannot be tracked to other parts of the rug. You may have to sponge the area with clear water.

Following are ways to lift spots from all carpet fibers:

Oil stains (butter, grease, ball-point pen ink) Lift excess material with a wad of absorbent cloth or paper towels. Apply dry-cleaning fluid sparingly.
Dry with vacuum cleaner air stream or electric fan.
Brush up the pile.

Foodstuffs (coffee, tea, milk, cream, gravy, egg, chocolate, ice cream, vomit) Lift excess.
Sponge with a solution of 1 teaspoon mild detergent, 1 quart warm water and 1 teaspoon white vinegar.
If the spot persists, dry and use dry-cleaning fluid in small amounts.
Dry and brush up the pile.

Starches and sugars (soft drinks, alcoholic beverages, candy)
Blot up excess.
Sponge gently with the detergent solution and blot it.
Dry.
If the stain is still there, repeat.
Brush up the pile.

Acids and inks (washable inks, urine, fruit, excrement) Remove the excess.
Sponge gently with the detergent solution.
Dry thoroughly and brush up the pile.

126

Heavy grease and gums (candle grease, paint, lipstick, crayon, chewing gum) For both gum and candle grease "freeze" by wrapping an ice cube in a paper towel.
Hold the ice on the spot until it hardens.
Lift off the substance.
Cleaning fluid may be needed afterward.
For other spots, use dry-cleaning fluid followed by detergent solution.
Dry thoroughly and brush up the pile.

To give the rug or carpet an all-over cleaning, buy one of several good rug shampoos that you can apply yourself. One type of shampoo is combined with water to make a high foam which is then applied to the rug with a brush or sponge. When it is thoroughly dry, the pile is restored by vacuuming or brushing. Another type comes in an aerosol can that sprays to make a foam on the rug. This, too, must be sponged in with a damp sponge-mop. The drying time is about four hours, and a brush or vacuum will restore the pile. A third type of shampoo is made for an electric rug shampooer. When using a shampoo do not wet the rug too much. All of these products are good, but none can penetrate deeply enough to lift the deep, ground-in soil. Only a professional cleaning can reach it.

Professionals will clean carpeting in your home or take removable rugs to their plant for the most thorough job of all. They use two methods: dry cleaning by absorption and wet shampooing. Your rug is brushed and vacuumed with a very heavy-duty machine to get out all the deeply imbedded grit and soil. For the dry-cleaning method they use a treated powder, sawdust or semi-dry foam, removing it when it has absorbed the soil. A wet shampoo is used for heavily soiled rugs. Professionals will replace missing tufts, rebind frayed edges, even dye your rug, if you wish.

To extend the life of your rugs and carpeting here are some suggestions:

1. Move heavy furniture once in a while, if only a fraction of an inch, to prevent permanent damage to the fibers from indentation. See that you have the right kind of casters—plastic wheels, not steel ones are needed for deep pile carpeting. Some householders place glass coasters under legs of heavy furniture.

127

2. Have the correct cushion or underlay for your rug. It will help cushion the rug from foot traffic. Buy the type and weight recommended by the carpet dealer. Small rugs should have non-skid backs.

3. Shift rugs for even wear. Rugs used over carpets should have soft, thin backs, not coarse, stiff backs. The abrasion will wear out the under rug.

4. Neglected stains, especially from food, may be a green light for insects. Stains from dog or cat urine may seem to disappear, but if they are not removed immediately and completely, they can suddenly reappear as yellow spots after an all-over cleaning.

5. Have your rug cleaned professionally at least once every two years. For a rug that withstands heavy traffic, have it done once a year.

Common complaints often heard regarding rugs and carpets seem to be:

FLUFFING OR SHEDDING
New rugs made of wool or wool blends fluff and shed a great deal when they are new, especially if they have deep pile. It is just the excess material left in the pile which has to work its way to the surface. In time and with frequent vacuuming, the shedding will stop. Rugs made from synthetic fibers tend to shed less.

PILLING
Small balls can appear on top of the pile. If they don't disappear after vacuuming, cut them off even with the pile.

SPROUTING
Tufts of pile suddenly appear above the surface. They are tufts that didn't get cut with the rest of the pile or have unraveled. Do not pull them out—cut them off straight across with scissors.

BUCKLING OR RIPPLING
This condition is caused by excessive humidity. If the condition does not disappear when the atmosphere changes, ask a carpet dealer if the rug has to be restretched. Too much humidity can also cause mildewing.

SHADING

An apparent change in color is often seen in plush or velvet rugs. The shading is light being reflected in varying degrees from the pile as separate tufts are shifted in different directions. It is more noticeable on solid-colored rugs than on those with patterns or texture.

CORNER CURLING

Correct the problem by holding a steam iron over (not on) the curled corner. Brush up the pile and weight the offending corner with books for a few days.

STATIC ELECTRICITY

Lack of moisture in the air causes it. It's not harmful, only a nuisance, but can be corrected by keeping pans of water under the radiator cover or applying an anti-static agent to the carpet surface.

SUMMER RUGS

Little care outside of occasional vacuuming or carpet sweeping is demanded from summer rugs made of sisal, rush or grass. You will find, however, that dust sifts through these rugs to the floor underneath which may require your attention. Rush and grass rugs can become dry and split. Give them new life by hosing them down.

THE CARE OF FLOORS

New developments in materials for floorings, floor finishes and wax products all help to reduce maintenance of floors. Problems can develop, though, from overwashing, overwaxing or using the wrong kind of wax.

All floors need scheduled care to keep them looking their best. Daily, those that are subject to heavy traffic should be swept or dusted to remove loose particles of dirt that might scratch or grind into the finish. Wipe up a spill promptly before it has a chance to set. A sticky spot will attract dirt and dust. Steer clear of oils on mops and dustcloths—oil softens the wax and can leave a sticky film to catch dust.

WASH A FLOOR

(except wood) when it begins to look dull and lifeless. Use a mild detergent in warm water (except on natural cork floors) applied with a clean mop, sponge, cloth or electric floor scrubber. Really scrub only where the dirt is firmly entrenched. Hot water and strong soap can fade and discolor flooring. Remove black heel marks with fine steel wool. Rinse with clear, cool water to remove all the detergent and wax. If the detergent is not completely removed it will leave a film. Do not flood the floor; too much water can lossen the adhesive which holds the flooring down. Mop up any excess water and let it dry.

WAX A FLOOR

(except wood) only when it is clean and dry. Wax forms a protective coating which can take much of the wear from the surface of the linoleum or tile. Dirt and grime will leave scratches on an unwaxed floor. Two thin coats of wax protect better than one thick one which may harden only on the surface. Apply the wax with long, even strokes, working in the same direction. It may be necessary to strip the floor of old, built-up layers of wax as it tends to get gummy and yellow. Twice a year is frequent enough for this harsh treatment. There are several preparations available to take up the old coats of wax, or you can make your own solution from detergent, ammonia and warm water. Consult the label on the wax you use to determine if it is detergent-resistant or not. A wax made to resist detergents will need more ammonia in the solution for its removal. Spread the solution on the floor and let it stand for several minutes to penetrate the old wax. Scrub any stubborn spots, then mop up the solution. Rinse with cool water and allow to dry completely before spreading on a new coat of wax.

The type of flooring you have will dictate the kind of wax you use. Floor waxes are either water-based or solvent-based.

Water-based waxes are easy to apply, will not yellow and should be used on all resilient floors (asphalt, vinyl and rubber tile, linoleum, asbestos and sheet vinyl) except vinyl cork or natural cork tile. Damage can be done to asphalt and rubber tile by the use of a solvent-based wax which can soften the binder of the flooring. Water-based waxes are marketed in three categories:

130

Clean-and-polish wax is a liquid form that is self-polishing and contains both detergent and wax. One step takes care of three steps—cleaning, waxing and polishing. Before using, sweep or vacuum the floor so all loose dirt is removed. The wax is spread with an applicator or clean cloth which has to be rinsed frequently to rid it of the dirt it has accumulated. If you have a large enough cloth you can refold it to a clean area. A wax of this type is good in areas where there is no heavy traffic.

Self-polishing wax is an easy-to-apply liquid wax that dries to a tough, shiny, scuff-resistant finish. Certain brands are even resistant to detergent washings, retaining their shine. When part of the floor has to be rewaxed, the whole floor has to be done. The floor must be clean and dry for best results before using this wax.

Buffable wax is a paste or liquid which is usually applied with an electric polisher. It will have only a slight sheen when dry, but buffing will bring out its high gloss. Because it is buffable, it is soft and will show marks that can be eliminated by buffing between wax coats. Touchups can be done where the wax wears thin.

Solvent-based waxes are used on cork and wood because water is a natural enemy to these flooring materials. The waxes come in liquid or paste, are self-polishing, buffable or of the one-step variety. You can always identify these waxes, because they have a definite cleaning-fluid odor and are marked "flammable."

WOOD FLOORS

Never use water on wood unless you have to mop up a stain or spill. If water is used, blot up the moisture immediately because it can warp and crack the flooring. If rain comes in the window, wipe up the puddle promptly. Clean wood floors with a dust mop (no oil) or vacuum. Hardwood floors are finished with lacquer, varnish, shellac, penetrating sealer or a tough plastic resin coating similar to that used on bowling alleys. All of these finishes, except the plastic resin, need a coat of solvent-based wax periodically to protect the wood and keep the finish from becoming scratched and worn. Paste and liquid waxes which must be buffed and applied

131

three or four times a year are considered the best for wood. Two thin coats, burnished to a hard brilliance, are better than one thick coat. The thicker the wax the harder it is to get a high luster and the slipperier the floor. Self-polishing waxes are less work but need to be applied more often—about once a month.

Hardwood floors with a plastic-resin coating are not to be waxed. The high luster achieved by this very sturdy coating will last for years with only dusting. Do not use water on this finish unless absolutely necessary.

Painted floors are treated in the same manner as hardwood floors. Dust and vacuum them—wax once in a while to save the painted surface.

RESILIENT FLOORS

Linoleum, vinyl, asphalt and rubber tiles, asbestos and sheet vinyl should be dusted or vacuumed daily, damp-mopped weekly and waxed monthly with a water-based wax.

Cork and vinyl cork are treated the same as wood with two thin coats of solvent-based wax.

MASONRY FLOORS

Ceramic, mosaic, quarry tile, marble, terrazzo, slate and brick floors make up this category. They come to more harm from too harsh, overzealous cleaning methods than from actual wear. Harsh alkaline cleaners are to be avoided since you can never rinse them off entirely. The simplest of care is required—dust once a week, wetmop with a solution of mild detergent and water, rinse and mop dry. Important in the care of all masonry floors is to wipe up stains immediately lest they penetrate the flooring. Even if the tiles are highly glazed, stains can sink into the grout between the tiles. There is little need to wax most of these floors because of their high glaze. Waxing white marble will cause it to yellow and become very slippery.

If quarry tile is not sealed it is sometimes waxed to bring up the luster. Use a water-based wax, preferably of the self-polishing liquid form.

Marble scratches easily. Be careful not to mar it with a metal part of the mop.

HOW TO CARE FOR CHINA AND GLASS

Whether you are lucky enough to have a dishwasher in your first home or have to rely on the standard wash-by-hand method of doing dishes, there are do's and don'ts for either method set forth by manufacturers of detergents, dishwashers and dinnerware. All of these suggestions are calculated to keep your china and glassware sparkling and clean.

All china and glassware need gentle handling and proper storing to prevent chipping and breaking.

One of the best ways to safeguard dishes and glasses is to scrape and stack them correctly after a meal. Acid foods (fruit and anything containing vinegar) left on fine china too long can change the color. Rinse glasses that have contained milk, alcoholic beverages and lemonade at once. Dishes should be scraped, and always with a rubber scraper or soft sponge, not with a knife or fork. Even though some dishwashing instructions say it isn't necessary, rinse the dishes and flatware before loading if you are not going to run the machine shortly. Some dishwashers have a pre-wash cycle which can rinse for you.

When washing dishes by hand, offset the hazards of chipping and breakage by using a plastic dishpan and countermat under the dish drainer. Lacking a countermat, lay a dish towel under the drainer so the dishes can't be chipped. Make a solution of mild detergent (better in hardwater areas) or soap and fairly warm water. Resist the temptation to dump any nearby dishes and glasses, helter-skelter, into the dishpan all at once. Without overloading the dishpan, in this order wash the glassware, silverware, dishes and cooking utensils. Rinse with hot water and place in the dish drainer, glasses upside down, plates carefully stacked on edge—silverware rinsed and spread out on a separate towel. If there are too many dishes for the drainer, stop and wipe the first batch, with a lint-free dish towel. Either let the rest dry naturally or dry them by hand. Dry the silverware by hand.

For you with the dishwasher, follow the manufacturer's instructions on loading. Select your dishwashing detergent with care, reading any recommendations on the label. Some detergents can cause noticeable fading of china in a short time. Decorations on fine china are particularly vulnerable to detergents and hot water

133

because they are applied over the glaze. Earthenware designs are put on under the glaze and cannot be harmed as much. Glassware can be broken easily in a dishwasher and should be placed with care. Some experts feel the harsh detergents can damage the surface of fine crystal and soften any gold and silver designs. To avoid softening, leave the glasses in the dishwasher until they are cooled to room temperature.

Too much detergent in the dishwasher can cause spots and streaks—use only as much as the manufacturer of the dishwasher recommends—no more. Filming can be caused either by hard water or by a residue of fat from food. A small amount of water softener can help.

To keep your dishes and crystal safe, store them correctly. Arrange your cupboards so the most used items are in front and on the lower shelves. Don't invite breakage by placing high glasses in front of short glasses. Cups are better hung for safety and space. To gain more cupboard space investigate the space-organizer racks which allow you to store a whole service of china in a relatively small area. Plate savers of felt or foam rubber are advisable between stacked plates of fine china. Use plastic hoods to protect seldom-used dishes against dust.

CARE OF SILVER

Your treasures of silver are meant to be used and displayed. The beautiful, satiny patina (made by many, many tiny scratches giving the silver character) can only be developed by regular use. The more you use both flatware and hollow ware, the less polishing it needs. Daily washing and drying prevents tarnish from accumulating. Tarnish is caused principally by a deposit of suphide, much of which is present in the air and builds up on unused silver. Don't use the same place setting over and over—alternate settings so the patina will become uniform throughout the whole silver service.

There are some foods that can be harmful to silver because they contain sulphur (eggs, mayonnaise and mustard) or are corrosive (salt). This is the reason why food particles should be rinsed from silver after using. Do not allow the knives to soak, though; immersion in water over a period of time can loosen the cement that holds the blade and knife handle together.

For hand-washing silver, use a mild soap or detergent. Do not use rubber gloves—contact with rubber will encourage tarnish. Rinse, spread the utensils on a towel and dry immediately and thoroughly. Moisture attracts tarnish.

Silver experts disagree on the advisability of machine-washing silverware. Some claim it causes too many unwanted scratches; others maintain there is no harm as long as you lay it properly (without the knives) and remove the silver as soon as the drying process is over. Do not store the silver, however, until it has reached room temperature.

There are several kinds of storage devices to help protect your silver—cloth bags, rolls, lined drawers, chests and cabinets. The principle is all the same—a treated material, some with tiny bits of silver imbedded in it, prevents sulphur in the air from reaching the silver. A special cloth can be purchased by the yard and you can make your own silver drawer. To store pieces of hollow ware have a bag roomy enough for the article with a drawstring top. Smaller pieces of hollow ware can be wrapped in kitchen plastic wrap which clings to itself, keeping out the air and moisture.

There comes a time, in spite of the best of care and storage, when silver has to be polished. The polishes fall into two groups: the pastes and liquids that clean and polish, and the tarnish-preventives that clean, polish and leave a shield to keep out tarnishing agents. *Pastes* are applied with a soft cloth in long, thin strokes. A small brush (old toothbrush) is used to clean intricate decorations. Rinse, dry and rub with a soft cloth or chamois to bring out the shine. If the tarnish doesn't come off it isn't tarnish. The piece may have to be replated or buffed professionally. *Liquid* polish is the easiest to apply and often doesn't have to be washed off. It's best for weighted articles such as candlesticks and vases which should not be immersed in water. It works equally well with flatware.

Tarnish-preventive polish (both paste and liquid) will lessen your polishing chores especially on the items that aren't washed often. It isn't too practical for much-used silver—after six or seven washings the polish must be applied again.

135

There are silversmiths' gloves, two-sided mitts made to restore the shine on silver. First rub the silver with the dark side which has a tarnish retarder, then buff with the other, untreated side.

Display pieces can be lacquered for an almost permanent tarnish-proofing. Do not use this silicone finish on any pieces that will be near heat or alcohol. Lacquers in the past have been known to eventually yellow and flake off, but new ones are being developed that are even heat-proof.

HOW TO CARE FOR OTHER METALS

COPPER AND BRASS

Decorative brass and copper are likely to be lacquered, which means they are immune to tarnish. They do not need polishing, in fact, polishing can crack the finish. Once the finish has cracked air will seep in under the finish and cause peeling and discoloration. The solution—remove the rest of the lacquer. To do this place the piece for 10 minutes in boiling water to which washing soda has been added (1 cup soda to 2 gallons of water). Sometimes copper cookware comes with a protective lacquer. This must be removed before using. Most manufacturers give full instructions with new products.

The treatment of copper and brass is the same. There are many metal polishes to choose from—paste and liquid, wash-off and wipe-off. The wash-off variety has an acid base and will stain if left on too long. For articles which should not be rinsed under water, the wipe-off polish is better. Polishing with a soft cloth will bring up the shine. A tarnish-resistant polish may help your pots and pans stay bright longer than before. A good homemade polish is a solution of salt and vinegar. Don't leave it on too long—it can pit the surface. After using, wash with soap and water, then buff.

Cooking utensils are hard to clean, especially on the bottoms where heat has caused considerable discoloration. It's worth the extra polishing effort to restore their beauty so you can display them proudly in the kitchen or as serving dishes. Follow a few simple rules to care for copper and brass cooking pans:

Always be sure there is liquid or fat in a pan; never place over heat dry. When melting butter, swirl it around the bottom of the pan and onto the sides. Soak a used pan in hot soapy water, promptly, to loosen food.

Do not use abrasives such as steel wool to clean inside or out.

Use a wooden spoon for stirring.

Replace the tin lining when scratches and discoloration appear.

Do not keep the pan on a high flame for long; lower the flame when the food starts to boil.

PEWTER

Modern pewter requires little cleaning. Dusting and washing occasionally with a mild soap and water to remove fingerprints and darkening is called for. Lacquer is unnecessary. Since pewter can tarnish near salt water you may want to use pewter or silver polish once in a while.

STAINLESS STEEL

Here is a metal beautiful and strong that needs little care, doesn't tarnish, won't wear off, won't chip or break, resists abrasion and is practically unaffected by food acids. Is it any wonder why it is so much in demand? It does water-spot and should be dried immediately after washing and rinsing.

Kitchen knives with stainless blades are very durable but must be treated with respect. Wipe after using, then wash, rinse and dry before storing. Knives should have a place of their own—a knife box or rack. Do not toss them in with the rest of the kitchen utensils. A blade's edge can be dulled that way, and a hand can be cut while searching for something else in the drawer. Sharpen the blade with a textured sharpening stone (found in good carving sets) or with an electric knife sharpener. If you have neither of these, see if your local hardware store hones knives.

Cooking utensils are a cinch to clean, also. They need no polishing and will withstand mild abrasives such as scouring powder and steel wool pads. Hardened or baked-on food can be cleaned more easily by pre-soaking. For hard-core cleanups (a blackened base from scorched food) soak the pan in a solution of baking soda and water. If a stubborn spot will not budge, make a paste of ammonia, scouring powder and water—lather it on with a steel wool pad. After washing and drying store the pans separately, either hanging or setting them separately in the cabinet.

ALUMINUM

For years aluminum has been a favorite for pots and pans because it is lightweight, resistant to corrosion and a good heat conductor. Two types are made into cooking utensils: cast aluminum, which is a heavy gauge, and sheet aluminum, whose thickness can vary. Both require the same care. The porosity of aluminum makes it a good heat conductor but also allows it to stain. To remove inside stains fill the pan with water, add two tablespoons of cream of tartar, simmer for half an hour, cool and scour with steel wool pads. Commercial cleaners will remove stains and the shine as well. Here are some don'ts:

Don't soak a pan in soapy water for long periods—the metal will discolor.

Don't pour cold water into a very hot pan—it can warp the pan.

Don't store pans covered—white spots can develop inside.

Don't drop pans—they dent rather easily.

CHROMIUM

Informally referred to as chrome, this is an electroplated finish on alloy steel. Many appliances are finished or trimmed with this hard, non-tarnishing metal that is quite resistant to corrosion. Hardware fittings in the kitchen and bath, electrical fittings, outdoor furniture, appliances and automobile trims—all of these are made from chromium. Because of its hard, shiny finish the only care chromium needs is a wipe-up with a damp cloth to erase fingermarks. Some chromium is very lightly plated; too much cleaning and polishing with abrasive agents can lift the chrome plating. Clean badly neglected chromium with a non-abrasive powder or chrome cleaner.

The trim on your car will deteriorate less if it is waxed periodically, particularly if the car is not garaged.

CARE OF COOKWARE

Other materials found almost exclusively in kitchen equipment (besides aluminum, stainless steel, copper and brass) require special techniques to keep them in the peak of condition.

CAST IRON

Cookware made from sturdy but heavy cast iron includes such pieces as skillets, griddles, popover pans and Dutch ovens (large covered pots). Cast iron heats evenly and retains the heat, making it excellent for long, slow cooking. The metal does have a tendency to rust from moisture condensation and must be kept properly seasoned to prevent the condition.

All cast iron cookware comes from the factory seasoned, which serves as a rust deterrent. Before using the first time, wash the pot in mild soap and water. Do not use a detergent—it can remove the seasoning.

When using a new pot, remove the cover after the cooking is finished so the steam will escape and not condense on the sides to rust. Cast iron should not be scoured; if you must, be gentle. The next time you cook with it, use a little extra grease to restore the seasoning.

Do not store cast iron with the lid on—it can sweat, causing rust to form. Store in a dry place only when the metal is thoroughly dry.

If signs of rust and discoloration appear, reseason the utensil. Scour with steel wool, spread unsalted shortening or salad oil on the inside, place the pot in a warm oven and leave for two hours. Remove and wipe off the excess fat with paper towels. Let it cool completely before storing.

PORCELAIN ENAMEL IRON

Cast iron cookware with a porcelain enamel finish is sturdy, almost chip-proof and attractive in decorator colors. It has all the virtues of cast iron without the rusting problem. It can be used for cooking on top of the stove or in the oven and can be transported to the table as a colorful serving piece.

There is no need to cook at high heat because the finished cast iron spreads the heat evenly and retains it. Let the pot get quite hot (on a medium flame) before putting fat in it. Do not subject a pot to extremes of temperature, such as bringing it from the refrigerator directly to the oven. Let the pot cool before washing and pre-soak to loosen cooked-on foods. Do not scour enameled cast iron; wash it with a mild detergent or soap. Abrasive agents will mar the surface. It can be washed in the dishwasher, however.

The same cleaning techniques are suggested for porcelain enamel on steel, which is a lighter-weight cookware.

CERAMIC

Glass ceramic will withstand extreme temperature changes. A casserole made of this material will go from the freezer or refrigerator to a heated oven safely. This is not true of all ceramic cookware—manufacturers warn that some will not take such drastic temperature changes.

You will find certain pots marked "flameproof," others "ovenproof." These terms do not mean the same thing. "Flameproof" means the pot can be used on top of the stove, under the broiler or in the oven. "Ovenproof" means the pot can only be used in the oven, not in direct contact with a flame. Some pots will withstand the heat of a gas flame but not the heat of electric coils. Obviously you must consult the label to know how to use a ceramic pot correctly.

Ceramic utensils are often guaranteed against chipping, breaking or cracking but they will stain from coffee, tea or mineral deposits caused by hard water. Take off stains by boiling a solution of water and vinegar in the pot for a few minutes.

A great advantage is ceramic's washability. No special soap is needed, and it is dishwasher-proof.

Earthenware pots, such as those from Mexico, although colorful, are not as strong as other types of pottery but are excellent for oven-cooking. Recently pottery cookware has been developed to stand the heat of a medium gas flame but not that of an electric coil.

NON-STICK FINISHES

Utensils lined with non-stick finishes are easy to clean, need less fat for frying and are, of course, stick-free. In order to retain this feature, care for these products properly from the beginning. Makers of certain coated cookware suggest that before cooking for the first time you wash the pan in warm water, dry, add a light coating of salad oil and wipe off the excess oil.

Pre-heat frypans before adding any fat, but don't allow them to become overheated. Non-stick finish can be affected by sudden temperature changes. Wooden spoons or spatulas are recommend-

140

ed when stirring in a finished pan so the lining will not be scratched. This does not affect the sticklessness, only the looks of the pan. Non-stick cookware must be washed with soap and water after each time it is used. If you cheat and merely rinse and wipe it dry, a burned carbon residue will build up, decreasing the efficiency of the coating. Do not scour this finish. The lining will not be harmed, however, by cleaning it in a dishwasher.

New developments are producing a non-stick finish, slightly rougher in texture, which is almost indestructible. The finish will even withstand the scraping of metal spoons.

GLASS

Cookware made of heat-proof glass is easy to clean, does not absorb odors or flavors and resists stains. Most glassware is designed for oven use only, but there is some which can be used on top of the range, also. Glass is breakable and cannot stand sudden changes in temperature. It is also a poor heat conductor; recipes specify a lower oven heat for pans made of glass than for those made of metal.

Glass can be scoured and washed by hand or in the dishwasher.

CARE OF LINENS AND BEDDING

TABLE LINENS

Like silver, linens should be used, not tucked away and only brought out on state occasions. Tablecloths and napkins do not lose their beauty and luster through usage if you care for them correctly. Stains and spots should be removed as soon as possible (see Chapter 8 on laundry and spot removal). Tears and raveled hems should be mended before laundering.

When storing linens which are infrequently used (such as large size tablecloths) keep them away from the light and as airtight as possible. Do not store white linen in a cedar-lined chest—the fumes will yellow the linen. Store linens with as few folds as possible. Roll tablecloths around a mailing tube or a facsimile made from brown paper. Fold napkins in quarters for storing and make the last crease just before using.

BEDDING

Air the mattress and pad once a week, and vacuum the mattress monthly, turning it over. Replace the mattress pad with a clean one.

Sheets and pillowcases need to be changed once a week; in hot weather, twice a week. Rotate the supply so all of your sheets receive equal wear. If you cannot wash your own sheets, find a commercial laundry that treats them gently.

Blankets with soft, thick nap are warmer but can shed a certain amount of fluff, especially when they are brand new. An occasional brushing, with the nap, can remove surface dust and excess fluff. To save blanket bindings make your bed so there is ample sheet turnback. And when the binding becomes frayed, change it for a new one. Many of the new blankets are washable. If your machine has a gentle action cycle and a large enough tub, wash your blankets, one at a time, at home. Launderettes sometimes have heavy-duty machines which you can use to wash blankets or area rugs.

CARE OF KITCHEN EQUIPMENT

REFRIGERATORS

Refrigerators have to be cleaned regularly whether they are frost-free or not. Save work by wiping up spills immediately before they solidify. Once a week empty the refrigerator—take inventory and see what must be thrown out before decaying or overripe foods develop odors. Wash the shelves, storage bins and door compartments with a solution of baking soda and warm water, then wipe dry.

If yours is a frost-free model, little else has to be done. Make sure the exterior is clean. A note to short brides—clean the top, too. Tall husbands can see where you can't. Follow the manufacturer's instructions on how and when to clean the ventilating panel at the bottom of the refrigerator. In most cases it must be done three or four times a year for maximum efficiency.

For you who defrost, do so before the frost builds up to the point where it impairs the refrigerating capacity. When the frost gets to be ½ inch thick it's time to defrost. Here is the easiest way. Turn off the current; empty the refrigerator. Wrap frozen food in newspaper for insulation. Remove the ice trays but leave the drip pan in place. In place of the ice cube trays, place flat pans of hot water. Do not use the ice trays for this purpose because they have a special finish which can be affected by hot water. Empty the drip pan as it fills with melted frost. You may have to refill the pans with more hot water, depending on how quickly you want to proceed. Never poke at the frost with a sharp instrument. When all of the frost is gone, clean the interior with the baking soda and water solution and dry thoroughly, then fill the refrigerator and turn on the current.

RANGES

The best way to take care of a range is to do it consistently—don't ever allow spilled food and grease to become baked on. If you clean each spill as soon as you can, wash the broiler after each using and give the stove a general cleaning once a week, you will have no range problems. Enameled surfaces are not washed when they are hot, nor should steel wool be used on them.

On gas stoves remove the burners and bowls underneath, wash in hot soapy water, rinse, and dry. Clean any clogged gas holes with a brush or wire. If carbon has built up on cast iron burners, boil them in a solution of baking soda and water for a short time; rinse and dry. Remove the drip trays under the burners and wash clean.

Electric coils lift up or unplug so spilled food can be removed. The heating unit is self-cleaning if something spills on it—burn it off and when the unit is cool, blow out the charred particles with the flat vacuum attachment tool. Never poke at the coils. Once a week, remove the chromium ring and bowl along with the drip pan underneath, for cleaning.

Always wash the broiler after each use to remove left-over bits of food from the rack and grease from the drip pan. Wipe up broiler spatters on the side so they have no chance to become baked on with subsequent use.

Cleaning the oven is only difficult when it is neglected. If food runs over, remove it soon after the oven has cooled. If the spill is left on and the oven reheated, the spill will become encrusted and

143

will be harder to take off. There are many good oven cleaners—some spray on when the oven is heated slightly, some are painted on with a brush when the oven is cool and have to be taken off with a solution of vinegar and water. Read the directions carefully when using these cleaners, because often certain precautions have to be exercised. A very effective and cheap cleaner is household ammonia. To use it, make a solution in a bowl or pan of ½ cup ammonia to 1 cup of water, place it in a cold oven, close the door and leave for two hours. Open the door (be prepared for strong fumes), remove the pan or bowl and clean the oven with steel wool, wiping clean with a soft cloth.

Certain ranges are made with ovens that clean themselves. There are two kinds: the pyrolytic which cleans at a high heat and the catalytic which has specially treated panels or liners that clean at a normal baking temperature. Follow the manufacturer's instructions if you have a range with a self-cleaning oven.

SINKS

Many sinks come with enameled surfaces that are sturdy but can chip or break slightly if heavy objects are dropped. Clean the enamel with a mild scouring powder to remove soil and stains from tea, coffee or acids in food. Rinse well to rid the surface of the gritty powder.

Stainless steel sinks don't chip or stain and require only light washing and rinsing to keep them in peak condition.

Never flush grease, coffee grounds or large pieces of food down the sink drain. Dispose of excess grease by pouring it into a container (an old orangé juice or coffee can) and discard in the garbage along with coffee grounds. After you have used the kitchen sink for a cleanup after a meal, run hot water to clear the drain trap.

6
Clothing and Its Care

CLOTHING, ONE OF the three basic needs of man, probably will cost you from 10% to 12% of annual income in an average year. In terms of your budget, clothing is considered a flexible category for several reasons—how much you spend will depend upon what you buy, what you need to buy and how you buy.

Under ordinary conditions a woman's clothing expenditures are less than a man's. Your husband's suits and coats can take a big bite out of the yearly clothing allowance, but, thankfully, his suits are apt to last longer.

A factor that always governs clothing expenses is what kind of life you lead. A college student doesn't have to be as well dressed as a businessman; a housewife, with no outside job, hardly requires the more extensive wardrobe of a career girl; a couple, vacationing in a rustic fishing camp, needs fewer and simpler clothes than if they were going on a cruise.

To help stretch the clothing dollar, plan to coordinate basics with what you have, acquire good shopping habits, always with an eye to quality, and take care of what you already have. Not everything has to be ready-made, either. Explore the fascinating world of home sewing. With a little know-how it's possible to make stunning outfits at a fraction of the cost of ready-to-wear and have the satisfaction of being creative and original. At least a working knowledge of sewing is very useful and economical when mending must be done and alterations are in order. Knowing how to care for your clothes is also a part of the budget battle—clothing which is treated with respect will look better and last longer.

To be an intelligent shopper you have to know something about the fabrics that make the clothes. With all the new fibers, blends and finishes which have revolutionized the textile field, it is difficult to identify one from another at times. Yet similar-appearing fabrics may perform in entirely different ways. The following section discusses the fiber and fabric families to help you become a more informed customer.

FIBERS

Fibers are the contents of threads or yarns which are then made into fabrics. There are two families: natural fibers and synthetic or man-made fibers. The natural fibers include: wool from sheep and similar animals; linen from the flax plant; cotton from the cotton plant, and silk from the cocoon of the silkworm. The synthetics or man-made fibers are derived from chemicals and have definite and unique characteristics. Rayon is man-made but an alteration of plant cellulose. Fabrics can be made from just one type of fiber or from a blend of fibers, either natural or man-made.

NATURAL FIBERS

Cotton A fiber dating back to Biblical times. It is extremely versatile, blending with other fibers while retaining its own good properties and taking to certain chemical and resin finishes. Cotton is inexpensive, washable, long-wearing, strong and not sensitive to heat. It resists abrasion, bleaches and takes dyes well. It does shrink and wrinkle, though, unless treated.

146

Linen Probably the first vegetable fiber woven into cloth by man. Fine linen is still considered luxurious and is fairly expensive. It is absorbent, cool and crisp with great strength and luster but with very little elasticity. Linen is washable and not sensitive to heat but must be ironed when thoroughly damp. It doesn't take dye as well as cotton nor does it hold it; it will wrinkle and shrink if not treated.

Wool A highly crimpled hair fiber with tiny scales which give it resiliency and form small air pockets for warmth. Wool is probably the first fiber to be woven into cloth by prehistoric man. It is very absorbent, takes dyes well, is wrinkle-resistant but will shrink unless treated. Dry-clean only, unless the label specifies that it is washable. Keep wool away from high heat or the scales will interlock causing it to felt and shrink. Wool blends well with synthetics or natural fibers.

Silk A fiber produced by the silkworm by spinning a cocoon which, when unwound, yields a strong, continuous thread. The production of silk was a well-guarded secret in China for thousands of years before it was smuggled to Europe in the 8th century. Cultivated silkworms eat mulberry leaves, giving the fiber a fine texture. Wild silkworms, feeding on oak leaves, spin a rougher, uneven silk known as tussah. Silk is lustrous, drapes very well, takes dye beautifully and retains it. It is washable if labeled; otherwise, dry-clean only. It is sensitive to heat and should be pressed with a moderate iron. Silk blends very well with either natural or synthetic fibers.

MAN-MADE OR SYNTHETIC FIBERS

Acetate Derived from plant cellulose, this inexpensive, lustrous fiber has a silk-like feeling making it look luxurious. Because it is soft it has excellent draping qualities. Acetate takes dye well but fades unless treated. The fiber is weak when wet and requires hand-washing or dry-cleaning if used alone in a fabric. Since it is sensitive to heat, press it on the wrong side with a moderate temperature iron. Acetate can be dissolved by acetones such as nail polish remover. You will often see acetate blended with other fibers.

Rayon The oldest and least expensive man-made fiber also has a cellulose base. It is absorbent, takes dye well and is quite colorfast. Rayon is durable, with excellent strength and many of the characteristics of cotton. Usually it is washable but, being weaker when wet, it should not be wrung or twisted, rather blotted with a towel. Iron on the wrong side with a moderate setting. Rayon blends well with all other fibers.

Triacetate A cellulose-base fiber which resembles acetate but is stronger when wet, machine washable, quick-drying and not sensitive to heat. It resists wrinkles and has good pleat retention. Triacetate takes dye well, holding its color. It blends with other fibers.

Acrylic A synthetic with the soft, resilient feel of wool. It is lightweight, usually with bulk, has good shape retention and resists wrinkles. An acrylic fiber takes dye very well, keeping its color. It washes best with gentle action and mild soaps and dries at a low heat setting. Acrylic fiber is sensitive to heat, so press with a low iron temperature. Because it pills in its pure form acrylic fiber is often blended to help do away with this tendency.

Modacrylic A more limited-use synthetic that is found mostly in high pile construction (fake furs and plushes). It is flame-resistant but not heat-resistant. The fiber softens at moderate temperatures and also is hard to dye. For deep-pile fabrics, dry-clean; for washables, use warm water.

Nylon This very versatile synthetic is blended with many other fibers so they may borrow its strength and abrasion resistance. By itself, it is extremely strong, lightweight, elastic, smooth and lustrous. It does not absorb moisture and has almost a clammy feeling, but it is wrinkle-resistant and pleatable. Nylon washes easily in warm water, dries quickly and requires a moderate setting to iron.

Polyester A strong, resilient, wrinkle-resistant fiber very often blended with other fibers for use in permanent-press garments. It is crisp and resists stretching and shrinking, is pleatable and absorbs little moisture. A polyester takes dye easily and retains the color. Although the fiber is sensitive to heat it washes well in warm water and needs a warm iron if any touchups are necessary.

Spandex Although it resembles rubber, this lightweight fiber is superior in its longer elastic life and resistance to sunlight, abrasion and oils. Spandex takes dye well and can be made into thinner fabrics than rubber. Wash it in warm water and tumble dry. Never use a chlorine bleach, and if ironing is needed, keep the setting low.

FABRICS

The fibers are made into a continuous thread or yarn by a spinning process in which they are drawn out, twisted and wound. How the fibers are treated when they are spun—to what degree they are straightened and twisted—determines the kind of texture and hand (the feeling) the finished fabric will have.

Fabrics are made by three basic methods: weaving, knitting or felting.

WEAVING

The process of weaving consists of interlacing two or more sets of threads at right angles—the lengthwise set (the warp) is stretched taut with the crosswise set (the filling or weft) passing alternately over and under the warp threads. Many, many variations are possible, depending on the way the interlacing is done, the size of the thread and the use of colors. Despite all the many effects that can be achieved, there are still only three basic weaves: plain, twill and satin. A *plain weave* is the strongest and has, as two major variations, the *basket weave* where two filling threads interlace with two warp threads, and the *ribbed weave* where one set of threads is thicker than the other. The *twill weave,* the second strongest, produces a diagonal effect thus: a filling thread goes over two warp threads, then under one with the next row of filling, shifting over one warp thread to create the diagonal ridge. By changing the direction of the diagonal other patterns can be made such as herringbone or broken diagonals. The *satin weave* is the weakest but most decorative. Threads in either direction

149

"float" or skip over several threads to produce a lustrous, shiny surface.

When buying fabric by the yard or in a ready-made garment examine the weave to make sure it is sturdy enough for the garment and that it will retain its shape.

KNITTING

An elastic and pliable fabric is made when the yarn is looped and the loops interconnect. A wide range of textures and patterns are possible with knitting variations. A knitted fabric drapes well, does not wrinkle and springs back after being stretched. It can sag, however, after long wear or if the knit construction is not tight enough and the garment is unlined. Fabrics used for dresses and suits are either double-knitted or backed with a permanently bonded coating to prevent undue stretching.

FELTING

Perhaps the oldest method of making cloth is felting, a process of interlocking wool or hair fibers through pressure, heat and moisture to form a fabric. Although other fibers can be used with wool they cannot felt by themselves without wool as a carrier. Felt is not strong and will tear but will not ravel. It can be molded into shape by the use of steam and heat but will not revert to its former shape. Felt, untreated for shrinkage, will shrink badly if subjected to moisture. Certain shaping materials which are used for interfacings are made of felted fabrics.

FABRIC FINISHES

Vat-dying The term refers to a group of dyestuffs that are applied mainly to cotton, linen and rayon. This group is considered the most colorfast, in every respect, to washing, bleaching, dry-cleaning and daylight. Yarns or whole pieces of fabric can be vat-dyed to give solids or prints.

Fluorescent dye A dye giving a luminous, brilliant appearance. It does not stand up in laundering or dry-cleaning.

Printing The surface of the fabric is decorated with dye in a variety of patterns and colors by several processes: block, screen, roller, burned-out, plissé, flock or shadow printing.

Napping A surface effect made by brushing up short fibers on the fabric to create a soft, fuzzy layer. Suedecloth, wool broadcloth and flannel (cotton and wool) are finished by napping. **Sueding** is similar except the fibers are cut closer to the surface.

Mercerizing An alkaline process causes the cotton fiber to untwist and swell, making it smooth. The woven fabric has a luster, feels silky and is stronger and more absorbent than untreated cotton.

Embossing The design is pressed onto the fabric surface by an engraved roller to create raised and lowered areas.

Crinkling A fabric can be given a crepe effect in three ways: the use of tightly twisted yarns, the use of tension and control of yarns in the weaving, or the impressing of crepe designs. The woven crepe does not lose its crinkle and is more resilient. All crepes are susceptible to shrinkage because of the high twist in the yarn.

Sizing There are temporary and permanent sizings. The temporary is a starch, gelatin or gum applied to the fabric to give it a stiff appearance, smooth surface or more compactness (in loosely woven material). Permanent sizing can be done by an acid treatment on sheer cotton, by a cellulose solution to seal the fiber ends or by a resin treatment.

Pre-shrinking A mechanical process to control shrinkage by giving dimensional stability, so the fabric will not stretch or shrink out of shape. When a fabric is woven the warp threads are held taut while the filling threads must crimp slightly to interlace with the warp. When the fabric is washed, the warp threads relax and crimp, thus shortening the garment and causing shrinkage. There are several patented methods used on cottons, woolens and synthetics. Most of them guarantee no more than 1% shrinkage.

Wash-and-wear A wrinkle-resistant finish is given to synthetic fabrics by heat setting. Cotton, linen and rayon are chemically treated with synthetic resins. When this finish is applied to fabrics they dry faster, wrinkle less, do not soil and need little or no ironing because the threads are coated smooth and cannot be penetrated. Seams can pucker, though, and become worse with wear.

Permanent press A process which permanently sets creases and pleats in fabrics and gives a permanent shape to the garment. The fabric is first treated with resin for a wash-and-wear finish. Permanent press setting is done in either of two ways—the garment is completely finished and then cured in a special baking oven or the fabric is cured at the mill, the garment is made up, then given a permanent hot head press. Once a crease is set it cannot be removed by pressing for possible alterations. Because cotton and rayon lose strength when they undergo permanent press treatment, they are often blended with synthetics for added strength.

Waterproofing Plastic film or a film coating makes fabrics able to repel moisture completely. The finish is permanent but can show wear and will stiffen in cold weather. Waterproof garments tend to be hot because no air can penetrate, therefore, no air can escape from inside.

Water-repellency Fabrics, treated chemically, which are able to resist wetting but are not able to repel a deluge of rain. Some finishes are durable and will last through dry-cleaning and laundering without having to be renewed. Others must be replaced with each cleaning. A garment finished for water-repellency will be cooler than one that is waterproofed, because air can flow through the fabric.

Spot- and stain-resistant Fluorochemical finishes guard fabric against oil and water stains which "bead up" on the fabric and can be rolled, wiped or blotted off.

Moth-resistant To prevent the vast damage done by moths to wool and other animal fibers each year, there are four ways your apparel can be protected. A chemical substance is applied to the fabric during manufacture; a chemical substance is applied during dry-cleaning; a wool protecting agent is used when the garment is washed in the final rinse water, or a chemical is sprayed on the garment.

Mildew-resistant Synthetics are highly resistant to mildew though the natural fibers are not. Chemical compounds can be applied when the fabric is manufactured and are also available for home use.

Anti-static A thermosetting resin can be applied to a fabric making a film around the fiber which absorbs or contains moisture. Because static electricity is generated when the air lacks moisture, the layer of moisture dissipates the electrical charge. Fabrics and finishes that absorb little moisture have a particular problem with static electricity. Fabric softeners, too, are effective anti-static agents.

Stretch fabrics In cotton fabrics the fibers are mercerized but are not held under tension thus allowing them to take on elastic properties and when woven, stretch either or both ways. Wool can be made stretchable by special weaving processes, by crimp-setting the yarn before weaving or by chemically treating the fabric and subjecting it to certain tensions.

Bonded fabrics A backing is fused to the finished fabric for stability or warmth. Laminating is very similar with the fused backing usually foam rubber.

Insulation A metallic coating is fused to the back of a finished fabric to keep out the cold or heat. Its effectiveness depends upon how good the base fabric is. This finish is used on fabrics for linings and draperies.

FAMILIAR FABRIC NAMES

Batiste A sheer, soft cotton fabric with a close, plain weave, often used for baby clothes, soft dresses, blouses and linings for lightweight fabrics.

Bengaline A cross-ribbed fabric in which the ribbed effect is made because the filling yarn is coarser than the warp. The fiber content is rayon, silk, cotton or wool, and it is found in ribbons, suitings and coatings.

Bouclé A very tightly curled novelty yarn that makes either a knitted or woven fabric in man-made or natural fibers. Good for sweaters, suits and dresses.

153

Broadcloth A closely woven fabric with a luster, it can be made of cotton, wool or silk. Wool broadcloth has a definite nap to it. Men's underwear, shirts, blouses, and dresses are made of cotton. For wool and silk dresses, suits and coats.

Brocade A very decorative design woven with part of the pattern raised against the background. Its threads can contain almost any of the fibers, sometimes metallic yarns. Used for more decorative garments such as evening dresses.

Calico A cotton fabric with a very distinctive, small, all-over design of peasant or flower motifs. For blouses, skirts and dresses.

Camel's hair The hair of the camel is blended with wool to make a natural-colored, lightweight, napped coating fabric. This expensive but rather fragile material is found in coatings and suitings.

Cashmere A soft, luxurious fabric that contains the hair fibers of the Kashmir goat blended with fine wool. It is fragile and can be found knitted or woven for sweaters, suits or coats.

Challis A very fine, soft, lightweight wool or blend of wool and cotton printed with a small design. It's used for soft blouses and dresses.

Chambray A fine, lustrous fabric which appears frosted because the warp threads have color while the filling threads are white. Usually it is made of cotton but sometimes of silk or rayon. Used for work shirts, dresses, and sportswear.

Chiffon A sheer, lightweight fabric made from a highly twisted yarn that gives it a crepey appearance. It is difficult to work with because of its elasticity and drapeability. Rayon, silk or a blend make up the fiber content. Fine dresses, blouses, scarves and overskirts are made from chiffon.

Chino A lustrous, sturdy cotton fabric woven with a plain or twill weave. It's popular for summer sportswear, men's slacks and uniforms.

Chintz A closely woven cotton made crisp with a glaze finish and usually printed with floral designs. It is primarily used for slip covers and draperies, sometimes for dresses and beachwear.

Corduroy A light-to-heavyweight cotton pile fabric with ridges or wales running lengthwise. The wales can come in varying widths. This durable fabric is a great favorite for sportswear and outerwear of all kinds.

Crepe A lightweight, soft fabric characterized by the pebbly or crinkly surface effect. Of rayon, silk, wool or synthetics, it is made into dresses, separates and some loungewear.

Damask A satin weave forms the decorative design in lustrous damask, much the same way as in heavier, more elaborate brocade. Damask, however, is almost always woven in one color. The fabric can come in several weights for table linen or dress fabrics and is made of linen, cotton, rayon or a blend.

Denim A strong, twill-woven cotton with a colored warp and a white filling thread. Heavyweight denim is used for overalls and jeans; lightweight denim is a favorite for sportswear.

Dotted Swiss A sheer cotton with woven dots suitable for children's clothes, blouses and dresses.

Drill cloth A medium-weight cotton which is very durable and closely woven. Khaki and ticking are made of drill cloth.

Duck A heavyweight cotton, closely woven and durable. The heaviest is canvas. Lighter weights are made into trousers and some sportswear.

Faille A flat coarse rib is woven into this rayon or silk fabric. The rib is finer than bengaline, but similar. Used for dresses, suits and evening wear.

Fake fur A pile fabric made from synthetic fibers, either knitted or woven, and dyed to resemble an animal fur. It is used for jackets, coats, loungewear and linings.

Felt The pressed fabric of wool and/or blends made by the felting process. It's used in millinery, sportswear and home decorating.

Flannel A slightly napped or brushed fabric of wool, cotton, rayon or synthetic, it can be made in many weights and can have a close or loose weave. Its uses: sleepwear, sportswear, men's wear, dresses, coats and suits.

155

Gabardine A twill-woven fabric with definite diagonal lines which can be made from wool, rayon or cotton. Gabardine is strong, closely woven and sometimes lustrous. Its uses: dresses, separates, men's wear, suits and coats.

Gingham A medium-weight cotton of plain weave which has a distinctive pattern of stripes, plaids or checks. The better gingham is yarn dyed, soft and tightly woven. Its uses: dresses, blouses, children's wear.

Homespun A plain woven fabric of wool or cotton which appears to be hand-woven. It is usually moderately heavy with a variation in yarn thickness. Its uses: skirts, jackets, suits and coats.

Hopsacking A coarse, loosely woven fabric of cotton or wool, sometimes with a basket weave. It's used for skirts, dresses and suits.

Jersey A plain knit of wool, rayon, cotton or synthetic blends with a smooth surface. It drapes very well and comes in several weights. It's used for sportswear, dresses, suits and occasionally coats.

Lace A hand or machine-made openwork fabric of cotton, linen or blends with intricate designs. It's used for trimming and elaborate garments.

Lamé A fabric with metallic threads woven into it to either make a design or weave an overall glitter. Primarily used for evening wear.

Lawn A very fine, sheer, plain-woven cotton with varying degrees of crispness. It is used for children's wear, sleepwear and fine blouses.

Madras A plain-woven cotton of plaid, stripes or checks which "bleeds" when it is washed, thus giving the desired faded look. The fabric is named for the section in India where it originated. Its uses: sportswear, blouses and skirts.

Matelassé A decorative fabric woven on the Jacquard loom with a raised quilted effect. The fibers may be silk, rayon, cotton, wool or synthetics. Its uses: evening clothes and specialized rainwear.

Melton A stout, smooth, dull wool fabric with the nap cut very close. Excellent for jackets and coats.

Mohair A soft, sometimes loopy, wool fabric with the brushed nap formed by the hair of the Angora goat. It is used for sweaters, scarves, mittens and sometimes suits.

Moiré A wavy, watery-like finish applied to a slightly ribbed taffeta fabric which can be made of rayon, silk or synthetics. It is used for evening garments.

Organdy A sheer, plain-woven cotton usually finished to make it permanently stiff. It is used for blouses, decorative skirts, some children's wear and evening wear.

Organza The same as organdy except in rayon, silk or a synthetic.

Ottoman A cross-ribbed fabric of wool, cotton, silk or rayon similar to bengaline or faille but with a much heavier rib. Its uses: suits and coats.

Oxford cloth A medium-weight cotton fabric similar to denim in plain or basket weave. The white filling thread is twice the size of the color warp thread. It uses: shirtings and some shirtmaker dresses.

Paisley A fabric made from any fiber which is printed with a distinct scroll-like overall design, which originated in Scotland. Blouses, dresses and some sportswear are made of it.

Peau de soie A silk fabric with a dull, satiny finish. Made into wedding dresses and other formal attire.

Pima A strong, long-fibered cotton which weaves into a fine-textured and lustrous cloth. It is used in good sportswear, shirting, dresses and blouses.

Piqué A medium-weight cotton fabric with cords running through it. Novelty weaves can produce lengthwise ribs, a waffle effect or a diagonal birdseye pattern. Some piqué is embossed and can be pressed out. It is used for dresses, blouses, skirts, children's wear and accessories.

Plissé A puckered finish which is applied to a lightweight cotton. It is used for sleepwear, children's wear and some blouses.

157

Polished cotton A glazed finish which is applied to a medium-weight, plain-woven cotton. Its uses: separates, dresses and children's wear.

Pongee A raw silk in natural beige which is lightweight but uneven in texture. It's used mostly for blouses and dresses.

Poplin A sturdy cotton, usually, in which the filling is heavier than the warp. It can also be made from wool, silk or rayon. It is used for sportswear, dresses, blouses and suits, depending on the fiber content.

Pure-dye silk A silk fabric which has a minimum amount of weighting or metallic finish to give the silk body and crispness. It can be used for any of the more luxurious clothes.

Raw silk A fabric made from the silk fiber of the wild silkworm which produces a heavier, uneven fiber. It is made up in dresses, suits and coats.

Rep Any fabric from any fiber with a ribbed effect.

Sailcloth A durable, closely woven cotton which is heavyweight. It is mostly found in sportswear.

Sateen A cotton fabric made lustrous because it is woven with a satin weave. It is made up into dresses, blouses and children's wear.

Satin A silk or rayon fabric, heavier than sateen but with the same high luster produced by the satin weave. Its uses: evening wear and linings.

Seersucker A light or medium-weight cotton or synthetic in which puckered, vertical stripes are produced on a plain weave background. Uses: summer clothes of all kinds.

Serge A very sturdy wool, silk or rayon fabric with a twill weave. The threads are tightly twisted to give the fabric a hard, tight appearance. Its uses: tailored suits, skirts, and men's wear.

Shantung A silk, rayon or cotton fabric in which the rough, irregular filling threads make slubs to give texture. Its uses: dresses, suits, blouses and sometimes coats.

Sharkskin A crisp, chalky, medium-weight fabric of rayon, silk, wool or synthetics sometimes made with a basket weave. It's used in sportswear and suits.

Taffeta A smooth, crisp, sometimes lustrous fabric, closely woven, from rayon, synthetics or silk. Evening wear and linings are made from it.

Terry cloth A cotton fabric woven with a third thread, besides the warp and filling, which makes loops on both sides and is highly absorbent. Besides toweling it is found in beachwear and some loungewear.

Tricot A fine knitted fabric of rayon, silk or cotton with a slight wale. It is used for underwear, sleepwear and gloves.

Tulle A sheer, netlike, stiffened fabric made of rayon, nylon, silk or synthetics. It is used for formal wear over another fabric and for veiling.

Tweed A nubby, rough-textured fabric of several colors which looks as though it were homespun. Tweed can be made of wool, cotton, silk or synthetics. It's used for sportswear, men's wear, suiting and coating.

Velour A pile fabric with a heavy, close-clipped nap to give a soft, luxurious feeling. It can be made from wool, cotton or synthetics. Its uses: millinery, loungewear, casual sportswear, suits and coats.

Velvet A pile fabric with a longer nap than velour and more luster. The back can be plain or twill woven, usually of cotton. The pile is made of silk, rayon or synthetics. Its uses: evening wear, loungewear and millinery.

Velveteen A pile fabric, duller than velvet, with a short, thick nap made entirely of cotton. Its uses: blouses, skirts, loungewear and evening wear.

Voile A lightweight, soft, sheer fabric similar to lawn which drapes very well. It is usually made of cotton, silk and sometimes wool. Its uses: summer wear of all sorts.

Woolen A soft, wool fabric easily draped. Because the fibers are short and the yarn is not tightly twisted this fabric can have a slight nap. Used for suits, coats, skirts, dresses and men's wear.

Worsted A hard-finish wool fabric in which the yarn fibers are tightly twisted to give a crisper feeling. Worsted will not drape as well as wool but will take a better crease. Widely used for men's wear, suits, dresses and coats.

HOW TO BUY CLOTHES

Wardrobe problems have been plaguing women for centuries, but at least they can be solved with less effort today with all the tempting clothes in the stores. Judicious planning is needed, however, with an eye to the budget and a realistic analysis of what your wardrobe requires.

Here are suggestions to help you get the most out of your clothing dollar.

1. Analyze yourself in front of a full-length mirror. Be critical. Are you buying the right kind of clothes for your figure, and are they suitable for your way of life now? Is your husband proud of the way you look in general?

2. Analyze your wardrobe carefully—plan basic items which will supplement it to advantage.

3. Coordinate colors with what you already have.

4. Choose accessories with care for quality, type and color.

5. If your budget is tight steer clear of expensive faddish clothes and accessories which are bound to be outmoded quickly.

6. Look for good value along with good quality. When buying an essential such as a winter coat or basic suit put quality first.

7. Look for the wardrobe stretchers, the separates, which will mix and match for numerous changes.

8. Buy the right size that fits you now. Don't kid yourself about losing weight next week so the dress won't be tight any longer.

9. Make your own alterations to save money, at least the simple ones.

10. Watch for sale notices from reliable stores. Some of the best stores in town may have the most remarkable "buys." Watch for "end-of-season" and "special events" sales to stock up on essentials.

After deciding to buy a garment look for these signs of quality in fabric, construction and workmanship.

1. Check the fabric. Plaids, checks and stripes should match at the seams. The weave and texture should be such that the fabric

won't snag, sag or pill. Consult the hangtag for information on the fiber content, possible colorfastness, finishes (shrinkage and wrinkle resistance) and suggested care. Look for any obvious flaws.

2. The seams and darts should be carefully sewn with no puckers, no broken stitches and with the proper stitch gauge. Darts are tapered to a fine point. Seams have a generous allowance so they won't pull out and fray.

3. Hem allowance must be adequate enough to allow for alteration in dresses, skirts and pants—2 inches for dresses and shirts and 1½ inches for pants. Seam binding is firmly woven and caught to the body of the garment so it is invisible from the outside.

4. Buttons are sewn securely, preferably with a slight shank and reinforced with a patch on the back if they are not attached to a facing. On heavier fabrics (coats and men's suits) buttons have smaller buttons on the back for extra strength. Snaps, hooks and eyes are also firmly attached.

5. Stress points are reinforced. Seam tape holds the shoulder and waistline seams from stretching. Extra stitches are taken at points of strain near pocket edges, openings, pleats or slits. Gussets (bias pieces under the arms) are reinforced at the corners.

6. The buttonholes are neat, evenly spaced and straight with no sagging. They are firmly stitched, reinforced at the corners and the correct size for the buttons used.

7. Zippers are flat with smooth plackets, easy to use, long enough and of the right color.

8. The collar lies flat or rolls, as the design demands. Interfacing of a suitable weight holds the collar and lapels to the desirable shape. The edges of both the collar and lapels match and are pointed if they are intended to be.

9. Trimmings, plus the buttons and sewing threads, are compatible with the garment.

10. Linings give shape to the garment and are smooth, of the appropriate fabric and carefully sewn in (invisible from the outside). When a coat or jacket is worn the lining should be generous enough to allow the garment to hang correctly. An expansion pleat in the lining back gives more ease. The linings are sewn in by hand on quality garments. Dresses, straight

skirts and sometimes slacks made of unbonded fabrics have an underlining sewn in with the seams to prevent bagging and stretching.

BUYING FOR YOUR HUSBAND

Does your husband like to shop for all of his own clothes or does he only venture into a store for suits, coats and shoes and ask you to buy the rest? If his shopping habits place him in the second category, you have a whole new field of shopping ahead of you. The same information about fabrics, finishes and basic construction details holds true for his clothing. You do need to know more—how a man's size is determined in each area of clothing and what his style preferences are.

Shirts The sizing of men's dress or business shirts is calculated by neck measurement and sleeve length. A 15-32 (or 15-2) shirt means the collar measures 15 inches buttoned and the sleeve length is 32 inches long. The collar shouldn't be choke-tight but have a little "give" for comfort. The sleeve length is actually the measurement from the base of the neck at the center back to the wrist with the elbow slightly bent. Many men find dress shirts with short sleeves more comfortable for summer wear.

The collar of a dress shirt can be buttoned down or not, require a collar pin or have hidden stays to help it remain in place. It can also be pointed or round. The cuffs are made double (or French, requiring cuff links), single (or barrel with a button) or convertible (using the available button or cuff links).

Shirts come in a wide range of colors and designs besides the ever-faithful white. Although there are expensive silk shirts, most are made of cotton in a variety of weights and weaves such as broadcloth, oxford cloth, batiste, chambray, even fine piqué. Wash-and-wear shirts are a wonderful convenience for the bride who must wash her husband's shirts.

Work shirts are sized in the same way as dress shirts, but they are cut fuller and longer to allow for more freedom of movement.

Slacks or pants Men's pants, trousers, jeans or slacks are sized according to the waistline measurement and the length of the inseam (length of the seam from the crotch to the finished edge at the bottom of the pants). Some pants come pre-cuffed while others—dress slacks and trousers—are unfinished and need to be measured for cuffing or hemming. Blue jeans and casual slacks are classified as slim or regular, designating the proportion of the cut.

Underwear Ribbed undershirts are sold by chest measurement. Some brands label: small (34-36″), medium (38-40″), large (42-44″) and extra-large (46″). Other brands label by each size from 34″ to 46″. Be generous with the size when you buy undershirts and be sure they are long enough (a full 8 inches below the waistline). There are men who prefer to wear T-shirts or plain knit undershirts with sleeves. These are sized in the same way.

Underwear shorts are made in the boxer style of cotton broadcloth or the knitted brief. Both styles are sold by waist measurement.

Pajamas Chest measurement determines the sizing of pajamas. Letters serve to classify the range: A (34-36″), B (38-40″), C (42-44″) and D (46-48″). Pajamas should hang loose from the shoulder and be roomy for comfortable sleep. They come in a range of fabrics: fine silk, rayon, synthetics and blends, but most of all cottons. Synthetics and some finishes tend to be hot in the summer because the fabrics don't "breathe" and do not absorb perspiration.

Socks The size of socks corresponds to the size and width of a man's shoe. Consult available charts on labels or displays. Be generous with the size—a sock should extend ½″ beyond the longest toe of the foot. Regular socks range in sizes from 9 to 13, plus outsize. Stretch socks are often sized to cover a scope of several regular sock sizes.

Five types of socks are made: dress hosiery, in ankle, garter and knee-lengths; casual socks, in ankle and knee-lengths; athletic socks, in ankle-length; work socks, in lengths of 10½″ to 14″, and boot socks, in 12″, 15″, 16″ and 18″ lengths.

Men's hosiery can be found in a wide selection of colors, textures and designs. The most popular ones are made of wool, combed cotton, lisle (a fine, strong cotton), nylon and acrylics.

Nylon is often blended with wool to give added strength and long wear. Acrylics are warm, lightweight and shrink-resistant but, like all synthetics, not very absorbent.

CARE OF CLOTHING

It's not enough to buy clothing of good quality—it must also be cared for properly to give its best performance.

1. Hang clothes straight on a hanger or fold them after wearing, especially if they contain wool.
2. Brush dry-cleanable clothes after wearing to remove lint and dust.
3. Remove spots and stains immediately if you can. Do not let them "set." They are harder to remove after a period of time—some never come out.
4. Give all-wool apparel a 24-hour rest after wearing to allow the very resilient fibers a chance to resume their normal shape.
5. Send clothes to the dry cleaners on a regular basis even though they may not appear to be dirty. The overall soil may be invisible to your eye but is becoming more imbedded with each wearing.
6. Do not press clothes with spots or stains still in them—heat may "set" them.
7. Launder washable clothing using the right soap and the correct wash cycle for the fabric and finish (see Chapter 8).
8. Mend rips, broken stitches, loose buttons or sagging hemlines before the garment is cleaned or worn again. If you delay, the situation is likely to get worse.
9. Store clothes without crowding so they won't become crushed. Use shoulder protectors over fragile garments or store them in garment bags to shelter them from dust and soil.
10. Protect your clothes when you are wearing them. Prevent stains by using an apron or a napkin. Wear a raincoat or carry an umbrella on a rainy day. Dress appropriately for any kind of manual labor or chores.
11. Unless they are treated, store wool garments with mothproofing during the summer months.

7
A Sewing Primer

MAKING YOUR OWN clothes can be as creative as painting a picture. Many women look upon sewing as an art form and not only make all sorts of original apparel but also save money by stitching up curtains and draperies. What could be more challenging than choosing a design and fabric and making it into a one-of-a-kind outfit that really fits? Granted, this kind of sewing takes a certain know-how, but it isn't that difficult to acquire the skill. Good sewing courses are offered across the country by adult education programs, department stores, fabric shops and sewing machine centers. The courses teach basic sewing techniques and advanced methods. They also help to sharpen your fashion sense by showing you how to select a dress pattern and the right kind of fabric. Your county home extension agent can supply you with information on classes and pamphlets on how to sew.

If you haven't the time or inclination to make clothes, learn to sew well enough to make simple alterations—be able to change hem levels and mend minor tears. You'd be surprised how much can be saved on tailor's bills.

EQUIPMENT

Find a niche or a corner which can be equipped as a sewing center. It can be small enough to house only a large sewing basket or, if you're a serious seamstress, it can be large enough to hold a sewing machine, a full-length mirror along with storage space for fabric and paper patterns.

To equip a full-fledged sewing center you will need:

Sewing machine	Tailor's chalk in two shades
Bent-handle cutting shears	Tracing paper and wheel
Pinking shears	Mirror, preferably full-length
Trimming shears	Skirt marker
Small snipping scissors	Cutting board or equivalent surface
Dressmaker pins	Seam bindings and tapes
Pincushion	Iron and ironing board
Tape measure	Pressing cloth
Six-inch ruler	Tailor's clapper
Yardstick	Tailor's ham or cushion
Needles and thread	Velvet board
Thimble to fit	Clothes brush

The home sewing machine, made by a reputable manufacturer, is sturdy and long-lasting, demanding the normal care of cleaning and oiling. Factory servicing for the motor may be necessary periodically. Since buying a sewing machine can be considered a long-term investment think about future needs as well as those of the present. The first decision you have to make is which type of machine you want, the straight-stitch machine or the zigzag stitch machine. Both types sew with a lock stitch of two threads (one thread from the top and one thread from the bobbin, below the needle). Both machines come in portable models as well as cabinet styles. A portable, usually quite sturdy, is ideal as a space-saver because it can be stowed in a closet when not in use.

The cabinet model will be more expensive because you are paying for a piece of furniture, but it will also offer more storage space in drawers, will have supported leaves for added work surface and sometimes have a bigger sewing head than the portable. Cabinet models come in a variety of woods and styles to fit with any type of home furnishing.

THE STRAIGHT-STITCH MACHINE

Less expensive and can sew forward or backward by adjusting a lever. The needle moves up and down in a stationary position as the fabric is fed under the pressure foot. If your sewing interests lie in tailoring and dressmaking with occasional mending or patching, this is the type of machine for you. It is easy to use and can sew almost any weight of fabric. Attachments are available—by substituting one for the pressure foot you can ruffle, bind, pipe or make buttonholes.

THE ZIGZAG OR SWING-NEEDLE MACHINE

More versatile and more expensive. It can sew like the straight-stitch machine or it can make all sorts of decorative stitches without attachments when the needle is freed, by lever or dial, to swing from side to side. If you enjoy embroidering, making unusual designs, appliqués, buttonholes and seam finishes, all by machine, this is the type for you. A word of caution—be sure you know how to operate the machine before buying it. Some brands need only a twist of a dial to select the desired stitch while others are built to use various templates (cams) to make the intricate patterns.

THE COMMERCIAL PATTERN

KNOW YOUR FIGURE TYPE

Before buying a dress pattern make sure you have selected one in the right size range. All pattern companies use size ranges with standardized sizes within them. Patterns in a size range are designed and proportioned for a specific type of figure at a given height. For example: the Misses' range is meant for a well-proportioned woman, about 5'6" tall. Within the Misses' range you can buy sizes from 6 to 20. The counter pattern catalogue in the store will list the size range and a description of the figure type they will fit. Sizes for women can usually be found in these ranges: Women, Misses, Half-Size, Petites, Juniors and Teens.

KNOW YOUR EXACT MEASUREMENTS

Buy the pattern according to your bust, waist, hip and back (base of neck to waist) measurements. Consult the measurement chart in the pattern catalogue to determine your right size. There is some "ease allowance" in all patterns.

KNOW YOUR SEWING SKILL

Unless you are experienced don't attempt to make a complicated design with numerous pattern pieces. Stick to the simpler patterns which are labeled. It's better to have a simple, well-made dress than one of complex design which looks painfully homemade.

CHECK YOUR PATTERN ENVELOPE

On the front are several views, marked numerically. Decide which view you are going to make and turn to the back of the envelope. Here you will find all sorts of valuable information: suggested fabrics suitable for the design; required notions— thread, zippers, seam binding, trim and button sizes—and the yardage needed according to the width of the fabric. If a lining or interfacing is called for, its yardage will be listed, too.

THE FABRIC

The pattern design and the fabric must be suited to one another if the garment is to be successful. Suggestions made by the pattern company are a guide to the fabric type, weight and degree of softness the pattern designer had in mind for the garment.

If you are considering a pile fabric or one with a one-way design make sure the pattern specifies yardage "with nap" (see fabric and sewing terms, page 170) or plan to buy extra yardage.

Before making a purchase, study the fabric carefully and check the hangtag to see if it has any special finishes or care instructions.

Ask the salesperson about shrinkage and colorfastness. Make a few elementary tests of your own which can reveal how a textile behaves:

1. Crush a small portion of a corner of the fabric in your hand to see if it wrinkles badly or springs right back to its former state. Sometimes this is a good way to find out if a cotton has been excessively sized.
2. Gently pull the corner diagonally to see how much stretch the fabric has. A stretch fabric should be pulled lengthwise and crosswise, also, to see how much it stretches and whether it springs back without puckering.
3. Rub the fabric briskly to see if small fiber balls (pills) appear. This condition can mean the textile has poor abrasion resistance.
4. Check the weave. Is it firm enough? Will it be hard to control or will it ravel? Make sure any fabric with much surface texture will not snag too much.
5. If the pattern design calls for pleating crease the fabric into pleats and see how it reacts.
6. If the pattern design calls for softness gather it in your hand or drape it over your arm to get an idea how it will look.
7. Be sure any printed fabric is printed straight with the weave.
8. When the salesperson is measuring the yardage you need, examine the fabric for any possible flaws.

FABRIC AND SEWING TERMS YOU SHOULD KNOW

To judge fabric and understand pattern instructions better, here are definitions of common sewing terms.

SELVAGE—The narrow, closely woven edge that runs lengthwise along both sides of a woven fabric.

GRAIN—The threads that run lengthwise and crosswise, referred to as "lengthwise grain" and "crosswise grain." The lengthwise grain is also known as the "straight grain."

ON GRAIN—This means that the lengthwise and crosswise threads meet at exact right angles.

OFF GRAIN—The grain threads meet on a slant and have to be straightened before cutting.

169

BIAS—The diagonal of a square. If you want a true bias, fold one corner diagonally across to where the crosswise threads run in the same direction as the lengthwise threads. The bias offers the maximum amount of stretch in the fabric.

WITH OR WITHOUT NAP—Fabrics with a definite nap (corduroy, velvet, velveteen, wool broadcloth and satin) or those with a one-way design require that all pattern pieces be cut with their tops pointing in the same way. Napped fabrics will shade differently if they are not cut this way. A special cutting diagram is needed as well as extra yardage. You do not have to take this precaution if a fabric does not have a definite nap.

UNBALANCED PLAID—Some plaid designs do not have the same color stripes on either side of the main strip. Check the design in both directions—lengthwise and crosswise.

SEAM ALLOWANCE—The amount of space from the cutting line to the stitching line on the pattern piece. Usually it is ⅝″ unless otherwise stated on the pattern piece.

FOLD GRAIN—The pattern piece is to be placed on the fold which follows the grain exactly, either lengthwise or crosswise.

BASTE—A way of holding two pieces of fabric together, temporarily, so they won't slip. You can hand-baste (taking long, even running stitches), pin-baste (placing straight pins perpendicular to the seam line at intervals) or machine-baste (using the longest stitch on your sewing machine).

STAY-STITCH—A line of stitching on a single thickness around a curve to keep the fabric piece from stretching out of shape while you are assembling the garment. Use it around the armhole, neckline and waistline curve.

GATHERING—Drawing in or puckering the fabric into a smaller space. For best control of gathers use the longest stitch on the machine. Make a row of stitching on the seam line and another row about ¼″ from it on the seam allowance. Pull both bobbin threads gently to gather evenly. On very heavy fabrics you may have to hand-gather by using a small running stitch.

EASE—A way of allowing extra room in certain places. Easing is a form of gathering but with much less fabric to draw in and no gathers to show. It can be done by pin-basting or with a gathering thread.

TRIM—As a sewing term it means to cut away extra fabric from the seam allowance after stitching to make it narrower. The seam of a collar point is trimmed very close to the stitching so the collar can be turned to a sharp point.

CLIP—The curved surface of the seam allowance is cut into, almost to the line of stitching. Example: a rounded collar must be clipped so it will curve naturally when it is turned and not be held back.

TACK—A few hand-stitches, sometimes invisibly, are made to hold one surface against another.

TOP STITCH (also called edge-stitching)—A row of machine stitching is made on the outside, very near the edge after the seam has been made, turned and pressed. It serves to hold a facing or seam in place or as a decorative stitch.

UNDERSTITCH—A row of top-stitching made on the outside of the facing, very close to the seam line to keep the facing rolled to the inside. Neither the seam nor the stitching should show.

BACK-STITCH—A way of securing thread at the end of a seam or dart so it will not loosen and ravel. To back-stitch on the machine, use the reverse stitch lever and restitch on the seam line. If your machine will not sew backward, stop at the end of the seam leaving the needle in the fabric, pivot the fabric and stitch back over the seam line. In hand-stitching, take a few tiny stitches over each at the end of the seam.

SEAMS AND FINISHES

Choose the type of seam that will be the most compatible with the fabric. Sew the seam straight and smooth, using the appropriate stitch length. Press each seam open or to one side, depending on the type, before joining or crossing another. There are many different seams and ways to finish them. Here are some of the most common.

171

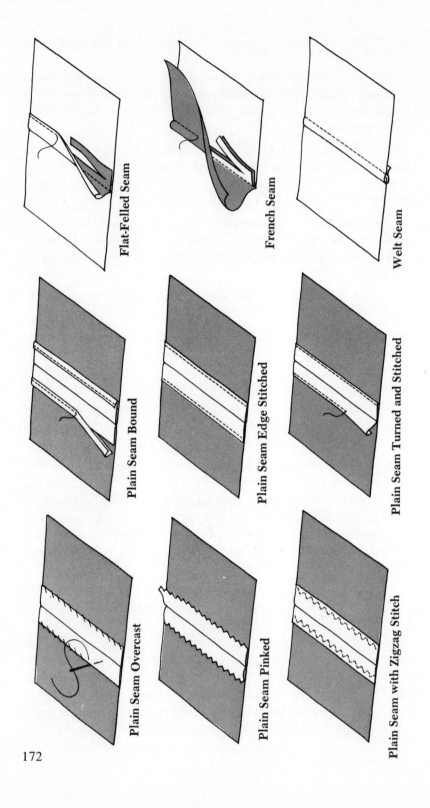

Flat-Felled Seam

French Seam

Welt Seam

Plain Seam Bound

Plain Seam Edge Stitched

Plain Seam Turned and Stitched

Plain Seam Overcast

Plain Seam Pinked

Plain Seam with Zigzag Stitch

PLAIN SEAM OVERCAST—A seam, pressed open, is finished to prevent fraying by a hand-overcast stitch on both sides of the seam.

PLAIN SEAM PINKED—With pinking shears finish the stitched seam, then press open. This is excellent for fairly firm-woven fabric.

PLAIN SEAM WITH ZIGZAG STITCH—The seam is stitched and pressed open, then a zigzag stitch is applied on both sides close to the edge. This is excellent for loosely woven fabric.

PLAIN SEAM BOUND—The same edge is enclosed in bias binding. If the seam is pressed open, bind both sides separately. If the seam is pressed to one side, bind both sides as one. This finish is used for unlined jackets and fabrics that tend to fray badly.

PLAIN SEAM EDGE-STITCHED—A row of stitching is made about ¼″ from the edge on each side to prevent fraying.

PLAIN SEAM, TURNED AND STITCHED—Raw edges of a pressed open seam are turned under and machine-stitched close to the edge. This is excellent for lightweight, unlined jackets and fabrics that fray.

FLAT-FELLED SEAM—A sturdy seam used for plain, tailored garments such as pajamas and shirts. Make a plain seam, on either the inside or outside of the garment. Press the seam to one side; trim the underseam allowance; turn under the edge of the upper seam allowance so it covers the trimmed underseam and top-stitch close to the turned edge. Do not use a flat-felled seam on fabrics with much bulk.

FRENCH SEAM—A sturdy but delicate-looking seam used on finer garments, especially sheer ones. Make a plain seam on the right side, allowing ⅜″ seam allowance; trim the seam allowance close to the stitching; press so the seam line is flat; turn to the inside and crease along the seam line; stitch just beyond the raw edges so they are enclosed.

WELT SEAM—A good flat seam for heavier fabrics. Make a plain seam; trim one side of the seam allowance and press to one side with the untrimmed side on top; turn to the right side of the garment and stitch about ¼″ from the seam line.

173

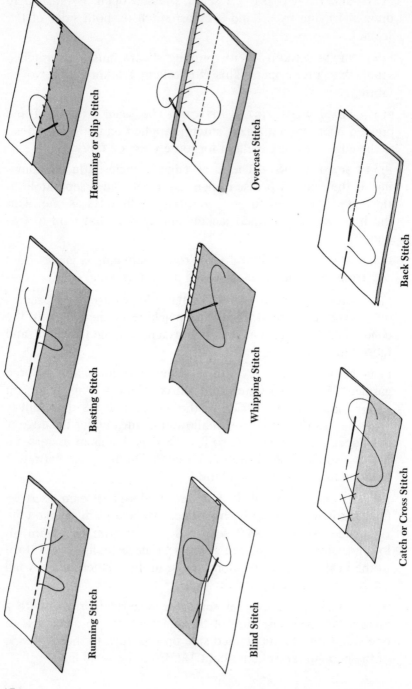

Hemming or Slip Stitch

Overcast Stitch

Back Stitch

Basting Stitch

Whipping Stitch

Running Stitch

Blind Stitch

Catch or Cross Stitch

BASIC STITCHES

Below are some of the most common basic hand-stitches used in home sewing.

RUNNING STITCH

A fine, simple stitch used for delicate garments. Use a fine needle and take a series of very small, uniform stitches, filling the needle before drawing the thread through. Repeat.

BASTING STITCH

The same technique is used as in the running stitch but with a longer needle and longer stitches (about ½"). It's easier to identify the basting stitches if you use a contrasting color of thread to the fabric.

HEMMING OR SLIP-STITCH

To make this stitch on a hem catch only a thread or two under the fold (the outside of the garment), bring the needle and thread out through the hem edge and repeat, keeping the space between the stitches uniform.

BLIND STITCH

Much like the hemming or slip-stitch, this one can be almost invisible on both sides. Pick up only a thread under the hem fold, slip the needle into the fold of the hem and come out ½" beyond; repeat, keeping the intervals uniform.

WHIPPING STITCH

A fine, close stitch used to hem linens. The edge is turned twice, then folded back against the right side so the edge of the hem is up. Make very fine, continuous close stitches over the crease, catching the folded hem and the body of the linen. When the hem is pressed no stitches should show on the right side.

OVERCAST

To keep raw edges from fraying make slanting stitches about ¼" deep, coming out on one side of the edge, going up and over the edge and coming out again. Repeat, not holding the thread too tight or the edges will curl.

CATCH OR CROSS-STITCH

A loose but secure stitch used to invisibly hold flat, raw edges of hems, facings and interfacings. Working from left to right, catch one thread on the top layer of fabric with the needle pointing left; catch a thread on the other lower layer the same way so the threads cross each other. Do not draw the threads too tight and keep the lower stitches the same distance from the raw edge.

BACK-STITCH

In hand-stitching this simulated machine-stitch is the sturdiest of all. The top shows a stitch about $\frac{1}{8}''$ long but underneath it is twice as long. Insert the needle into the seam line and take a stitch $\frac{1}{8}''$ long; bring the needle out on top and insert again where the first stitch was started; this time bring the needle out $\frac{1}{4}''$ farther ahead or one stitch as it appears on top. Always insert the needle down where the last stitch is visible from the top.

TO MAKE A SIMPLE DRESS

Assuming that you are going to make a basic dress, one with short sleeves and a waistline, here are the principal steps to take:

1. Shrink the fabric before cutting unless it has been preshrunk or has a shrinkage-control finish. For washables (cotton, linen and some rayon) soak in hot water for an hour, dry and press. For woolens, pin the selvages together and lay the fabric flat. Wet a lengthwise folded sheet thoroughly, wring it and place on top of the wool fabric; fold the wool loosely over the sheet so most of the wool surface is exposed to the moisture; leave overnight; remove the sheet and let the wool dry flat; press if needed.
2. Straighten the fabric according to pattern instructions.
3. On the pattern instruction sheet circle the correct cutting layout, the one that corresponds to the right dress size, view, fabric width and nap requirements.
4. Lay the fabric on the cutting board or table after checking whether it should be opened to a single layer or folded to a double thickness. If a double thickness is required, fold with the right side in and make sure the selvages are together and parallel.
5. Sort out the pattern pieces you need for the view you are making. Since almost all commercial patterns are now printed,

the cutting and marking information is printed on each pattern piece. Check for possible alterations. If you need to lengthen or shorten, there is a horizontal line on each major piece showing where to do it. To shorten, say 2″, you need to fold only 1 inch because it is doubled over. To lengthen, cut the pattern along the line and insert another tissue paper underneath or allow a precisely measured space at that point between the top and bottom of the pattern piece.

6. Place the pattern pieces on the fabric, according to the instruction sheet. The top and bottom of the arrow, designating the lengthwise grain, must be exactly the same distance from the selvage because this determines if the dress will be "on grain" and will hang well when it is finished. After measuring the arrow tips, pin the rest of pattern to the fabric.

7. Cut around each piece carefully, cutting notches out instead of in to the seam allowance. If there are two or three notches in a row, cut them as a single unit. Use your bent-handle cutting shears, never pinking shears, for cutting notches.

8. Mark all darts, gather lines and possible buttonhole or pocket place marks with tailor's tacks or tracing paper on the wrong side of the fabric.

9. Remove the paper pattern from the fabric just before sewing it.

10. Thread the sewing machine with the correct shade of thread and make sure the machine needle is the right size for the fabric and thread.

11. Starting with the bodice (waist) baste or pin-baste and machine-stitch darts; press and sew shoulder seams. Following the instruction sheet attach the collar and/or facing. Stitch the side bodice seams allowing for a placket on one side or in the back; sew the underarm seams of the sleeves. Press. Leaving the sleeve right side out, work from the inside of the armhole and pin or baste the sleeve into place. Ease the cap of the sleeve by pin-basting or gathering. Sew and press.

12. Sew skirt darts or make gathers; press. Stitch the side seams of the skirt, allowing for a placket either on the left side or in the center back; press. Working from the inside, attach the bodice to the skirt, stitch and press.

13. Baste the zipper into the placket, according to instructions, stitch and press.

14. Finish the sleeve edges and the seams in the appropriate manner. If other fasteners are needed, sew them in place.

15. Let the dress hang overnight before measuring for hemming so the fabric will be able to settle. Mark the hem and finish.

MENDING

It is possible to extend the life of clothes, socks and sheets by mending holes and tears when they are small so they can be controlled.

Darning socks is made easier if you work over a darning egg to keep the tension of the darning threads even. With matching yarn make lengthwise threads, starting well back from the edge of the hole so the thread will have a good anchor. Weave cross threads over and under the lengthwise threads just as fabric is woven. If the hole is too big, don't attempt to darn it. Sweaters are darned much the same way with an exception—the loops must be picked up at the top and bottom of the hole so they can't ladder or run after darning.

Mending is often done to repair a small corner tear on a sheet or garment. Baste the tear against a piece of paper on the back to hold edges in place. If you have a zigzag machine, use the closest zigzag stitch sewing back and forth perpendicular to the tear. Remove the paper and basting stitches after sewing. To mend by hand use very short running stitches, sewing back and forth in the same manner as the sewing machine. Iron-on tape is great for mending small rips. Just put the tape on the wrong side, apply a hot iron and the rip is mended.

Patching can be a tedious job if the hole is large. Fortunately there are patches which iron-on in the same way as mending tape. Sometimes repeated laundering will cause the patches to lose their grip, however.

To patch, cut away the frayed portion of the hole making it as uniform in size as possible. If there are corners, clip them diagonally in ¼ inch. Cut out a patch of matching fabric at least two inches wider and longer than the hole. Baste the patch into position under the hole; turn under the edges of the hole and machine- or hand-stitch. Turn to the inside of the garment and machine- or hand-stitch the edges of the patch. With careful stitching and precise matching a patch can be almost invisible.

8

Laundry, Spot and Stain Removal

WASHDAY ISN'T WHAT it used to be. The revolution in synthetic fabrics, along with new blends and finishes, has brought about drastic changes in laundry equipment and cleaning agents in the last 25 years. Even the methods have been updated to make washing simpler for you. But, in spite of the many innovations, the basic principle still remains—dirt must be removed from clothes, either by hand or by machine.

Many brides will have access to laundry facilities in their apartment houses or to a nearby launderette. Even if you aren't contemplating buying a washing machine and dryer, you should know how to operate them to get the best results.

For those of you who want to buy but have a space problem, washing machine manufacturers have good news for you. They have designed equipment that will fit into the smallest apartment. A compact washer with a 1½ lb. load capacity can be set in the sink or bathtub for use and stored on a shelf when idle. New

179

stackables, with the dryer mounted on top of the washer, take up little space and only have to be placed near a hot and cold water supply and a drain. A portable washer, which is tucked under a cabinet or in a closet when you don't need it, can be rolled to the sink, the casters locked, the hoses connected, and you're set to wash with an automatic machine. The best part about these space-savers is that they rarely need extra electrical wiring or installation.

CLOTHES WASHERS

A clothes washer is considered a major appliance with a lifetime of about 10 years, depending on use and care. The price range is considerable with the cost determined by the type of machine and how elaborate it is. Three types are on the market: automatic, semi-automatic (automatic action) and non-automatic. Also there is a combination washer-dryer.

AUTOMATIC

A power-driven machine which takes the clothes through the complete washing cycle (wash, rinse and spin-dry) with only one setting. After the initial selection no manual controls are needed and a thermostat automatically controls the water temperature for each operation. It must be installed, temporarily or permanently, near electric current, hot and cold water faucets and a drain.

SEMI-AUTOMATIC OR AUTOMATIC ACTION

Another power-driven washer which cleans the same as the fully automatic, but one or more of the operations has to be started manually.

NON-AUTOMATIC

Although it, too, is power-driven, this washer requires each operation to be done by hand. The tub is filled manually, for washing; the water is extracted from the clothes either by hand-feeding them through a wringer or placing them in a spinner. With both types the rinsing is done in a separate tub.

WASHER-DRYER COMBINATION

This space-saving appliance can wash and dry clothes in one continuous operation automatically. Either the washer or dryer action can be used without the other. The machine is front loading and the drying time is considered slow by comparison with standard automatic dryers.

The most advanced, and expensive, clothes washers offer a choice of eight to ten wash cycles with controls programmed to meet the needs of almost any fabric or fabric finish that is washable. Next best, and slightly cheaper, are models made with fewer wash selections but enough cycles to adequately launder sturdy, delicate and wash-and-wear fabrics. Economy washers have only one cycle with a choice of hot or warm water. The more combinations your machine has, the more diverse fabrics you can wash and the more complicated your machinery is. Experts feel that a machine that offers five wash-and-rinse combinations is more able to take care of the average family's laundry.

CHECKPOINTS TO CONSIDER BEFORE BUYING A WASHING MACHINE

1. The water requirements Automatic washers vary greatly in the amount of water used, a concern for anyone who has to pay high water bills or has a septic tank. Ask the salesperson how much the machine uses for a complete wash cycle including hot water and a combination of hot and cold water. Some machines have water savers in which used water is recycled.

2. The tub capacity The size of the tub, or wash basket, governs how many pounds of clothes (calculated dry) the machine will efficiently wash at one time. The range can be anywhere from 6 to 16 pounds. Some makers claim their machines will hold 18 pounds. A machine with a larger tub could reduce the number of loads you have to do plus the overall consumption of water. If you have the room for a larger machine, consider buying one with a mini-basket that slips over the agitator and holds delicate items, handling them with a gentler action.

181

3. The water level If you live in a low water pressure area or in one where pressure fluctuates, it's wise to buy a metered-fill machine which continues to fill until it reaches the level you have selected as opposed to the time-filled machine which fills for a fixed amount of time.

4. The controls They should be clearly marked and convenient to read with a light behind them. Be certain the machine you choose has the wash cycles you want. Some machines come with automatic dispenser for detergents, bleach and fabric softener—you put them in the designated dispensers, start the machine and the cleaning agents are automatically added to the wash at the correct time. Check to see if there is a lint-control or a filter that must be removed to be cleaned.

5. Safety There should be some device that automatically stops the machine if it is opened during the spin cycle. In one brand the lid locks during the spin; many other makers provide for the machine to stop if the lid is opened during this operation. Overload and unbalanced loads can be a problem for the wear of your machine and some makers have installed a convenient buzzer to summon you to adjust the clothes.

6. Installation Be sure of your dimensions. Don't buy an appliance that can't be squeezed into the space you planned. Ask if there are charges for installation. If you are buying a machine that recycles water, check to see if there are any special requirements.

7. The warranty Know what is covered and for how long. If there is a service contract, make sure it is with a company within your area.

8. The construction The outside is either porcelain or baked enamel while the inside can be porcelain or stainless steel. The surface of both outside and in should be smooth and easy to clean. The door on a front-loading machine must have a strong catch. A washer loading from the top should have small rubber gaskets on the corners so it won't bang when closed abruptly. Some top-loading doors open flat so you can use them to place the laundry basket as you are loading or unloading the laundry.

CLOTHES DRYERS

An automatic clothes dryer, either gas or electric, is more than a year-round convenience—it is a saver of time and clothes. It will dry and de-lint a full washerload of clothes with even heat and tumbling action that helps to de-wrinkle all clothes, especially those with permanent-press finish. An old matted-down towel can come out of a dryer looking fluffy and nearly new. Some desirable features: a moisture-sensing control that will shut off the heat when the load is dry; a signal that alerts you when the drying cycle is almost over so you can remove permanent-press clothes immediately; a fluff cycle that has either no heat or no tumble action for certain fabrics and pillows; a damp-dry setting; a foot pedal to operate the door, and an ozone light to freshen the air. Each time the dryer is used the lint tray should be emptied; if allowed to build up, lint can lessen the efficiency of the dryer.

A dryer that is powered by gas is more expensive to buy but less expensive to run. Installation necessities must be taken into account—the gas dryer requires an electrical circuit of 115 volts to power the drum, timer and light and a connection to a gas-supply line. It must be vented to the outside, with a metal duct, to carry off excess heat and moisture.

An electrical dryer, which is more expensive to operate, requires a heavy-duty electrical circuit of 230 to 240 volts. Some dryers will run on 115-volt circuits but take twice as long to dry the clothes. It is recommended that venting be used here, too.

LAUNDRY AIDS

An array of laundry aids, almost bewildering, can be found on most supermarket shelves. There are soaps, detergents, enzyme detergents and pre-soaks, bleaches, fabric softeners, water conditioners, starches and bluings. It's a question of choosing the right products for the kind of washload you are doing. These aids are available in various forms—bars, tablets, flakes, granules and liquids. Some accommodate heavy-duty and some delicate washing needs.

SOAP

A product of animal fats, any form of soap sudses well and works best in soft to relatively soft water. It tends to curd and form a scum in very hard water, a condition which can be rectified by adding a water softener. Soap is gentle on all fabrics, excellent for hand-washables, a "must" for washable leather gloves. Being a natural product soap is easier on sewage disposal systems because it breaks down into elements which can be absorbed readily into soil or water.

DETERGENT

A synthetic washing aid which is popular because it is unaffected by hard water and has excellent cleaning power. It is designed for either heavy-duty or delicate laundry, for hot or cold water, and comes in all of the various forms. Heavy-duty detergent either can be of the concentrated (or controlled low-suds) variety or can come with regular sudsing action which produces massive bubbles. In spite of the effective cleaning action of the normal sudsing detergent, it concerns conservationists because it is not absorbed easily into the soil or water when disposed of and the bubbles go on and on. Front-loading machines can only use low-sudsing, concentrated detergents. Read the package label to determine if other aids have been added to the detergent—possibly bleach, water softeners and/or brighteners.

BLEACH

A chemical used to whiten white clothes, brighten colors, remove simple stains and deodorize. There are two types, chlorine and oxygen. Some are combined with bluing. Both are marketed in liquid and powder form. Bleach with chlorine as an ingredient is stronger, more effective against stains and can also fade colors that are not colorfast. It works well with soaps and detergents with the exception of those containing enzymes. Do not, however, use chlorine bleach if your water is especially rich in iron—it will mark the clothes with rust streaks. An oxygen bleach is milder and also safer on most fabrics. It does not perform as well in removing stubborn stains but does not fade colors, either. Consult package directions on how to use bleach. All should be diluted before adding to the wash and never poured directly on the clothes. When using bleach for hand-washing, rinse thoroughly.

FABRIC SOFTENER

A chemical agent added to the final rinse water which fluffs, softens and sometimes brightens the laundry as well as decreasing the static electricity. Other additives such as bluing are not to be used in the same rinse. A softener should not be poured directly on fabrics. Either it is dispensed automatically into the washer or diluted as package directions say.

WATER CONDITIONER

An ingredient that softens the water, prevents soap scum and rust stains and helps the soap or detergent to do its job better.

STARCH

A fabric finisher which gives a crisp appearance to untreated cottons and linen and can retard soiling and staining. Starch comes in the form of powder, cubes, liquid or spray. Vegetable starch, a by-product of corn, washes out and has to be replaced each time in a separate operation after the final rinse. The degree of stiffness can be controlled. A plastic starch, in liquid form, lasts through several washings. Probably the most popular and easiest to apply is the liquid which is sprayed on when you iron; it moistens, gives a good finish and makes ironing easier.

MISCELLANEOUS

Less soap or detergent is needed if washing soda or borax is added to the wash load. Either one serves as an excellent teammate to remove stains and imbedded dirt, whiten without bleaching and sweeten the wash. For heavy stains follow directions on the package.

WASHING PROCEDURE

PREPARATION

Close zippers, unbutton buttons, fasten hooks, and empty pockets for possible handkerchiefs, facial tissues or metal objects. Turn down pants' cuffs and brush out loose dirt. Tie or buckle belts to prevent tangling. Pretreat stains and imbedded dirt (like that around collars and cuffs) by pre-soaking or rubbing a cleaning agent onto the soil. Turn washable sweaters inside out to diminish pilling. Mend small rips and partially falling hemlines so the washing process does not extend the tears.

SORTING

Separate into one pile everything that must be hand-washed. This will include delicate lingerie, nylons, panty hose, good sweaters, fragile blouses and dresses along with any non-colorfast garment which might "bleed" on to another article in the washing machine.

Sort the machine-washables into logical groups that can be laundered together:

1. White or light colorfast cottons and linens—shirts, blouses, table and bed linen, handkerchiefs, towels and cotton underwear. Soap or a heavy-duty washing detergent and bleach can be used.

2. Colorfast medium-colored garments of cotton, linen, blends and synthetics—shirts, dresses, blouses, bath towels, colored table and bed linen. Wash with detergent or soap. If bleach is needed use one with an oxygen base.

3. Dark washable, other than wool—dungarees, socks, shirts and work clothes. If they are heavily soiled a pre-rinse may be called for. Some makers of cold-water, heavy-duty washing detergents recommend them for heavily soiled, dark clothes. A heavy-duty detergent along with one of the washing aids will also remove the soil.

4. Wash-and-wear. If there are drip-dry garments in this group, they can be removed before the spin operation begins and hung on the line.

5. Any washable woolens and wool blends—blankets, socks, skirts, slacks, shirts and dresses. A mild soap or detergent will do the trick.

6. Delicate fabrics need a mild soap or detergent. For the use of the mini-basket follow the manufacturer's instructions.

MACHINE-WASHING

You're not going to have a full machine load of wash from each sorted group every time. To solve this problem either put off washing a group until you have enough laundry to fill the load or combine two groups. If you are going to delay washing, pile the sorted dirty clothes of a group into a pillow case and return to the hamper until you have enough of the same for a washer load. Certain groups can be combined, without disastrous results, if you are careful in the selection. The white group can be washed with the colorfast medium-colored clothes using milder bleach. Wash-and-wear garments combine with delicate fabrics providing all are colorfast, not too soiled and the detergent is mild enough for all.

The wash cycle selected has to do with the fabric and dye necessities. Hot water, at 140 degrees F., gives the quickest and best cleaning for white and colorfast cottons and linens. For woolens, synthetics, wash-and-wear and some non-colorfast fabrics, warm water at 110 degrees F. is best. Cold-water detergents need a water temperature of 80 degrees or less to operate most efficiently and cut down on any possible shrinkage. Wrinkles are reduced in wash-and-wear fabrics if a cool-water rinse is programmed. For wash-and-wear, woolens and delicate fabrics the spinning time is slower and less than for the hardier cottons and linens.

To load the washing machine, fill with one of the sorted loads, making sure that all the contents are free to circulate and that there is an even distribution of large and small items. Don't overload the washer—for a cleaner wash follow the manufacturer's instruction on its capacity. Pile the clothes lightly to the brim of a top-loading machine, halfway up a front-loading one. For a non-automatic, fill to three-quarters full. Add the soap or detergent and any other aids that are dispensed automatically, select the wash cycle, close the lid and start. In an automatic, uneven distribution or overloading can cause thumping, heavy vibrating or trigger a mechanical buzz. If this happens, shut off the machine, rearrange the wash if a heavier piece is causing the imbalance or remove an article to reduce the load.

After the clothes are washed in a non-automatic they are put through a wringer to force out the water and transferred to a rinse tub to be wrung again after rinsing. Feed the clothes into the wringer so they are evenly spread across the wringer surface and with buttons and metal zippers folded inward so they won't pop off. For the non-automatics with a spinner, clothes are transferred to the rinse tub, then back to the spinner basket to be whirled damp-dry.

HAND-WASHING

The delicate articles washed by hand need to be pampered. They require a mild soap or detergent, lukewarm or cold water (depending on the soap) and gentle squeezing so the suds go through the garment. Rinse thoroughly, pressing and squeezing out the excess water—don't wring. Blot out more moisture from sweaters and nylons by rolling them in a Turkish towel and pressing gently. Wool, in particular, is very fragile when wet and has to be handled with care. Dry all delicate things away from direct heat and away from direct sunlight. To dry a woolen sweater, lay it flat on a Turkish towel and mold it into the correct shape. To be absolutely certain that you block a sweater to its original shape, make an outline of it on paper before washing, for reference.

DRYING

With an automatic dryer this process is simply one of selecting the correct time and temperature for the type of load. Do not overdry. As soon as the tumbler has stopped, remove the clothes immediately to avoid wrinkles. If you have the special setting for damp-drying, remove the clothes at that time and prepare for ironing.

For drying otherwise, in the basement or out-of-doors, shake each piece, once or twice, before hanging to smooth out any possible wrinkles. To hang sheets on a line fold double, hem to hem, turning the hem side over the line slightly and securing with clothespins. Hang shirts and blouses by the tails, towels by the two corners on the short side, dresses by hems, slacks and trousers by waistbands. Hang white articles in the sun (except for synthetics), colored garments in the shade. For basement drying, if you have no lines, use a collapsible rack with plastic-coated or rubber rungs that will prevent snagging.

IRONING

The job of ironing has been all but eliminated from the round of household chores. With all of the new no-iron fabrics and finishes it would seem that there is no ironing left to do. It's not quite that simple; many of the synthetics and finishes benefit with a slight all-over pressing or at least a touchup of the collars and cuffs. Untreated cottons and linens still have to be ironed, and many a just-married budget won't stand for the relatively high cost of good commercial laundries. But, with the new spray-on speed starches and fabric finishers, ironing shirts and linens isn't nearly as difficult or time-consuming as it once was. It does help to have the right equipment and know-how.

IRONS

New combination irons with both steam and dry settings are considered to be the best for all-purpose laundry needs. Some models also have a spray feature that releases more steam on areas that need more moisture. A thermostat controls the temperature you select for the type of fabric being ironed. Some models have a non-stick coating on the soleplate (ironing surface) to prevent starch build-up.

Dry irons, without steam features, are cheaper and just as effective, though not as convenient. Both steam and dry irons have the thermostatic temperature controls for ironing various types of fabrics.

Dry ironing is hotter and requires dampening to remove wrinkles. To press or iron clothes that are dry and those with textured or pile weaves, the cooler temperature of the steam iron is better. Either iron should be well-balanced and not weigh more than four pounds. Moisture and heat take out wrinkles—not a heavy weight.

Before using a steam iron read the directions carefully. Tap water is recommended for some makes, while others require distilled water. It is never advisable to put very hard water into a steam iron—the mineral deposits can clog the steam vents. You can buy distilled water or you can collect it from the melted frost of your refrigerator.

Take good care of your iron. Don't drop it and don't scratch the soleplate by ironing over sharp-edged objects or by removing any build-up from starch or scorch with a knife. To remove build-up on a hot iron, apply a wet, wrung-out bunched up towel which has been sprinkled with scouring powder to the soleplate and rub. When it is clean, turn the towel to a clean surface and press the iron over it to clear of scouring powder. To remove build-up from a cold iron, use mild scouring powder and steel wool. Don't ever leave the iron connected when you are called away, even for a few moments. Let the iron cool before storing and wrapping the cord around it. Don't ever leave water in a steam iron for more than half an hour because it may rust the inside.

PREPARE FOR IRONING

Sort the laundry for ironing in the same way as you did for washing. Fold and hand-smooth articles you won't be ironing, such as no-iron sheets (regular ones, too, if you're not fussy), knitted and T-shirts, Turkish towels, bed pads and underwear. If cottons and linens are not damp, sprinkle (don't soak) them with warm water, roll, wrap in a pillowcase, tea towel or plastic bag and put in a cool place, preferably the refrigerator. This makes them easier to iron and prevents any possible mildew from developing. When a steam iron is used, most articles with wash-and-wear finishes do not have to be dampened. Linen tablecloths, napkins and clothes that are heavily starched must be dampened thoroughly, rolled and left for several hours so the dampness is distributed evenly. The ideal way to achieve uniform moisture is to remove the articles from the dryer or the line before they are completely dry and iron immediately or roll, cover and store.

Select a comfortable place to do the ironing with good light and a mat or rug under your feet. Have an ironing board at a comfortable height. New ones are adjustable and can even be made low enough for you to sit and iron. Do not buy too narrow a board—it just prolongs the chore by requiring excessive shifting of the garment. A silicon-treated ironing board cover is the best because it will not burn or stick. You can buy a heavy cotton cover with a pad or use a clean, old sheet, doubled and tacked underneath. Spread papers on the floor around the board to protect large pieces from soil. Most important, allow yourself some amusement while you iron—have a radio nearby or set up the ironing board where you can watch a movie on television. A little diversion makes the time go faster and the work seem lighter.

HOW TO IRON

Choose the right temperature for the fabric and finish as suggested by the selector. It's a good idea to iron all the articles requiring one temperature at the same time, then advance to the next group which requires a higher setting. Iron collars, cuffs and sleeves first on any shirt, blouse or dress before proceeding to the body of the garment. Iron dry as you go and there will be less need for touchups at the end. Be careful about placing a hot iron on a zipper or button—it might melt. Be gentle, don't poke, when ironing in and around tucks, gathers and buttonholes. Press lightly to smooth. When ironing double thicknesses, press on both sides. Do not iron elasticized garments or plastic—again, the melting problem. If you must iron corduroy or any heavily napped fabric, do it lightly with steam, preferably from the wrong side.

Linens are ironed with a dry iron (they require high heat) and are pressed dry. Have a damp cloth handy to redampen any section which dries out before you can iron it. A long tablecloth is folded lengthwise once, with the ends and sides even. If they aren't even, gently pull them to shape before ironing. Iron first one side, then the other to insure a lustrous finish. Fold once more lengthwise and press gently. For storing, fold across two or three times to make a rectangle but do not iron in these creases. If you are going to store the tablecloth on a roller, crease it only once.

191

Any table linen with padded embroidery or open hemstitching has to be treated with extra care. Press the embroidery, right side down, with a soft Turkish towel underneath to act as extra padding. Remove the towel and gently iron around the embroidered design, being careful not to poke the iron into or through the stitching. Damask napkins are treated much the same way as tablecloths. They are ironed and creased into quarters for storage with the final folds made at the time they are used.

Most washable slacks and trousers are made either of synthetic fabrics or wash-and-wear finishes for a minimum amount of pressing. Use a "cool" iron and press the pocket linings on the inside and on the outside, around the pocket welts and fly front. Smooth the pants' legs to make crease lines down the center front and back. If the crease lines are set, be sure to press along the same line so you don't make a double crease.

To iron a shirt, wash-and-wear or cotton, spread it on the ironing board so the yoke is on top, the back toward you, the front hanging over the other side of the board. Iron the yoke first, along with a few inches of back and side fronts, then the back side of the collar. Turn and iron the front side of the collar. The sleeves are next, one at a time—iron the cuff inside, pressing up into the tucks or gathers, turn and iron the outside of the cuff and rest of the sleeve. For the body of the shirt, iron the left side (buttonhole side) first, the back next and finally, the right front. Either place the finished shirt on a hanger or fold it thus: button the top and next to bottom buttons in front, turn the shirt, from down, fold back both sides with sleeves in lengthwise thirds, smooth the sleeves, fold the tail up over the cuffs and making a center crosswise crease, fold the bottom to the top.

Pressing woolens or blends requires a slightly different technique than ironing does. Heat and steam are needed to give a crease or remove a wrinkle. For best results use a steam iron, set at "wool" temperature, and a press cloth. The iron is not slid back and forth, rather it is lowered to the press cloth, then lifted and lowered again. You can buy a specially treated press cloth which generates higher temperature when sponged, or you can use an old cotton or linen tea towel as long as it is lint free and colorfast. Dip the whole towel in warm water and wring out. Bunch the towel, roughly into quarters, and run the hot iron over it to generate steam and partially dry the towel. Fold the towel in half and place it on the garment where you want to press. The double thickness protects the garment from the intense heat of the iron, avoiding possible scorching and shining, but allows the steam to penetrate to the fabric. If the press cloth seems to dry out, redampen it. The garment is not pressed dry and should be carefully hung after pressing. Do not wear it until it is thoroughly dry.

SPOT REMOVAL

The best way to cope with spots and stains is to take quick action. The sooner you deal with a fresh spot, the better your chances are of removing it. Don't wait for the spot to dry or set—blot it promptly and treat any stain which remains. A great many stains will come out when sponged with cool water. Some stains are actually set with heat—through washing, pressing or just sponging with hot water. If a spot has grease in it, a soap or detergent should be used after the cold water on a washable fabric, then sponge-rinsed.

Knowing the fabric content of a garment can make spot removal simpler. Save hangtags that come with clothes for helpful information on their care and washability. If you are uncertain about the fabric content in a stained garment, take it to a reliable cleaner and tell him the source of the stain. Sometimes even he can't tell, with all the new synthetics and blends, but he can run tests to see if the fabric will tolerate certain cleaning procedures.

The removal of spots calls for a gentle hand and no hard rubbing. Scrape off excess solids carefully with a dull knife or spoon or blot up any excess moisture. When applying a liquid cleaner work from the outside to the center so the stain won't spread more, placing a paper towel under the stain to blot it. Pat, don't rub. Directions on commercial spot removers should be read and followed carefully—many contain warnings to use adequate ventilation.

STAIN-REMOVING AGENTS

Bleaches Hydrogen-peroxide, chlorine bleach.

Absorbent powders Cornstarch, fuller's earth, French chalk, salt.

Solvents Denatured alcohol, turpentine, dry-cleaning fluids, trichloroethane, spray spot-lifters.

Washing agents Detergents, soap, enzyme detergents or presoaks, ammonia, vinegar, washing soda, borax.

Here is a list of spots and stains most commonly encountered and what to do about them.

Adhesive tape Sponge with trichloroethane.

Alcoholic beverages and soft drinks Sponge with cold water and if needed, follow with a mixture of cold water and glycerine. Launder washable fabrics.

Ball-point ink Gently rub in petroleum jelly and apply a dry-cleaning fluid.

Blood Sponge with cold water. If the stain remains or is set in a washable fabric, soak in a solution of 2 tablespoons of ammonia to 1 gallon of warm water, then wash.

Butter Remove any excess. For washable fabrics sponge with soap and water and rinse. Apply dry-cleaning fluid, spray spot-lifter or use an absorbent powder on dry-clean-only fabrics.

Candle wax Rub with an ice cube, scrape off excess. Place the cloth between two blotters or folded facial tissues and press with a warm iron. Use a dry-cleaning fluid if the wax color persists.

Carbon paper Sponge with cleaning fluid.

Chewing gum Rub with an ice cube until the gum can be rolled off, sponge with dry-cleaning fluid.

Chocolate Use trichloroethane or another dry-cleaning fluid, sponge with a solution of soap and warm water, rinse. If the stain remains, use a mild bleach on washable garments, otherwise have the garment professionally cleaned.

Coffee and tea Soak fresh stains in cool water. If the beverage contained cream, sponge with trichloroethane or dry-cleaning fluid. Some sources recommend pouring very hot water from a height of 2 feet through the stain.

Curry For washable fabrics apply warm glycerine, rinse, apply a few drops of ammonia, rinse, and if the stain persists, add a few drops of hydrogen peroxide and rinse. Non-washables almost always have to be professionally dry-cleaned.

Dye If the spot is small and fresh it can be flushed out with cool water. For larger stains a color remover has to be used and the garment redyed.

Egg Sponge with cold water, then trichloroethane or a dry-cleaning fluid. Do not use heat of any sort until the stain is completely removed.

Fruit Rub the fresh spot with cold water and a few drops of glycerine, let stand for 2 hours, add a few drops of vinegar, sponge and rinse. This treatment can be used on stains caused by cherries, peaches, pears and plums. For the removal of other fruit stains, see coffee and tea removals.

Glue Let stand in soap and warm water solution until the glue dissolves, then rinse.

Grass Sponge with denatured alcohol or use an enzyme pre-soak product. Launder. If the stain remains use a mild bleach.

Greasy foods and oils (includes gravies, cream and salad oils) Remove the excess, sponge with trichloroethane, a spray spot-lifter or one of the absorbent powders. Launder, if the fabric is washable.

Ice cream All fabrics should first be sponged with cold water to remove the sugar. For washables, if it's chocolate or coffee ice cream, sponge also with trichloroethane and launder. For non-washables treat with trichloroethane or denatured alcohol after the cold water has been applied.

Ink So-called washable ink can sometimes be removed with cold water and if the stain remains, use one of the absorbent powders.

195

Lipstick Rub with glycerine to remove the grease, then sponge with a dry-cleaning fluid. If the garment is washable, launder with a detergent. Non-washables may have to be professionally cleaned.

Liquid Makeup Brush away powder and sponge with a dry-cleaning fluid.

Meat juice Sponge with cool water, then with a dry-cleaning fluid or an absorbent powder.

Mildew Usually these spots will come out in the laundry if they are fresh and the fabric is washable. If the stains persist, use a mild bleach. Non-washables should be taken to the dry cleaner.

Mud Let it dry, brush off the excess. Sponge with denatured alcohol.

Mustard Work glycerine into the stain, sponge with denatured alcohol. Washables are laundered using a mild bleach.

Nail polish Sponge with alcohol or a thinner. Nail polish remover can be used on sturdy cottons but rinse right away so it doesn't make holes.

Paint If it's a water-based paint sponge with cold water but don't let it set more than 3 hours. For oil-based paint sponge with turpentine, then use trichloroethane.

Perspiration Sponge with a diluted solution of vinegar and water, then launder. If color has changed, expose the area to ammonia fumes, preferably when the garment is damp. Have non-washables professionally dry-cleaned to remove odor and stain.

Rust Apply lemon juice on the stain but do not let it dry. Rinse in warm water and launder.

Scorch If a washable fabric is slightly scorched the stain will probably disappear when laundered. If the stain remains, use a mild bleach. A deep scorch can well mean that the fibers have been ruined. It's virtually impossible to remove scorch from silk or wool.

Shoe polish The base is grease and will come off with trichloroethane or a dry-cleaning fluid. If it is ground in, apply glycerine to loosen it; scrape off the excess. Launder washable fabrics. For woolens, use denatured alcohol.

Suntan lotions Sponge with trichloroethane, then soak in a detergent solution to which vinegar has been added. If the stain remains use a mild bleach in the laundry.

Tar Soften the stain by rubbing in petroleum jelly. Allow it to stand for a few minutes and follow with a treatment of cleaning fluid. Launder washable fabrics.

Wine Pour salt or club soda on a still damp stain until it has absorbed all of the color. Wine that has set is difficult to remove—in washables it may be removed by bleaching alternately with vinegar and ammonia solutions.

9

Good Food—Planning, Shopping and Cooking

YOUR FIRST KITCHEN may leave much to be desired in the way of space and decor. Despite limitations of any kind, give the kitchen a vital personality—make it a center of hospitality, love and creative cooking. The tantalizing aroma of good food can help change the blackest mood to a lighter shade and relax the most harried husband. The kitchen may have the proportions of a closet but, with skill and deftness, you can turn out a feast fit for a king—or a husband. Even the most modest meal which has been well prepared, shared and savored can produce results best described as pure contentment.

The bride who already has explored the fine art of food preparation has a distinct advantage over the newlywed who "can't boil water." But the novice should not despair. Preparing a meal is all a matter of timing, organization and experience, with some help from a good basic cookbook. To become a first-rate cook you need to have a genuine interest in food, imagination, a flair for experimentation—and it helps to have a husband who appreciates and encourages your efforts. Cooking, like sewing, can serve as a creative outlet for you. Look upon it as an art.

Apartment dwellers usually have little to say about the kitchen except for the color of the paint, and landlords seldom permit structural changes. Therefore it is up to the bride to exercise ingenuity if space is at a premium or the arrangement is awkward. Storage can be found on a blank wall or behind the kitchen door. Mount a pegboard and hang pots and pans or smaller cooking utensils. Build a shallow cabinet (4 to 6 inches deep) behind the kitchen or closet door, tailoring it to fit your needs. Enclose space above kitchen cabinets with doors to store seldom used equipment and supplies. Put up a pot rack, available in hardware stores, which has hooks for hanging pans conveniently out of the way. These racks are often made of wrought iron and come in circular or semicircular shapes. To gain counter space have your husband attach a shelf, work height, on a blank wall. Install it permanently, if space permits, or make it with a drop-leaf construction which can be lowered when not in use. Take advantage of all the new cabinet accessories to help organize dead storage space in cabinets or directly under them. On the market are turntables, roll-out drawers which are self-stacking, slide-out lid racks and stacking vegetable bins. A small, inefficient pantry or closet can be converted into a roomy storage place by the installation of space-saving, swing-out sections with shallow but convenient shelves. Buy cookware that serves a dual purpose to save more space—a double boiler when not used for that special purpose can act as two pots; a casserole with a raised lid can be separated to give you an uncovered casserole dish plus a shallow skillet. Look for these features when you buy cookwear and serving dishes.

EQUIPMENT FOR THE KITCHEN

The major appliances which are considered necessary to equip a kitchen are a range and a refrigerator (or combination refrigerator-freezer). The automatic dishwasher is not quite as essential but, if you can afford it and have the room, by all means buy it for convenience and time-saving qualities.

Before buying any or all of these basic appliances study your needs, present and future, estimate the space problems and calculate how much you can afford to spend. Shop carefully. Look in more than one store—prices can vary drastically. Examine more than one brand to get the features you really want. Note that colored appliances cost more than white ones. Buy a well-known brand from a reputable store that will guarantee installation and servicing. Read the instruction book thoroughly so you understand what the appliance is capable of doing. Ask to have a demonstration. Check on the warranty and guarantee. And when the appliances are installed make sure they are level, even if your floor isn't, to provide the best performance. The temperature of an oven should be checked for accuracy when installed. All appliances should be in top working order and be free of defects when they are installed.

THE RANGE

Many models and types of stoves are on the market, using either gas or electricity. Both do a first-rate job of cooking and feature many of the same conveniences. Your choice will depend on your personal preference, the cost and convenience of installation and operation. Since the range you choose can be a very good friend for years, weigh carefully all the features you deem essential along with the ones you think desirable before making a final decision.

To install an electric range, a heavy-duty electric circuit is required. A gas range needs to be connected to a gas outlet (either natural or mixed) or have suitable connections to consume bottled gas. A gas stove is considered more economical to operate in most sections of the country. It heats quicker but will cause spattering and leave flame marks on the pan bottoms. Electric heat is slower, more even and cleaner. The surface units do burn out, though, and must be replaced periodically.

Many "extras" are available on ranges, but they do add to the initial cost. Range tops usually have four to six surface units grouped to provide a working area in the center or at one side. A glass ceramic cooktop has a radiant surface with electric elements heating in sunburst spots to provide controlled temperatures. Top surfaces come with built-in griddles, well-cookers; gas stoves can even have "burners with brains" controlled thermostatically to regulate temperature and flame.

Various models feature different types of ovens. Some have two ovens, an extra-wide oven, a wall oven, a warming oven, a self-cleaning oven. Almost all have controls which regulate the temperature. Of great convenience is the oven with the "keep-warm" temperature setting as low as 140 degrees F. A more expensive model has an oven with a clock control; set the control for the cooking time, the cooking temperature, and the clock automatically does the rest. This feature is a great boon for the wife who works part-time.

The broiler size can vary in gas ranges, no matter how large the oven. Broiling is done at the top of the oven in the standard electric range under the top heating element, making it impossible to bake and broil at the same time. To accomplish this you must have two ovens.

Ranges come with clocks, signal buzzers, rotisseries, outlets for other appliances, timers, storage compartments and built-in venting systems. Below are the standard types of ranges you can buy.

Free-standing range The complete stove stands independently and consists of the surface units, the oven and the broiler. It's available in a wide range of sizes, colors and extras.

Eye-level oven range Stands independently and is a complete unit with the oven over the cooking top. Some models are mounted on a cabinet base while others have a second oven below.

Built-in range The cooking top is mounted on a base cabinet, completely separate from the oven and broiler, which allows flexibility in placing them where the kitchen plan permits.

Drop-in or slide-in range A one-piece unit which is set between two cabinets to appear built in. The drop-in is suspended from the countertop or mounted on a base. The slide-in rests on the floor. Either model may or may not have finished sides.

Range with warming shelf A free-standing one-piece unit with the oven and broiler below the cooking top and either a warming cabinet or shelf above the cooking surface.

Ranges are finished in baked enamel, porcelain, chrome or
stainless steel. Check to see that the controls are placed well and
easily read. The broiler and grid should be made of aluminum or
porcelain enamel and should adjust to several positions. The oven
door should fit tightly and have a lock stop; the inside shelves (at
least two) should be adjustable to several positions and have lock
stops to prevent tipping. There must be an oven vent to expel
greasy vapors.

THE REFRIGERATOR

How often you shop for food can depend partially on the size
and efficiency of your refrigerator. With plenty of storage space
and a good freezing section it may be necessary to visit the
supermarket only once a week. Today's refrigerators are classified
two ways—the conventional and the combination.

The conventional has only one heavy outside door which
encloses both the refrigerator and freezer sections. Storage bins
hold meats and fresh produce. The freezer section, separated
from the refrigerator by a lightweight door, can make ice cubes
and hold frozen foods for a period of a week or more. It cannot
reach a temperature low enough to sharp-freeze fresh foods so
they will keep for long periods of time.

The combination refrigerator-freezer has two heavy outside
doors which enclose the refrigerator and freezer sections separately. The refrigerator has all the same features as the conventional type but the freezing section is larger and is capable of
reaching a temperature of 0 degrees F. The low temperature
means fresh foods can be sharp-frozen to keep longer. The
freezer section can be located at the top, side or bottom.

Refrigerators are sized by interior cubic footage. Some brands
utilize the footage better than others by the way the interiors are
designed and the shelves are spaced. Many shelves are adjustable,
some pull out and some swing around for greater accessibility.
Door shelves add to storage room and convenience.

A real time-saver is the "frost-free" model which never needs
defrosting. While it costs more initially, many housewives think
the extra expense is well worth the freedom from defrosting. This

feature does not mean the refrigerator doesn't have to be cleaned out, though.

If you have a space problem and the refrigerator has to be set into a definite area, take careful, accurate measurements and match them with the outside dimensions of the model you are considering. To be able safely to push a refrigerator back against the wall the heat from the condenser coils must be discharged in the front. You must allow room for air to circulate if the heat is discharged from the back. Some doors, when swung open, have hinges which adjust to become flush with the side of the refrigerator while other hinges allow the open door to extend inches beyond the refrigerator side. This can be an important factor if you are placing the refrigerator in a corner and need every inch you can save. While standard refrigerator doors are hinged right-handed (meaning the opening is on the left) you can order a model with left-handed hinging if it is more convenient to your kitchen plan.

The outside finish is of porcelain, baked enamel or stainless steel. The interior is finished with porcelain enamel, plastic or aluminum. Baskets and shelves are made of rust-resistant metal and plastic. The door closes tightly with the help of a rubber gasket around the inside edge. Several brands have magnets for door closings and, if the refrigerator is leveled properly, the door will swing shut gradually by itself. Check to be sure all controls are placed so they are easily read with a light located nearby.

THE DISHWASHER

An appliance well worth having is a dishwasher. Though your kitchen is small you may be able to find a place for a portable model, one of which comes with a handy chopping-block top. Other types are the free-standing and the under-counter model. Both need to be permanently installed. Dishes washed in automatic dishwashers can be more sanitary than dishes washed by hand because many have hot water boosters or heating units to insure very hot water. A certain water pressure is required for maximum efficiency—ask the salesman if this can be a problem in your area.

The capacity of the dishwasher is measured by how many place settings it will hold, with the size varying from 6 to 18 settings. Shop carefully, though—some dishwashers load to a greater advantage than others no matter what their capacity is supposed to be. Look for plastic-coated racks to hold the dishes flexibly, yet firmly enough so they cannot knock together and chip. Besides washing, rinsing and drying, some dishwashers will have cycles for pre-washing and plate warming. It is helpful to have a control switch which allows you to stop the dishwasher after it has started, to remove or add dishes. Some brands are quieter in operation than others because of special insulation which deadens sound.

SMALL APPLIANCES

Small electric appliances are popular as shower and wedding gifts. Any duplications or unnecessary items should be returned or exchanged for other merchandise. If you are buying on your own, select the appliance carefully on the basis of what it will do, how often you will use it and whether you can store it where it will be accessible when you want to use it. Be sure the appliance you are considering is not a duplication of something you already have. For example, if the stationary mixer has a juicer attachment you don't need a separate juicer.

Classified as small appliances are toasters, coffeepots, waffle irons, portable mixers, stationary mixers, skillets, blenders, can openers, electric knives, knife-sharpeners, broiler and roaster ovens, rotisseries, deep-fat fryers, vertical broilers, buffet servers, automatic juicers, ice-crushers, hot trays and multi-purpose hostess centers.

Look for appliances which are immersible for easy washing, either because they have removable heating controls or because the controls are sealed. Some appliances have interchangeable controls. Of course you can only use one at a time but there is only one cord to store and the purchase price is cheaper.

COOKWARE

Pots, pans, casseroles and mixing bowls are made from a variety of materials in a wide range of colors and designs. Don't be tempted, however, to buy a set of pots and pans because they look pretty. Different culinary techniques call for utensils made from different materials. A set may also include items which you really don't want or need. Look for quality in cookware—handled properly, it will last for years. Buy pots with lids that fit tightly to prevent water loss. Look for handles that are firmly attached, comfortable to handle and well insulated. Some, made of a high-heat-resistant resin, can withstand oven heat without melting. The pans should be seamless, well-balanced with rounded corners and smooth edges for easy cleaning. Many utensils are now coated with non-stick finishes, some tough enough to resist scratching and staining.

Common materials made into cookware include:

Aluminum Lightweight metal, excellent for conducting heat quickly and evenly. It is inexpensive, dents easily and can stain when subjected to strong soaps and some acids.

Stainless steel A tough, durable, lightweight metal that is difficult to harm and simple to clean. It's a moderately good heat conductor. It is used for mixing bowls as well as cookware.

Aluminum-clad stainless steel The combination of metals gives excellent heat conductivity and is easily cleaned.

Copper A durable and attractive metal that is lined with either tin or stainless steel for cooking pots. It is an excellent heat conductor but discolors with exposure to air and gas flames. Special cleaning is required. Copper mixing bowls are favored—egg whites beat to a greater volume in them.

Copper-clad stainless steel A combination of metals that gives excellent, even heat conductivity and beauty.

Cast iron A durable, heavy metal good for long, slow cooking. It heats slowly, evenly and retains heat. Special cleaning care must be taken to keep cast iron seasoned and free of rust.

Ceramic A colorful pottery, glazed on the inside, that conducts heat poorly, can be fragile and is used for casseroles. It's good for slow oven cooking and cleans well. New pottery has been developed that will withstand the heat of a moderate gas flame but not that of an electric unit.

Glass A poor heat conductor and breakable but it is easy to clean, resisting stains and acids. The transparency of glass allows you to see the food being cooked. Check the label for information—whether it is flame-proof as well as oven-proof.

Glass-ceramic A non-transparent material, more durable than glass. It's a poor heat conductor, easy to clean and doesn't stain. Some brands can take the extreme temperature changes (from freezer to oven) with no danger of breaking. Mixing bowls are often made of this material.

Porcelain enamel on cast iron With the enamel applied to both the inside and outside of a utensil, it's durable, heats evenly, cleans well. This colorful cookware has all the advantages of cast iron without its problems of rusting and seasoning. Food can be cooked, served and stored in the same pot or casserole.

CUTLERY

A good sharp knife that holds an edge is worth its weight in gold to the dedicated cook. It can help you prepare food efficiently and quickly. A dull knife is a bad tool. When you are shopping for cutlery, buy for quality; a cheap knife is no bargain. Good cutlery, properly treated, should last for years depending on how thick the blade is and how often it is sharpened. The thinly ground cutting edge can be reduced by too much sharpening.

Steel, plus carbon, is the basis for knife blades—the higher the carbon content, the better the blade. In the past decade stainless steel has been developed with a high carbon content to give knives edge-retaining properties so they seldom have to be resharpened.

The tapered or straight-edge knife is used for slicing and chopping; the knife with a serrated edge (with tiny, saw-like teeth) is used when a slight sawing or tearing motion is required, as for cutting bread and cheese. The knife with the scalloped edge is becoming very popular, slicing smoothly and evenly with the cutting edge behind the scallops wearing well.

A knife should have good balance and fit your hand correctly. The weight is balanced either in the handle or in the blade, depending on the job function. For example: the weight of a boning knife is concentrated in the handle, to help give leverage for cutting meat away from the carcass; a chef's knife, used primarily for chopping, needs the weight centered in the blade for more efficient action. Use a wooden board for chopping, and, if possible, for carving.

There are different knives for various tasks.

1. Paring knife with a short handle and blade for peeling and paring.

2. Utility knife with a slightly longer blade for peeling when the paring knife is not large enough.

3. Small serrated or scalloped-edge knife for slicing fruit, cheese or tomatoes.

4. Boning knife with a medium long, slim blade used to remove meat from the carcass.

5. Bread knife with an edge serrated or scalloped about 8″ long.

6. French chef's knife with a heavy triangular blade about 10″ long. A cook's knife is fashioned the same way but with an 8″ blade.

Paring Knife

Utility Knife

Fruit Knife

Boning Knife

Bread Knife

French Chef's Knife

Butcher's Knife

Ham Slicer

Carving Knife

Grapefruit Knife

207

7. Butcher's knife with a heavy thick blade for cutting raw meat.

8. Ham or cold slicer with a long slender blade (10″) which cuts easily through cold meats.

9. Carving knife or hot slicer with a long blade thicker than the ham slicer, used for carving hot meats.

10. Grapefruit knife has a short curved blade serrated on one or both sides.

A basic carving set consists of a carving knife, a fork with a guard or thumb rest and a sharpening steel to hone a sharp edge. Deluxe sets often have two knives, one for carving and one for slicing, along with a wide-pronged fork.

Electric knives are very useful for carving quickly and neatly. Two serrated edges move back and forth at a very high speed when activated by a lever in the handle. They are convenient—you just place the knife where you want to cut and press the lever—but they do tend to tear the meat if it is sliced too thin. Because the controls are in the handle, some electric knives are awkward and cumbersome to handle.

STOCKING THE KITCHEN

The kitchen has to be stocked with certain basic items before you can cook the simplest meal. Here is a guide to show you what is needed in the way of cookware, utensils and general cooking supplies.

Cookware and utensils Three lists are compiled in this category to guide you: the first, a group of essentials needed for a working kitchen; the second, fill-ins to be added as you become more proficient in the culinary arts, and third, items for the expert cook who also has plenty of storage space. Small electric appliances are not included.

THE ESSENTIALS

1 6″ frying pan	1 paring knife
1 10″ frying pan	1 8″ cook's knife
1 Dutch oven (5 or 6 qts.)	1 slotted mixing spoon
1 double boiler	1 wooden spoon
1 can opener	1 kitchen fork

1 medium saucepan
1 graduated glass measuring cup
1 set of measuring spoons
1 casserole
1 coffeepot
1 set of tongs

1 rotary beater
1 rubber scraper
1 pancake turner
1 rectangular baking pan
1 corkscrew
3 graduated mixing bowls

THE FILL-INS TO BUY SOON

1 pepper mill
1 large saucepan
1 small saucepan
1 wire whisk
1 grater
1 spatula
1 ladle
1 large strainer
1 sifter
1 pastry brush
1 rolling pin

1 cookie sheet
2 pie plates
3 layer cake pans
2 cooling racks
1 loaf pan
1 chopping board
1 asbestos mat
1 set measuring cups
1 kitchen scissors
1 tea strainer
1 timer

1 shallow baking pan
1 pair poultry shears
1 meat grinder
1 potato masher
1 utility knife
1 carving set
1 serrated bread knife
1 cheese knife
1 roasting pan with rack
1 tea kettle
1 canister set

FOR THE EXPERT

Kitchen scales
1 chopping bowl with chopper
1 mortar and pestle
2 more casseroles
1 paella pan
1 chafing dish
1 pastry tube
1 omelette pan
1 meat thermometer
1 crepes pan
1 wok with ring
1 fish poacher
1 steamer
1 fondue pot
1 large au gratin pan
1 French chef's knife
1 boning knife
1 ham slicer
1 balloon whisk
1 espresso coffeepot

Nest of soufflé dishes
Spring forms
Molds for pastry or gelatin
6 individual ramekins
6 custard cups
1 tube cake pan
1 garlic press
1 cleaver
1 vegetable mill
1 set of long skewers
1 set of short skewers
1 pair spaghetti tongs
1 basket for deep fat frying
1 colander
1 lemon juicer
1 wooden mallet
1 pastry blender
1 metal meat tenderizer
1 bulb baster
1 butter melter

Basic cooking needs Every kitchen must have a stock of staples, spices and condiments in the cupboard to form a foundation for cooking. It's handy to have some shortcut foods on the shelf, too. It may surprise you how much it costs to lay in these basic supplies, but you'll find many of the items will last for a long time. Before buying in quantity, make sure you have the storage space and that you'll be able to use up the ingredient while it is still good.

STAPLE LIST
Granulated sugar
Confectioner's sugar
Brown sugar
Coffee, ground and instant
Tea
Baking powder
Baking soda
Cornstarch
Vegetable shortening
Vegetable oil
Cereal
Unsweetened chocolate or cocoa
Rice
Spaghetti and noodles

HANDY SHORTCUT FOODS
Bouillon cubes
Pudding mixes
Flavored gelatin
Spaghetti sauce
Salad dressings
Biscuit and pie crust mix
Bread crumbs
Pancake mix
Crackers
Concentrated soups

SPICES AND CONDIMENTS
Prepared mustard
Dry mustard
Iodized salt
Pepper
Catsup and/or chili sauce
Olive oil
Vinegar
Worcestershire sauce
Tabasco sauce
Jams and jellies
Vanilla extract
Mayonnaise
Soy sauce
Garlic and garlic salt
Onions
Cinnamon
Nutmeg
Celery salt and seed
Herbs

MENU PLANNING

The food you eat supplies your body with energy for work and play, nutrients for growth and health. To maintain good health you need *protein* for growth and repair of body tissues; *minerals* and *vitamins* for proper body functions, and *fat* and *carbohydrates* for energy. No one food contains all the nutrients needed, but most foods contain more than one nutrient. For this reason foods should be chosen wisely from a variety of different kinds to insure a balanced diet.

There are four broad groups of food. Plan the main part of your daily meals around foods from each of these groups for a sound diet and add other foods for appeal and satisfaction. The four groups offer a wide range of food so there is no reason for monotonous menus.

MEAT GROUP

For protein to build and repair body tissues. It includes beef, veal, pork, lamb, organ meats (liver, heart and kidney), poultry, eggs, fish and shellfish. Dried peas and beans, nuts and peanut butter can be substituted for the meats as other good sources of protein. Daily you need two servings from this group. A serving consists of 2 to 3 ounces of meat, fish or poultry without bone; 2 eggs; 1 cup of dried peas or beans, or 4 tablespoons of peanut butter.

VEGETABLE—FRUIT GROUP

For vitamins and minerals for growth and upkeep of the body. Included are all vegetables and fruits, rich in vitamins A and C as well as minerals. Daily you need four or more servings from this group—at least one serving of citrus fruit rich in vitamin C and at least one serving of a green leafy or deep yellow vegetable rich in vitamin A. A serving consists of ½ cup of any fruit or vegetable or a whole piece of fruit such as an apple, orange or banana.

MILK GROUP

Along with the protein and vitamins in this group, minerals are a vital source of calcium which is needed to maintain good teeth and strong bones. Included are milk in any form (fluid, skim, buttermilk, evaporated or dried), cheese and ice cream. Cheese or ice cream can replace part of the daily milk requirement. Daily you need two or more 8-ounce glasses of milk or the equivalent. Some of the equivalents are: ½ cup of cottage cheese-1/3 cup of milk; 1 inch cube of cheddar cheese-½ cup of milk; ½ cup of ice cream-¼ cup of milk.

BREAD—CEREAL GROUP

For protein, iron vitamins and food energy. Included here are all breads and cereals made of whole grain, enriched or restored—cooked cereals, ready-to-eat cereals, macaroni, rice, spaghetti, noodles, rolled oats and cornmeal. Daily you need four servings from this group. A serving consists of 1 slice of bread; ½ to ¾ cup of cooked cereal, macaroni, noodles, spaghetti or rice.

OTHER FOODS

These are the ones which satisfy, give energy, and add appeal to round out a meal. They are added to other foods or included in recipes and include unenriched, refined cereals and breads, sugars, flours, butter, margarine and other fats such as vegetable oils.

TO KEEP YOUR WEIGHT WHERE YOU WANT IT

In our weight-conscious society everyone knows about calories, the units of fuel contained in food which, if burned, yield a certain amount of energy. All food calories are alike and all foods contain calories, but some foods are high in calories without being high in nutritional value. If you eat the foods high in calories and do not burn up the energy, you will gain weight. The number of calories your body needs per day for adequate fuel depends on your age, your body frame, your sex and how active you are. A person with a large bone structure is going to weigh more and need more food for fuel than a person with a very slight frame. An active person will burn up more calories in exercise than one who sits at a desk all day long. As an adult grows older he needs less to keep the body functioning. Men need more calories than women, and after a long illness everyone needs more fuel to rebuild the body. If you don't already have one, buy a calorie counter or chart to be a guide on your daily requirement, along with the caloric values of many common foods.

The best way to maintain the weight you want is to develop good eating habits. If you splurge over the weekend with rich desserts and other foods high in calories, be conscious of calories during the week and cut down to simple, protein-rich dishes.

Watch in-between-meal snacks which can be laden with calories. Overeating is the basic cause of overweight.

Before proceeding with a serious diet get a medical checkup and follow the advice of your doctor on dieting. Beware of fad diets or the so-called crash diets which are supposed to take off pounds and pounds in no time. Many can be dangerous to your health, creating a nutritional imbalance. Others simply represent a water loss which will return in the way of pounds once you resume your normal eating habits.

MEAL PLANNING

With the four essential food groups as your main outline, plan daily menus for a week at a time, taking into account planned guests and nights out. Make them flexible enough so you can take advantage of unexpected food bargains or allow for unexpected guests. For the sake of your budget, plan some dishes that use less expensive cuts of meat, meat substitutes and leftovers. Here are some points to keep in mind:

1. Plan a meal with color as a factor as well as nutrition. Don't plan to have mashed potatoes, cauliflower and roast pork all in the same meal. Brighten the menu with a green vegetable.
2. Plan for a variety of textures. When you are having noodles, contrast them with a crisp salad.
3. Plan meals that you can handle with the equipment at hand. Two oven dishes that need vastly different temperatures cannot be cooked at the same time in one oven.
4. Plan a whole oven meal at once, taking into account the temperature needed to cook each food. For example, have a meat loaf and baked potatoes at the same time.
5. Vary the flavors. When one food is very spicy, have a bland one for contrast. Some foods demand other flavors—for example: ham with sweet potatoes.
6. Plan for variety each day and, at least once a week, introduce a new food or recipe. If you both like it, add it to your menu repertory.
7. Consult a good cookbook for new ideas on how to present basic food in a new way. Make a file of the ones you both like for future use.

213

8. Plan for a food rich in protein at each meal—meat, poultry, fish, eggs, milk or cheese.

9. Combine sizes and shapes of food. Don't serve two creamed foods such as mashed potatoes and creamed peas together.

10. To save time and money plan some meals with leftovers which can be used as casseroles or in other forms for other meals.

11. Plan well-balanced meals. After a heavy main course, serve a light dessert.

While you are deciding on the week's menus make a shopping list. Check the staples to make sure you have everything on hand that the recipe needs. Ideally, you should jot down on a shopping list anything which needs replenishing during the week as it becomes low. Also check the refrigerator to see if there are leftovers which must be used while they are still usable. Since every household should have an emergency shelf of sorts, check it for possible replenishing.

SHOPPING

With shopping list in hand you are ready to go to the market. One weekly trip to the market should suffice if you have planned carefully and have good storage facilities at home. You may find it necessary to fill in with fresh vegetables and fruits during the week. Some tips on how to get the most from your food dollar are:

1. Check the newspapers for specials. Many weekend specials start several days before so you can manage to shop at other times to avoid the crowds. Clip any newspaper article that offers money off on an item. Do not buy it, though, unless you need it or can use it in the near future.

2. Shop at supermarkets. Because they deal in volume they can afford to sell at a cheaper price than smaller shops. Many have their own brands in canned and frozen foods—some are excellent, some are mediocre—but they are usually cheaper. You'll have to experiment to see if they suit you. For special brands and cuts of meat you may have to go to specialty stores.

3. When you have found a store you like, stick to it. Unless you have lots of free time it will save you aggravation and energy to patronize one store where you know where everything is located.

4. Invest in an inexpensive hand-checker or pocket-counter which you can carry in the palm of your hand and, by means of pushing buttons, add up what you are spending. It can prove to be a useful way to stay within your budget.

5. Buy vegetables and fruits in season. They are cheaper and better.

6. Don't overbuy, especially when it comes to perishable foods. Spoiled food is a waste of money.

7. Compare prices.

8. Compare weights, size of containers and water contents.

9. Read the labels. According to law, canned goods labels must say the common name of the product, the form of the product (whether it is diced, sliced or whole), the ingredients, the approximate number of servings and the name and address of the manufacturer and/or packer.

10. If your store offers trading stamps ask yourself if you pay extra for the stamps. If the prices are higher than those in other stores, then you do pay for them and they can hardly be a saving.

11. Resist impulse buying and don't pick up anything unless you really want or need it.

12. Use variety meats frequently, such as liver, kidneys, tongue and heart.

13. Buy milk by the half-gallon or gallon container rather than by the quart.

14. Buy sugar, rice or flour more cheaply by the bag than by the box. The packaging costs less. If you have the room, buy in a larger quantity.

15. Economy sizes are not always cheaper than smaller sizes. Figure the cost per ounce to determine which is cheaper.

16. The outside color of eggs does not affect their inside taste. Buy the cheaper color.

17. Butter by the pound in bulk is cheaper than butter prewrapped into quarters.

18. Sliced cheese is more expensive and dries out faster than cheese bought in bulk form and sliced by you at home.

19. Concentrated frozen orange juice is cheaper than a comparable amount of fresh orange juice.

20. Frozen vegetables can cost less than fresh ones and be more nutritious, especially if you buy them in city markets where the vegetables may have been picked days before. Frozen vegetables in large plastic bags cost less than the smaller amounts in boxes. Again, it's the packaging which costs.

21. Chickens cut up are more expensive than whole chickens.

22. Pre-stuffed cuts of meat and pre-breaded cutlets can be more expensive than if you stuff and bread the cuts at home.

23. Non-fat dried milk is much less expensive than fluid milk and just as nutritious.

24. Evaporated skim milk is cheaper than evaporated whole milk and also contains fewer calories.

25. Less expensive margarine can be substituted for butter in cooking, even for a spread.

26. Large boxes of unsweetened cereal are more economical than small, pre-sweetened, individual boxes.

27. Less expensive cuts of meat can be made tender by being marinated for several hours before cooking.

28. Most convenience foods are more expensive than it would cost you to produce them at home. Packaged seasonings for gravies, salad dressings and specialties are very expensive.

29. Regular rice costs less than the pre-cooked variety or special rice blended with other ingredients.

30. Basic pasta shapes (spaghetti, macaroni and noodles) cost less than the specialty forms.

BUYING MEATS AND FISH

Many of you will be buying your meat pre-packaged at the supermarket instead of custom-cut from a friendly, helpful butcher. It is very difficult to choose from all of the attractive packages, except by price, unless you know something about the cuts of meat and how they should be cooked.

Beef is the meat most often graded; that which is shipped across state lines must be inspected by the federal government. Lamb and veal are sometimes graded but pork is not. Many states and cities have their own inspection laws, but not all do. You will know if the meat is graded and inspected by the round purple stamp marked "U.S. Inspected" which is affixed to the meat certifying that it is safe, untainted and free from disease. The grades and what they stand for are:

USDA Prime The best and most expensive quality of meat; tender, juicy and well textured with good marbling (fat distribution) through the lean meat. The fat encasing the outside is thick and creamy white. Most of the prime quality meat goes to the best restaurants and hotels but you may be able to find some in the better butcher shops.

USDA Choice The next best grade with less fat but still very tender and juicy. Good butcher shops and supermarkets will carry this grade.

USDA Good A good quality of meat with less fat and relatively tender with little or no marbling. It has a mild flavor but lacks the juiciness of the two top grades.

USDA Standard Meat from young low-quality animals which is less tender, less flavorful and with very little fat.

USDA Commercial Meat coming from older animals. It has flavor but is tough and coarse.

The most tender and expensive cuts of beef (sirloin, T-bone, porterhouse and prime rib roast) are better cooked by the dry heat methods: broiling, roating, pan-broiling and barbecuing. Heat seals the surface, preventing the juices and nutrients from escaping. The less tender cuts, those with connective tissue and fiber (chuck, brisket and short ribs), need to be cooked longer in moisture—stock, wine or water—to become tender. Moist meat methods include braising, stewing, pot-roasting and poaching. Chopped meat can come from the scraps of any number of cuts—sirloin, round, chuck or a hodgepodge which is unidentified by cut. Chopped sirloin and ground round will have less fat than chuck.

Liver, one of the variety meats, is an excellent source of iron, with pork being the most nutritious, beef next and calves' liver the least. Most people buy the more expensive calves' liver because it

217

is flavorful and tender. Almost as tender is steer liver, from the young animal, if your butcher will slice it thin for you. Liver is usually sautéed, somtimes broiled. Other variety meats are: sweetbreads, kidneys, brains, tongue and heart. Be sure they are fresh before you buy because they can spoil quickly.

Veal is the meat of a calf from 6 weeks to 3 months. The meat should be pale, almost white, tinged with pink. It has no fat, no marbling and is at its best in late winter or early spring. Roasts and chops are cut from the leg, shoulder or loin. Stew meat and ground veal come from the scraps of any cuts. If you are buying the thin scallops for an Italian dish buy the ones which come from the leg for the tenderest meat. Veal should be cooked thoroughly but gently so it will not toughen.

Pork is available in either fresh or cured meats. Fresh pork is at its best when it is pale pink, firm and fine grained without too much fat. Roasts are cut from the leg, shoulder and loin, needing *long, slow* cooking. Chops and cutlets are sautéed or braised until they are thoroughly cooked. Smoked ham and bacon are cured pork. Ham can be parboiled and baked or just baked with or without a glaze. Bacon, best with a minimum of fat, is sautéed or broiled.

Lamb is a young sheep, the younger it is the more expensive the meat. As the lamb matures the meat gets darker. Mutton is the meat from a sheep over a year old. There are many cuts of lamb, but the most popular are leg of lamb and lamb chops from the loin or shoulder. The tender morsels of lamb in shish-kebab are cut from the leg and then marinated. Lamb and mutton should be cooked slowly and thoroughly.

Poultry is sold dressed, ready to cook and should be creamy white to yellow in color with no visible pinfeathers, no blemishes and fairly plump. Do not buy a chicken with any distinguishable odor. Chickens are sold whole or cut up. They are an excellent buy and are cooked in many ways: broiled, fried, barbecued, roasted, fricasseed and boiled. Chickens are sold as broilers (young, under 2½ lbs.); broilers and fryers (young, 2½ to 3½ lbs.); roasters (young, 3½ to 5 lbs.); capons (castrated males, 6 to 8 lbs.), and fowl (hens about 5 lbs.). Capons are usually roasted while fowl are good for stewing and fricasseeing. Other poultry in the markets are ducks, geese and turkeys. Young ducks may be called ducklings and are roasted. Geese are roasted and can be tough and greasy unless you know how to cook them well. Turkeys are classified much like chickens: fryer-roaster (from 5 to 8 lbs.); young hen or young tom (from 6 to 24 lbs.), and the mature, a less tender, older bird. Turkey is almost always roasted, with or without stuffing. There are some very good boneless turkey roasts available which are handy for serving at buffet parties.

Fish must be fresh or frozen to be safe and good. Both deep sea and fresh water fish are seasonal and, if fresh, should have bright bulging eyes, reddish gills and scales still firmly attached. If you are planning to freeze the fish at home ask the butcher if it has been frozen before and thawed. Shellfish include both mollusks and crustaceans—shrimp, lobsters, mussels, oysters, scallops, crabs and clams. Many are sold alive, except for scallops and shrimp. If you are buying live ones with shells be sure they are tightly closed, and not cracked. Lobsters should either be bought alive (and still wiggling) or cooked. Shrimp are sold with the heads removed, either fresh and unshelled or cooked, with or without the shells. It will cost you more to buy them cooked. They also come frozen and uncooked but shelled, which can be worth the extra cost.

To buy meat intelligently here are some guidelines:

1. Look for the inspection label on the meat.
2. Larger cuts are often sold as "specials." If you have the storage room, buy them and have the butcher cut the meat in two. A leg of lamb can serve as a roast as well as being cut into steaks or cubes for stewing. Many stores offer combinations—so much chopped meat with a roast or steaks, however you want the meat cut.
3. The tender cuts of meat come from the section where the least movement and muscle buildup have occurred in the animal.
4. Boneless meat, although more expensive to buy, may prove less expensive per serving because there is no waste.
5. If you are buying from a butcher, watch the scales with him.
6. When buying poultry look for the bird with a well-filled-out breast for the most white meat.
7. You know better what you are buying if the pre-packaged meat has a transparent tray so you can see on both sides.

BUYING CANNED GOODS

Read the label for information of the contents of the can, whether it is whole, diced or sliced, the water content and what has been added. There are different qualities—if you are using the contents to make a salad or as a serving alone you want to buy the best quality for uniform size, shape and color. On the other hand, the less expensive or second quality is sufficient in cooking with other ingredients.

Besides giving the net weight the label usually tells you the number of cups the can will yield if the contents are in fluid or semifluid form.

BUYING FRESH VEGETABLES AND FRUITS

Fresh fruits, vegetables and salad greens are cheaper and of better quality when they are in season. Look for freshness— bruised, limp-looking produce is not a good buy.

FOR VEGETABLES AND SALAD GREENS:

Asparagus Stalks are tender, not woody, tipped with white. The tips are close and compact. The size has little to do with tenderness.

Beans If they are snap beans, they should snap. Crisp, small beans with a good green color are best. Avoid large bumpy ones which indicate tough seeds inside.

Broccoli A good dark green color with small, compact flowers.

Cabbage The head is firm and heavy with tight leaves, either red or pale green. Watch for discoloration and possible worm-holes.

Cauliflower A firm creamy white head with no soft spots or discoloration.

Celery The stalks and leaves appear to be crisp and fresh with no discoloration or rust marks.

Corn The husks and silks are fresh and moist, not dried and withered. The kernels are plump and juicy; immature kernels are undersized; overripe kernels are hard and indented.

Cucumbers Best when they are slender and firm, with a good green color and no signs of wrinkling or withering.

Eggplant Best when it is firm with a good purple skin showing no signs of wrinkling or withering.

Lettuce Although there are many kinds, some crisp and some soft, all varieties should appear fresh with no signs of wilting or discoloration. Avoid iceburg lettuce showing any signs of rust which can permeate the whole head.

Onions They are clean and hard with no discoloration or softness at the stem end. If you are buying by the bag make sure there aren't any spoiled ones in the center. Mild-flavored onions are flat in shape while global-shaped onions are more pungent in flavor.

Parsley The color is a uniform dark green with no yellow discoloration. Although parsley can be revived in ice water at home, look for a fresh, unwilted bunch.

Peas The pods should be well filled but not splitting open, a sign of overmaturity. Fresh peas have a good green color with no discoloration.

Potatoes The best ones are firm, smooth and free of blemishes, cuts and sprouts. Potatoes with green skin tend to be bitter. Those harvested early in the season are less mealy. New potatoes are small, roundish and have very thin reddish-brown skins.

Root vegetables Include carrots, radishes, beets, turnips and parsnips. All should be firm and smooth. Oversize ones are pithy or woody inside. The condition of the tops has little bearing on the flavor of the vegetable.

Scallions Are fresh and crisp with white tips and green tops showing no signs of withering or discoloring.

Spinach Large, fresh appearing leaves, either crinkly or flat, sold loose or in a package. Watch for withered, discolored leaves.

Tomatoes Are plump, uniform and unbruised with a good color (pink, red or yellow). Avoid the ones with growth cracks and scars. Vine-ripened tomatoes have the best flavor and can be completely ripened at home if left at room temperature.

Watercress Look for bunches with good dark green coloring, unwilted and with small, tender leaves.

221

FOR FRUITS:

Apples Good color is indicative of good flavor. Look for bruises and possible worm marks.

Bananas The best are firm and yellow with no bruises or broken skin. Bananas speckled with brown are ripe and ready for use. Those a little greener can be ripened at room temperature.

Citrus fruits A smooth skin means the fruit has more juice. Buy the fruit which seems the heaviest for its size. An orange with a slight tinge of green can still be ripe. Deep yellow lemons are milder than the more tart green-yellow ones.

Grapes Should be plump with a good healthy color, unbruised and firmly attached to the stem.

Melons (not including watermelon) Ripe when they have a fruity aroma and are slightly soft at the blossom end. Avoid excessive softness and obvious bruises.

Peaches The yellow or reddish-yellow ones which are fairly firm but not bruised are your best buy. Avoid the very soft and the very hard.

Pears A slightly hard pear can be ripened at room temperature. If the pear is firm but yields to a slight pressure it is ripe and ready to be used. According to the variety, the color range can be from light yellow to yellow-bronze.

Pineapple Like melon, a ripe pineapple has a fruity aroma. Buy the one which seems heavy for its size. Avoid any that seems soft or shows signs of decay or mold.

Watermelon For the best quality, the surface color is dull with the rind, directly below, cream colored. The inside is red, firm and with few immature seeds among the other seeds.

BUYING EGGS

Eggs are graded by federal standard with a grademark on the carton. If they are handled properly after the grading and kept refrigerated there should be little loss in quality. Eggs graded AA (fresh, fancy) and A are both excellent for all purposes, especially where appearance counts. Grade B eggs are better used in cooking. The nutritional value, however, remains the same. The color of the shell makes no difference in the interior contents.

Size determines the way eggs are classified, no matter what their quality rating is. The weights per dozen are as follows: U.S. Extra Large, 27 ounces; U.S. Large, 24 ounces; U.S. Medium, 21 ounces, and U.S. Small, 18 ounces. The size will not affect most recipes with the exception of sponge and angelfood cakes where eggs are the sole leavening agents and the number may have to be increased if you use small eggs.

If you are planning to hardboil eggs, they should be at least three days old so the shells can be peeled without breaking the cooked white.

BUYING MILK AND CREAM

Almost all milk has to be pasteurized to be sold locally or across the country. This is a process of heating the milk to kill certain bacteria. Milk is sold in liquid or powdered form. The cream can be separated from the milk and processed separately. Various forms of milk are:

Whole milk A fresh milk in fluid form with at least 4% butterfat. If allowed to stand, the cream will rise to the top and can be skimmed off.

Homogenized milk Fresh fluid milk processed so the fat in the liquid is broken down into small particles to stay in suspension and not rise to the top.

Skim milk Fluid milk in which the butterfat (cream) has been removed but almost all the nutrients remain.

Buttermilk A commercially made product from skim milk with added particles of clabbered cream or butter.

Evaporated milk A whole or skim milk from which half of the moisture has been removed before canning. The flavor is vaguely that of caramel. The cans are convenient for storage, needing no refrigeration until opened.

Sweetened condensed milk The same as evaporated milk with the addition of sugar.

Dry milk solids Air-dried milk particles in powder form of either whole or skim milk which can be reconstituted into liquid by the addition of water. Stores conveniently and is inexpensive.

Light cream The liquid which rises to the top of the whole milk and contains 18 to 20% butterfat.

Heavy cream The liquid with slightly more butterfat content which rises to the top of whole milk and when separated can be whipped into stiff peaks. If overwhipped it will form a sort of butter.

Half and half Richer than whole milk, it is part milk and part cream.

Sour cream Cream which is allowed to ferment or sour either naturally or, in the case of pasteurized cream, a commercial culture is added. Sour cream now comes in several versions which contain fewer calories.

BUYING CHEESE

Cheeses are available either natural or processed. The best and most expensive is the natural cheese which is aged slowly to give an excellent flavor. A processed cheese is one which combines natural cheese with milk or another liquid. Originally cheeses were named after their place of origin but this hardly holds true today. You can buy both imported and domestic cheeses of varying quality and price in the supermarket.

Cheeses fall roughly into three categories:

Hard Parmesan, Provolone and Romano, all grating cheeses.

Semi-hard Edam, Gouda, Swiss, Port du Salut, Muenster, Gorgonzola, Jack, Cheddar, Blue, Brick, Gruyère, Limburger, Stilton, Roquefort, Tilsit, Feta and Bel Paese.

Soft Farmers, Pot, Cottage, Cream, Ricotta, Neufchâtel, Camembert, Brie, Mozarella and Liederkranz.

BUYING SUGAR

There are many forms of sugar and each has its own power to sweeten and flavor. Follow directions in the recipes and on labels to use each one to its best advantage.

Granulated A fine-grained sugar made from beet or cane, used in an all-purpose way for cooking and flavoring.

Super-fine A sugar ground finer than granulated, used for light volume cakes and to sweeten fruits.

Confectioners' In its finest form, sugar has the consistency of powder. It is used for uncooked cake icings, berry sweetening and in some candies. Do not substitute it for granulated sugar in baking.

Brown A less refined sugar with more moisture and a stronger flavor, it is available in light and dark shades. It lumps easily and dries out if not kept in a tightly sealed container after opening. Some brown sugar has been refined to be pourable at all times but it hasn't the strong flavor.

Lump A conveniently molded granulated sugar cut into cubes for use in hot drinks.

Corn syrup A liquid simple sugar, either light or dark, which is sometimes used with granulated sugar to prevent crystallization in cooking.

Honey Another liquid sugar with a unique flavor of its own, used for sweetening cereals, fruits and often as a spread.

Maple syrup A very sweet syrup from the sap of the sugar maple tree, used for flavoring in cooking, candy making and alone as a syrup.

Molasses A byproduct of sugar making with a strong, heavy flavor. It's used in cooking and baking often accompanied by pungent spices.

Sorghum A thinner, less sweet version of molasses used for baking.

BUYING FATS

Both animal and vegetable fats or oils are used for table spreads and cooking fats.

Salt butter Made from fresh or soured cream, butter must have a fat content of 80% with the rest made up of milk solids. Salt is added to the churned butter to flavor and help preserve it. Butter is highly regarded as a table spread and as a cooking fat because of its flavor and its ability to withstand high heat before burning. It will stand even higher temperatures if the milk solids are removed through clarification.

Sweet butter Made like salt butter but without the salt added. It is thought to have a more delicate flavor than salt butter but will spoil sooner.

Lard The rendered fatty tissue from pork which is considered a solid fat. It is white in color, relatively inexpensive and sold in package form. Lard is excellent for flaky piecrusts and biscuits but not good for cake baking.

Margarine Similar to butter with 80% fat and the rest milk solids, its base is a vegetable oil—corn, cottonseed or soybean. Almost all brands are enriched with vitamins and minerals. Margarine is interchangeable with butter, but it will burn at a lower temperature.

Solid vegetable shortening Hydrogen is added to refined vegetable oil to make a solid, white shortening. Sometimes emulsifiers are added to give a higher volume when used in baking. This kind of shortening is blander than butter, margarine or lard.

Oil Either one or a combination of vegetable oils. The oil is pressed from the seed or fruit of olives, corn, cottonseed, peanut, sesame, safflower, soybean or sunflower. Olive oil is thought to have the best flavor for salad dressing and cooking, but it is expensive. The oil becomes semisolid when refrigerated but will return to its liquid form when held at room temperature. Oil is 100% fat and cannot be substituted for a solid shortening in cooking unless the recipe specifies it.

BUYING FROZEN FOODS

The frozen food section of your supermarket abounds with a broad choice of foods—frozen juices, vegetables, TV dinners, meats, fish, foreign specialty foods, even waffles and garlic bread. Don't put too much stock in the number of servings some packages claim to contain—most adults feel they are skimpy for a healthy appetite. Buy only unstained, unbroken, solid packages. Any of these signs can indicate the food may have defrosted in transit and was refrozen, thus losing quality. Select your frozen food toward the last of the shopping so it won't be away from the freezer too long.

STORING THE GROCERIES

If you have other errands to do after grocery shopping on your way home make sure the food is not left in the sun or near a heat source. When you get home unpack and store the food immediately.

1. Store the frozen foods in your freezer at once.
2. Store the meat in the coldest part of the refrigerator or in the meat drawer. The transparent wrapper on packaged meat will hold it for several days in the refrigerator but it should be loosened so the meat can breathe.
3. Meat wrapped in paper from the butcher shop should be removed, the meat covered loosely with wax paper or aluminum foil and placed in the meat drawer.
4. If fresh meat is to be frozen, remove the store wrapping and place it in the special heavy duty plastic freezer bag (closed with a twist tape) or wrap it in aluminum foil making sure all the air is expelled and the edges securely locked or taped.
5. Wrap cold cuts, luncheon meat and sliced cheese in a plastic wrap to insure longer freshness, and stow in the meat drawer.
6. Cured and smoked meats such as ham, bacon and frankfurters can be stored in the refrigerator in their original wrapping. Use them within a week.
7. Most of the newer refrigerators have a special tray or swing-out case for egg storage. Place eggs in it, large side up, to maintain their peak quality.
8. Wash salad greens thoroughly and drain. Wrap in paper kitchen toweling to take up the excess moisture and store in the crisper drawer.
9. Wash and drain fruit that has an edible skin. Stow it in the medium cold section of the refrigerator unless some is held at room temperature to complete the ripening process. Bananas are not refrigerated.
10. Put away the staples in the refrigerator and cupboards.

HOW TO COOK

To become a good cook you must first learn the basics of assembling meals. Practical experience will help you get the hang

227

of cooking, of seeing what happens when an ingredient is changed or added. A sense of adventure will help you to become a creative cook. To start with the basics:

1. Get a good basic cookbook or two.
2. Referring to the menu for the meal, look up the recipes, the ingredients needed and the methods of procedure. Most good cookbooks are a fund of information. If you are cooking a roast and are not sure how you should proceed, look at the beginning section on that particular meat and read the author's suggestions.
3. Read the recipe carefully and thoroughly so you understand the whole procedure.
4. Assemble all of the ingredients, utensils and cookware necessary to the operation before starting.
5. Since timing is the key factor in preparing a meal, calculate how long it will take to prepare and cook each dish. Work out a schedule in your mind, or on paper, when each dish should be started and how long it takes to be finished. Some dishes can be cooked ahead of time and held to be reheated just before serving. A tossed salad can be completely assembled except for the dressing and refrigerated until just before serving. At the last minute you toss the dressing with the salad greens and serve.
6. Allow time for the oven to heat to the desired temperature. The average oven takes about 15 minutes to reach a broiling temperature, less for lower temperatures.
7. The best friend many a bride has is her timer. Use it if you have trouble remembering when something should be removed from the oven.
8. Start with the dish that takes the longest to prepare and/or cook.
9. Even the most experienced cook has trouble following a recipe in preparing a dish and carrying on a conversation simultaneously. Devote your whole attention to the task. Measure accurately. Dry ingredients are placed in a measuring spoon or cup and leveled across the top with a kitchen knife for complete accuracy. Measure fluids in individual cups or measuring cup, holding the cup at eye level so the measurement is level with the line.

10. There are some foods which must be cooked at the last minute such as scrambled eggs or broiled meats. If you have a hot tray or a warming oven, food will hold its heat for a short while. Cover the dish with aluminum foil to minimize heat loss.

11. Serve everything piping hot or ice cold, however the dishes are intended to be served.

12. Store leftover food in the refrigerator after the meal, covering any food which might leave or absorb odor. Transfer small leftovers from large dishes to small ones to utilize refrigerator space better.

Some cooking failures which could easily be avoided:

1. Cook all eggs gently. Start eggs for hard-boiling in cold water; as soon as the water boils, turn down to simmer and continue cooking. When the eggs are done, pour off the hot water and immerse in cold water to avoid the formation of the green ring between the yolk and the white. Scramble and fry eggs over medium heat, also, so they won't become stringy and tough.

2. Before beating eggs, let them stand until they reach room temperature. If they are to be separated, do so immediately after taking them from the refrigerator and then let each bowl warm. Eggs will whip to a greater volume this way.

3. Cook a sauce or custard containing eggs in the top of a double boiler with the water in the bottom pan hot but not boiling. If the sauce boils, the eggs will curdle and separate.

4. To add egg yolk to a hot sauce, add a spoonful of the hot sauce to the egg yolk mixture, blend, then add the egg yolk mixture to the hot sauce.

5. To make cream or white sauce successfully, melt butter or margarine in a pan and remove from the burner. Add flour and mix into a paste. Add milk and return to the burner, stirring until the mixture has thickened. Cook for another 5 minutes.

6. When thickening a sauce or gravy, never add the raw flour to the hot liquid. Make a thin paste of flour and cold water and add it gradually to the hot liquid, beating with a whisk or a slotted mixing spoon. Let it simmer gently for 5 minutes after thickening to take away the flour taste.

7. When cracking eggs, break each one into a small custard cup first before adding to a basic dish of ingredients. If, by chance, you have a spoiled egg it can be discarded from the custard cup without ruining the rest of the ingredients.

8. The water for pastry must be very cold. After mixing all the ingredients lightly, chill the dough for a few minutes so it is cold when you roll it. Actually you can mix the dough in advance and refrigerate it. Dust the board with a little flour and brush a bit on the rolling pin if it is not covered with a stockinette cloth. Roll the dough from the center out, turning the dough occasionally to prevent sticking.

9. When beating eggs be certain the bowl and beater are completely free from grease. Do not beat eggs in aluminum or plastic.

10. After you have made a cake containing eggs, flour and baking powder, bake it immediately. Some single-action baking powders can start leavening very quickly.

11. Do not shake a cake pan before putting it in the oven to bake. You can knock out all the air you beat into it.

12. Do not open the oven door too many times when baking. The cake may suffer because of the variation in heat.

Be careful while working in your kitchen—PLAY SAFE.

1. Wipe up any grease that falls on the floor with soap and water before you take a spill. Grease can be treacherous.

2. Have plenty of pot holders handy to remove anything hot from the stove.

3. Do not let long handles extend beyond the edge of the stove where they can be accidentally hit and cause a spill.

4. Hot grease spatters. Do not pour it into another container until it cools. Don't pour hot grease into a glass container—it may break.

5. Handle sharp knives with care and keep them in sheaths when not in use. Do not leave sharp knives immersed in soap and water in a sink. It's bad for the knives and could be bad for your fingers.

6. Do not leave boxes of matches where they can be accidentally ignited from the range.

230

7. After using the broiler, wash it so there will be no forgotten grease to smoke or catch fire the next time you use the oven.

8. If fat does catch on fire in the broiler or in a skillet, sprinkle salt or baking soda on the flame to smother it. You might also investigate purchasing a small fire extinguisher for just such emergencies.

9. Do not let curtains blow free near a stove where they can ignite over an open flame.

10. Follow instructions and precautions on the use of a pressure cooker.

11. If you should burn yourself slightly, run cold water over the burned area. For more severe burns have first aid supplies handy.

WEIGHTS AND MEASURES AND THEIR EQUIVALENTS
which may prove handy are:

3 teaspoons	=	1 tablespoon
4 tablespoons	=	¼ cup
5 ⅓ tablespoons	=	⅓ cup
8 tablespoons	=	½ cup
16 tablespoons	=	1 cup
½ pint or 8 fluid oz.	=	1 cup
1 ounce	=	2 tablespoons or ⅛ cup
8 ounces	=	1 cup or 16 tablespoons
1 pint	=	2 cups
2 pints or 4 cups	=	1 quart
4 quarts or 16 cups	=	1 gallon

EQUIVALENTS AND SUBSTITUTES for some common foods are:

Brown sugar	1 cup	1 cup granulated sugar
Butter, 1 stick (¼ lb.)	8 tablespoons	½ cup
Butter, 2 sticks (½ lb.)	1 cup	4/5 cup bacon fat
Butter	1 cup	7/8 cup vegetable oil
Cabbage	½ lb. shredded	3 cups
Confectioners' sugar	3½ cups	1 pound
Cheese, grated	5 cups	1 pound
Cottage cheese	1 cup	½ pound
Cream cheese	6 tablespoons	3 ounces
Chicken	2 cups cooked, diced	3½ lb. whole chicken

231

Chocolate	1 square	1 ounce (4 table-spoons grated)
Cocoa	3 tablespoons plus 1 tablespoon of fat	1 ounce of chocolate
Coffee	40 cups	1 pound
Granulated sugar	2 cups	1 pound
Flour	1 cup	1 cup plus 2 table-spoons cake flour
Milk	1 cup	4 tablespoons dried milk plus 1 cup water
Mushrooms	6 ounces canned	1 pound fresh
Peanuts	1 lb. shelled	2¼ cups
Potatoes	1 lb. raw, unpeeled	2 cups mashed

A GLOSSARY OF COOKING TERMS

A LA KING—A meat or fowl served in a rich cream sauce.

A LA MODE—Usually means to be topped with ice cream.

AU GRATIN—A topping of cheese, sometimes mixed with bread crumbs, over a casserole or vegetable.

AU JUS—Meat served in its own natural pan juices.

BAKE—To cook in the oven in a covered or uncovered pot or pan.

BARBECUE—To cook slowly on a spit or rack, basting frequently with a highly seasoned sauce.

BASTE—To pour melted fat, drippings or other liquid over cooking meat to prevent drying.

BATTER—A mixture of water or milk and flour, seasonings and eggs, thin enough to pour. It can be used to coat food for deep fat frying or for griddle cakes and waffles.

BEAT—By using a spoon, whisk, electric mixer or rotary beater, to incorporate air into ingredients or mix to a smooth consistency by turning over and through them over and over.

BLANCH—To immerse in boiling water for a short time to loosen the skin of fruits, nuts or vegetables for easier peeling. This can also be the preliminary step for food preservation.

232

BLEND—To thoroughly combine two ingredients.

BOIL—To cook in water or other liquid at a boiling temperature (212 degrees F. at sea level). Bubbles rise rapidly and continuously to the surface and break. For higher altitudes, higher temperatures are required to boil liquid.

BONE—To remove meat from the carcass of an animal.

BONED AND ROLLED—Meat cuts which have had the bones removed and then are rolled and tied for roasting.

BRAISE—To brown meat in a small amount of fat, then cook very slowly in a covered pan with the steam or meat juices for moisture.

BREAD—To coat with fine crumbs, either bread or crackers.

BROIL—To cook directly under or over the heat source, searing the natural juices in.

BROWN—To cook in fat until the meat is brown. Done usually in a skillet on top of the stove.

BRUSH—To daub butter or other cooking fat on the surface of the food with a pastry or cooking brush. Before cooking turkey you will brush the skin with melted butter.

CARAMELIZE—To melt granulated sugar over a low heat in a heavy pan until it turns to liquid.

CHILL—To refrigerate until the food is thoroughly cold.

CHOP—To cut up food with a knife or cleaver until it is of uniform small size.

CLARIFY—To clear a liquid of bits of solid or cloudy substance. Butter is clarified by melting slowly, letting it stand a few minutes and then removing the foam and solids from the surface by skimming.

CREAM—To work two or more ingredients together until they are blended, soft and creamy. Sugar and shortening are combined this way.

CUBE—To cut a food into small squares, about ¼ to ½ inch in size.

CUT IN—To incorporate fat into flour with knives or a pastry blender when making pastry until the mixture resembles corn-meal.

DEVIL—To combine sharp, tangy spices and seasonings to certain foods such as cooked egg yolks and ground ham.

DICE—To cut into very small cubes.

DISSOLVE—To mix a dry ingredient with liquid until it makes a solution.

DREDGE OR COAT—To lightly dust a food with flour, crumbs or crackers. Often the food is dipped in milk or a beaten egg before coating.

EN BROCHETTE—Marinated pieces of meat and vegetables are placed on small skewers and broiled.

FILLET—To completely remove the bone and skin from meat, fish or chicken before cooking.

FOLD—To combine two ingredients, such as beaten egg whites into a cake batter, very gently cutting down through the mixture with a whisk or spoon, turning over and repeating until they are mixed.

FRY—To cook in hot fat in a skillet on top of the stove. Deep fat frying means that the depth of the fat is enough to submerge the food in it. To sauté, or pan-fry, very little fat is used.

GRILL—To broil, often referring to cooking over charcoal.

JULIENNE—To cut into fine lengthwise strips (carrots and potatoes, mostly).

KNEAD—To press dough with the heel of the hand, stretch and fold it over and over until it is elastic and smooth.

LARD—To insert thin strips of fat into meat by using a special long larding needle or to place strips on top of the meat to make it self-basting when being roasted in the oven.

LEAVENING AGENT—An ingredient which makes a food rise when cooked. It can be baking powder, baking soda, salt, eggs, cream of tartar or yeast.

MARINATE—To let foods stand in a liquid (usually a mixture of oil and vinegar or wine) for a period of time to add flavor and tenderize meat. The marinade, the liquid, is often used to baste the food while it is cooking.

MINCE—To chop as fine as possible.

PAN-BROIL—To cook food in a skillet on top of the stove with little or no fat.

PARBOIL—To boil food until partially cooked.

PEEL OR PARE—To remove the outer peel or skin.

POACH—To simmer very gently in liquid so the food holds its shape.

POT ROAST—To cook large cuts of less-than-tender meat in a tightly covered pan by braising.

PUREE—To force cooked or uncooked foods through a food mill or put them in a blender so they become a thick liquid.

RECONSTITUTE—To restore a concentrated food to its original state such as adding water to frozen orange juice or dried milk.

REDUCE—To boil liquid rapidly until part of it evaporates, making it less in volume, more concentrated and richer as a sauce.

RENDER—To cook a solid fat slowly until it melts.

ROAST—To cook meat uncovered in the oven without water. This term can also refer to meat cooked on a rotisserie.

ROUX—A mixture of flour and melted fat used to thicken a liquid.

SCALD—To heat a liquid just to the boiling point without letting it boil.

SCORE—To make shallow gashes with a knife in a meat such as a ham, or to pierce the surface with a fork.

SEAR—To brown very quickly over a high heat. This is a way of sealing in all the natural juices.

SHORTENING—A term used for fats used in cooking.

SHRED—To cut into thin strips with a knife or shredder.

SIFT—To put through a fine screen to break down the lumps into powder and lighten with air.

SIMMER—To cook just below the boiling point.

SKEWER—A thin metal rod, either short or long, used to spear food for cooking. This is used in en brochette cooking. A skewer can also be a small pin which holds the stuffing in a fowl or fish.

SKIM—To take off, with a spoon or skimmer, the fat which rises to the top of a liquid either before or after it is cooled.

STEAM—To cook food in hot steam, with or without pressure. The food is placed on a rack in a covered pot or in a perforated pan over boiling water.

STEEP—To let stand in very hot water.

STEW—To simmer in liquid for a period of time.

STOCK—The juices derived from cooking vegetables, meat, fats, seasonings and sometimes water. Stock is used for the basis of soups and many sauces.

THICKENING AGENT—An ingredient which, when combined with fat or a small amount of liquid, will thicken a liquid when cooked. The agent can be flour, cornstarch, egg yolks or grated potato.

TOSS—A light mixing of ingredients by the use of a fork and spoon or two spoons. Green salads are tossed with the dressing to blend.

TRUSS—To tie back the legs and tuck the wings of a fowl so the bird will hold its shape when cooked.

UNMOLD—To remove a jellied dish from its mold either by dipping the mold briefly in hot water or by wrapping a hot towel around the bottom of the mold to loosen it enough so the contents can be turned out easily on a serving plate.

WHIP—To beat rapidly and thoroughly so the food increases in volume or becomes smooth.

EQUIVALENT OVEN TEMPERATURES:

Keep warm	140 to 200 degrees F
Very slow	200 to 250 degrees F
Slow	250 to 325 degrees F
Moderate	325 to 375 degrees F
Moderate hot	375 to 425 degrees F
Hot oven	425 to 475 degrees F
Very hot	475 to 500 degrees F

THE SEASONINGS

Herbs, spices and condiments have been used since the beginning of recorded history by man to enhance the flavor of the food he eats. If you know how to use them, seasonings can do wonders to a very mediocre dish by increasing its flavor tenfold. Although spices have little or no food value, they can make a dreary but nutritious dish taste exotic and appetizing. Ground spices, if not used within a year, should be replaced because they lose their pungency. Herbs often contain vitamins and minerals, especially if they are fresh. Many herbs can be grown in a small garden or even in a window sill box. Some herbs and spices are quite mild, others overpowering. Certain ones complement each other and go hand in hand with specific foods. To discover the magic of herbs, spices and condiments and how they should be used, read your recipes carefully and do a little experimenting on the side.

To help you become familiar with the many seasonings, they are defined thus:

Allspice A berry of the pimento tree whose flavor resembles a blend of cinnamon, cloves, nutmeg and juniper berry. Sold whole or ground, it is used in a few meat dishes, many desserts.

Anise A seed with the taste of licorice, sometimes found in cabbage dishes but mostly used on the tops of cookies and pastries. Crush the seed to release the full flavor.

Basil A leafy herb, easily grown, good for stuffings, soups, salads, egg dishes. Excellent for Italian dishes, especially those containing tomatoes.

Bay leaf A small aromatic leaf packaged whole or crushed which is an excellent flavoring for stews, stuffings, hearty soups, marinades, pot roasts and poultry. Use it sparingly and remove before serving. It is the basis for many a bouquet garni.

Bouquet garni A group of herbs tied into a small cheesecloth bag to be placed in a soup, stew or stock to flavor in cooking. Remove before serving. One combination: parsley, thyme, marjoram and bay leaf. Another group: leek, carrot, celery, parsley, cloves and bay leaf.

Capers Tiny buds from the caper bush, sold pickled in bottles and which resemble the taste of sharp gherkins. Excellent for garnish and used in tartare sauces, egg salad, potato salad and cole slaw.

Caraway A pungent seed used on the crust of rye bread and other breads, also in salads, cheeses and egg dishes.

Cardamom A plump, pungent white seed of the ginger family used in pickling and when ground in some baked goods. Include a seed in coffee for a delicious taste.

Catsup A thick, smooth tomato sauce with added spices. It serves as a base for barbecue sauces and flavors stews and broiled meats.

Cayenne A very hot red pepper to be used sparingly. It adds zest to bland dishes of seafood, eggs, fish and some salads.

Celery seed and salt A celery flavor with a faint bitter taste, sold in seed form or ground and combined with salt. The seed is excellent in potato and cabbage salad, in barbecue sauces and for pickling. The powdered form is very versatile, adding agreeable flavor to any number of foods such as dressing for salads, stews, meats and vegetables.

Chervil An herb with a delicate aroma often combined with parsley and chives in omelettes, salads, chicken, vegetable soups and veal. The flavor of chervil is much better when it is fresh.

Chili powder A strong peppery flavor which comes from the ground chili pepper of Mexico. This hot spice is used a great deal in Mexican dishes such as chili con carne.

Chili sauce A thick tomato sauce, similar to catsup but more highly spiced and with small bits of tomato left in. It's used to season some stews and combine with mayonnaise to form Russian dressing.

Chives A member of the onion family, the plant has thin, tubular leaves that are cut, chopped fine and added to omelettes, soups, stuffings and meats. This is an excellent window sill plant which will thrive on being cut for use.

Chutney A sweet pickled fruit with a mild pungent taste, often served with curries but also a good condiment for certain cold meats.

Cinnamon A spice derived from the aromatic bark of an East Indian tree. It's marketed either in stick or ground form and is used in pastries, sweet rolls, pickling and as a spread for toast. Many east Mediterranean meat and rice dishes call for it.

Cloves A spicy, dried bud of the clove tree, available whole or ground. It flavors ham, stocks and, in combination with other spices, is used in Oriental dishes for marinades as well as for pickling.

Coriander A seed with a sharp, unique flavor used in pot roasts, sauces and in Oriental, Mexican and Latin dishes. Sometimes it's used in meat balls or sausages.

Cumin A ground spice used in Mexican dishes, cheese appetizers and some breads. Chiefly it is blended with other spices to make curry powder.

Curry powder A mixture of spices, the blends depending on how hot the curry is. Cumin, coriander, turmeric, ginger and cayenne may all be a part of the blend. Curry is used for sauces which bear its name, Oriental dishes and marinades.

Dill A pungent herb used as a seed and a leaf. The seed is used mostly as pickling spice. The leaf, also known as dill weed, is good on salads, in sauces, particularly sour cream, in stews, chicken and fish dishes.

Fennel A licorice-flavored herb chopped fresh on salads. The crushed leaves go well in sausage, lentils, roast duck and fish.

Fines herbes A group of finely chopped herbs, usually including parsley and chives, which is added to omelettes, soups, stews and salads. Some combinations: parsley, chives and tarragon; parsley, chervil and chives, or parsley, basil and chives.

Garlic A close relative of the onion family, garlic grows in a tight bulb which is divided into sections called cloves. It has a strong, pungent odor and is widely used in meat and poultry dishes, stews and salads. Many people prefer to use it in moderation, rubbing a roast with a cut clove and then discarding it; cuisines from almost all of the Mediterranean countries use it liberally.

Ginger A root known for its pungent flavor available in several forms—fresh, candied and ground. The root and ground ginger are used in marinades, exotic sauces, Oriental dishes and for baking. Candied ginger can be a very subtle flavoring for meat stews.

Horseradish A very strong root, found most often grated and bottled. Added to hot dishes, sauces, shrimp cocktail sauce and some appetizers. A small amount added to apple sauce will accent the apple flavor.

Mace and nutmeg Both come from a tough-husked aromatic fruit. Mace is the outer bark; nutmeg, the kernel. Nutmeg, the more common, is sold whole for grating or in ground form. It's added to meat and seafood dishes, fruit, desserts and sprinkled over eggnog.

Marjoram A leafy herb with a full-bodied flavor, an old favorite to add to meat and egg dishes, salads, vegetables, poultry and salad dressing.

Mint An herb, actually spearmint, from the large mint family, which is tangy and fresh. The leaves are used to garnish fruit cups, mint juleps and other cooling drinks. It goes well with new potatoes, carrots and lamb. Mint is easily grown and a hardy perennial.

Monosodium glutamate A flavor enhancer with no detectable flavor of its own for meat dishes and on vegetables. Widely used in Oriental cooking.

240

Mustard A sharp, hot flavored seed, also available in powdered form. The seed is favored for pickling and in the powdered form is added to sauces, salad dressings and some fish dishes. Mustard made in the form of sauce is popular as a condiment for meats and fish.

Oregano A pungent herb related to marjoram but a little bit sharper. It's part of chili powder and is used widely in meat and pork dishes, stews and many Italian recipes with tomato contents.

Paprika A mild spice ground from the sweet red pepper. It's used as a garnish as well as flavor in many Hungarian dishes, in meats, eggs, stews, salads, sauces and fish.

Parsley An herb of many uses, rich in vitamins and minerals. It's found in bouquet garni, fines herbes, valuable as a subtle blender for other flavors. Parsley is cooked with many dishes, vegetables, fish, meats, stews and stuffings, also as a garnish, chopped or whole.

Pepper A berry from an East Indian shrub, yielding a strong bitting flavor. Both white and black peppercorns are marketed to be ground at home in a pepper grinder, or pepper can be bought in the ground form. Pepper is used almost as universally as salt as an all-purpose seasoner.

Pimiento A sweet red pepper, bought by the can or jar, used in salads, sauces and as a garnish.

Poppy seed A dried seed from the poppy with a mild nutlike flavor used on bread and rolls, in fish and meat dishes, on noodles and in some pastries.

Rosemary Strong, pungent, subtle needle-like leaves from a shrub. It blends well with meats, particularly with lamb, and is sometimes found in heavier marinades.

Saffron The very pungent, deep yellow dried part of the saffron flower. Only a pinch is needed to color and flavor rice dishes, some fish, sauces and a rare cake. Too much has a medicinal taste.

241

Sage A fragrant herb with a very decisive flavor which, when used cautiously, is very good in bread stuffings, stews and gravies.

Salt A seasoning with many powers besides its flavor. It firms cooking vegetables, toughens eggs, helps preserve food, acts as a leavening agent in baking and brings out the flavor of many foods. Coarse salt which is ground at home in a salt grinder is stronger in taste than the commercially packaged variety.

Savory An aromatic herb with a slight resin flavor often combined with other herbs in stuffings, poultry and meat dishes, omelettes, green bean salad and heavy lentil soup.

Sesame seed An oily, crisp seed with a nutlike flavor which tops breads and pastries. It's used in marinades, for coating frying chicken and flavoring Korean dishes. Some eastern candies are made of crushed sesame seeds.

Shallot A member of the onion family, this small bulb has a flavor close to garlic but more delicate. A shallot is often minced with herbs for fines herbes. Don't let a shallot brown in sautéing or it will become bitter.

Soy sauce A thin dark brown sauce made from soybeans and used extensively in Oriental cooking or as a condiment. Excellent as a marinade base.

Tarragon An herb which has a distinctive licorice flavor when it is fresh, but loses it when dried. Excellent in salads and sauces, mushroom, chicken and lobster dishes. Tarragon is a perennial bush which multiplies and is easy to grow.

Tabasco A very hot, thin sauce much like cayenne. Good in sauces and omelettes. Use a drop at a time.

Thyme A slightly pungent herb with a full-bodied flavor which lends itself well to meats, stews, heavy soups, poultry stuffing, creole and gumbo dishes.

Tomato paste A very thick concentrated paste made from tomatoes. A small amount can enrich the flavor of gravies and sauces. Dilute it for a tomato sauce.

Turmeric An herb of the ginger family usually marketed as a yellow powder with a mild, sweet flavor. It is one of the ingredients in curry powder.

Vanilla A pod (bean) or the liquid extract from the vanilla plant. This is a favorite flavoring for desserts, cakes, puddings and candies. The vanilla bean flavor can be brought out by heating it with milk. Make vanilla sugar by placing the bean in the sugar canister for a week.

Worcestershire sauce A piquant condiment which can be used on cooked meat, or in gravies, stews or marinades.

COOKING WITH WINE

Used with discretion wine can bring a subtle flavor to many a dish, helping to improve the taste of the other ingredients without dominating them. Besides being an excellent flavoring agent, wine is also a good tenderizer of meat. Certain recipes call for wine as a cooking ingredient or to be used in a marinade, but you can have fun experimenting with a small glassful in other foods. Wine, when heated, loses its alcoholic content very quickly and, if boiled, loses much of its flavor. If you are making a stew where the wine is to be added at the beginning of the cooking process, keep the pot covered and the heat low so the stew will simmer. In this way the elusive flavor of the wine will be retained.

Wines used most in cooking are sherry, dry Madeira, vermouth, Marsala, the white wines (chablis, sauterne and moselle) and the red wines (Burgundy and claret). Dry red wines flavor red meats, their sauces and occasionally a chicken dish. The white wines are added to fish, lamb, white sauces, cheese and chicken. Sherry is added to soups, shellfish, sauces and desserts; Marsala is a favorite wine for Italian recipes. The dessert wines, port, sherry and Madeira, along with liqueurs are better with dessert sauces, fruits and pastries.

HOW TO CARVE

Carving is a skill which can only be developed and polished by practice—and a good sharp knife. It helps to know a little bit about the animal's anatomy—where the bones are located—and how the grain of the meat runs. Most meats are cut against or

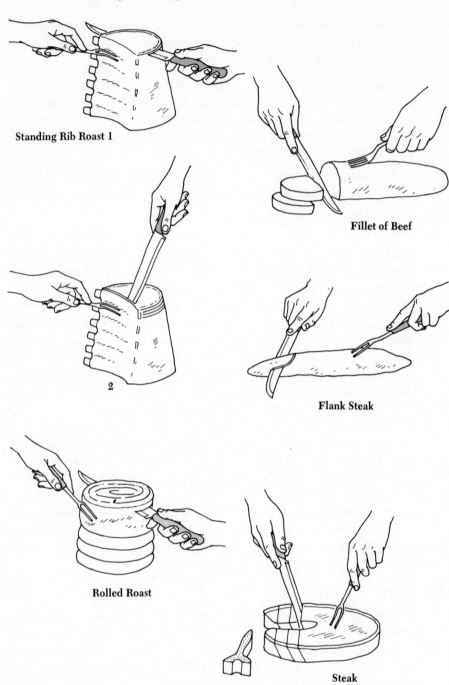

Standing Rib Roast 1

2

Rolled Roast

Fillet of Beef

Flank Steak

Steak

across the grain to insure juicy, non-stringy slices. There is a correct way to carve every type of roast and fowl—the way the meat is set on the platter, the way the knife is used and the angle at which the meat is sliced. Carve on a wooden board whenever possible so the knife will not scratch a good china piece. Have a small, warm platter next to the carver to hold the slices after they are cut. If the carving knife does not have a keen edge, sharpen it on the carving steel or stone before attempting to cut the meat. When carving use a long, light stroke, pushing and pulling the knife with a saw-like movement. Keep the fork behind the knife on the side next to you for better anchorage and protection. A good carving fork will have a thumbpiece or shield to protect you further.

To carve beef

STANDING RIB ROAST—Place the meat on the platter, ribs to the side, the larger end to the bottom for a firm base. Carve crosswise toward the bone, cutting the slices to desired thickness. Carefully cut along the bone to free the slices. Reverse each slice over the knife and place on the warm platter so more of the natural juice is saved.

ROLLED OR BONELESS ROAST—Carve across in the same way, cutting the slices as thick as you want them. Sever the strings and remove any excess fat with the point of the knife.

FILLET OF BEEF—Hold the fillet in place on a board with the back of the fork, not with the tines because of the tenderness of the meat. Starting with the widest end use the slicing knife to cut straight down and through in one motion. The slices are thick, from ¾″ to 1″.

FLANK STEAK—Use the slicing knife and, holding the steak firmly with a fork, start at the small end and slice very thin diagonal slices by holding the knife blade at an angle. If the meat is not cut across the grain it will be stringy.

STEAK—Cut out and remove the bone with the point of the steak or boning knife, holding one end with a fork. Slice crosswise at an angle to retain the juices.

To carve lamb

LEG OF LAMB—Place the roast, leg bone side down, on the platter with the exposed tip of the leg to the left of the carver.

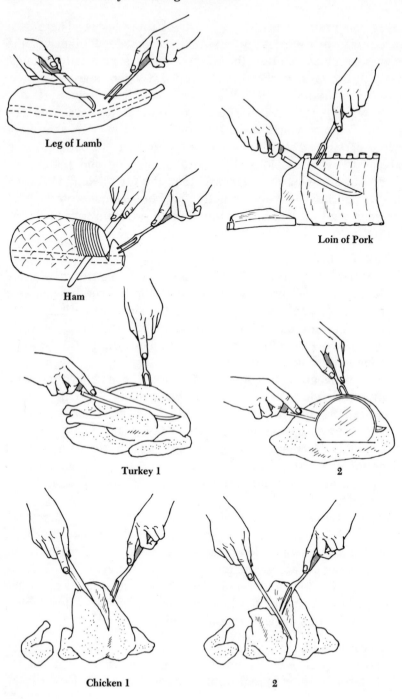

Leg of Lamb

Ham

Loin of Pork

Turkey 1

2

Chicken 1

2

246

Using the carving knife, start a third of the way down the leg, slicing across to take off a small shallow piece from the top. Continue across the top making thin slices. Lamb is cut with the grain of the meat.

To carve pork

HAM—Cut a parallel piece from the bottom to make the base flat. Turn over and place the ham on a board, preferably one with spikes for better anchorage. Cut a small wedge down to the bone near the shank end (where the bone is exposed), and remove. Continue slicing down, working toward the butt end. Free a series of slices from the bone at one time by making one parallel cut. For cold ham, angle the slices more and make them thinner.

LOIN OF PORK—Stand the roast with the ribs on top, where the backbone has been removed. Holding firmly with the fork, cut down between the ribs for individual servings. For thinner slices, cut down near the rib several times and free the slices from the bone with one cut.

To carve a turkey

Place the turkey on a platter, breast side up, drumsticks toward the carver. Cut down between the thigh and the body; push the leg away from the body with the fork to separate it at the joint with the tip of the knife. Place the piece on the warm platter and separate the thigh from the leg. Holding the drumstick by the bone, slice downward for servings of dark meat. To remove the wing slant the knife very low at the base of the same side and remove the wing at the joint. Make a horizontal cut at the base of the breast on the side so the breast slices will fall away easily. Starting at the front side, carve thin slices at a downward angle until reaching the widest part of the breast. Alternate carving from the side front and the side back to give even slices. After carving one side, spoon out the dressing from the body cavity.

To carve a chicken

A larger roasted chicken can be carved in much the same way as a turkey. A smaller chicken is quartered. The leg and thigh section is severed at the joint and removed to a platter. Starting from the top of the breastbone, cut down, as close to the bone as possible, press the meat aside and continue cutting until the wing is separated. The wing and breast will be all in one piece.

MENUS FOR TWO WEEKS

To help you along the road toward good, simple meal planning, here are menu suggestions for two weeks—attractive, nutritious, and easy on the budget. The weekday menus are designed to be simple so they take a minimum amount of your time to prepare and utilize leftovers. More elaborate plans, calling for more preparation, are scheduled for weekends—even one company dinner. You may have unexpected company and you may be invited out to dinner at the last minute. When these unscheduled changes occur, take them in your stride. Learning to cope is all part of being a homemaker.

Recipes are given for the dishes marked with asterisks.

FIRST WEEK

Sunday

Brunch:
Orange juice
*Scrambled eggs   Sausage
Sweet rolls   Coffee

Dinner:
*Baked ham   Sweet potatoes
Green beans   Celery and carrot strips
Fruit cup   Milk or coffee

Monday

Breakfast:
Grapefruit
Cereal, hot or cold
Toasted English muffin and butter, Jams
Coffee or milk

Lunch:
Ham sandwiches on rye bread with lettuce
Apple sauce   Milk

Dinner:
*Broiled chopped meat wrapped in bacon
Hash brown potatoes
Broccoli   Lettuce and tomato salad
Camembert and crackers
Coffee

Tuesday
_____
Breakfast:
Orange juice
Soft boiled eggs   Whole wheat toast
Coffee or milk

Lunch:
Tomato soup
Peanut butter sandwich
Apple   Milk

Dinner:
Cranberry juice
*Ham-broccoli-cheese casserole
Tossed salad
Ice cream   Cookies
Coffee

Wednesday
_____
Breakfast:
Tomato juice
Poached eggs on toast
Coffee or milk

Lunch:
*Split pea soup
Melba toast with cheese spread
Fruit gelatin   Milk

249

Dinner:
*Oven-fried chicken
Rice
Glazed carrots   Lettuce with Russian dressing
Sliced fruit
Coffee

Thursday

Breakfast:
Applesauce
Hot cereal
Muffins with jam and butter
Coffee or milk

Lunch:
Omelette
Carrot and celery strips
Cookies and milk

Dinner:
*Liver sautéed
Potatoes au gratin
Mixed vegetables   Green salad
Fruit gelatin
Coffee

Friday

Breakfast:
Cranberry juice
Scrambled eggs   Bacon
Toast
Milk or coffee

Lunch:
Tomato juice
Clam chowder (canned)   Crackers
Fruit   Milk

Dinner:
*Shrimp curry   Rice
Chutney   Side dish of coconut
Tossed salad
Ice cream   Cookies
Coffee

Saturday

Breakfast:
Orange juice
*French toast   Syrup
Bacon
Coffee or milk

Lunch:
Vegetable soup
*Open-face cheese sandwiches
Fruit gelatin   Milk

Dinner:
(For company)
Tomato juice   Cheddar sticks
*Roast beef au jus
*Browned potatoes
Lima beans
Celery, cabbage and watercress salad
Angel Food cake (make from a mix)

SCRAMBLED EGGS

4 eggs	One or two drops Tabasco sauce
4 tablespoons milk	¼ teaspoon garlic salt
½ teaspoon dried or	¼ teaspoon celery salt
1 teaspoon fresh, minced parsley	Salt and pepper to taste

Beat eggs, milk and seasonings together until well blended. In a heavy skillet heat 2 tablespoons butter over medium heat. When the butter bubbles (but doesn't brown) pour in the egg mixture, stir with a fork constantly until the eggs are done to your liking. Serve at once.

251

BAKED GLAZED HAM

Buy only ½ of a precooked smoked ham (shank end weighing 5 to 6 lbs.). Preheat the oven to 350 degrees F. Unwrap and wipe the ham with a damp cloth. Scrub the rind well with a stiff brush. Dry and place in a shallow roasting pan with a rack, fat side up. Insert meat thermometer into the thickest part, not touching the bone. Bake uncovered for about 1½ hrs. Take out of oven and score the fat diagonally about ⅛" deep to make a diamond pattern. Stick whole cloves into the corners of the diamonds. Blend together ½ cup brown sugar and 1 teaspoon dry mustard and moisten with ½ cup of orange juice. Spread over the fat and return the ham to the oven to finish baking. Spoon glaze over the ham twice more. The meat thermometer will register 160 degrees when done. Increase the oven temperature to 400 degrees during the last 15 minutes so the sugar forms a glaze.

BROILED CHOPPED MEAT WRAPPED IN BACON

1½ lbs. chopped meat (round or chuck)
1 teaspoon salt
Pepper
1 teaspoon Worcestershire sauce
½ medium onion minced
¼ teaspoon marjoram
¼ teaspoon garlic salt
4 strips lean bacon

Combine all the ingredients, except the bacon, until they are well blended and make into four meat patties about 1 inch thick. Wrap each one with a bacon strip around the side and secure the ends with a toothpick. Broil about 7 to 8 minutes on each side. The bacon is crisp and the meat cooked to a medium degree of doneness.

HAM-BROCCOLI-CHEESE CASSEROLE

1 package frozen broccoli spears
1 can cream of mushroom soup (condensed)
½ cup of milk
Leftover ham sliced thin
½ cup grated cheddar cheese

Preheat the oven to 350°F

Cook the broccoli according to directions until just barely done. Drain. Blend the soup and milk together. Grease the bottom of a casserole lightly. Arrange ham slices in the bottom, overlapping one another. Place the broccoli on top of them. Pour the soup mixture over the contents and sprinkle with the cheese. Bake for ½ hr. or until the cheese is bubbly.

SPLIT PEA SOUP

1½ cups split peas	2 carrots sliced thin
Ham bone	1 stalk of celery, chopped
1 onion stuck with cloves	1 bay leaf

3 qts. cold water

Rinse and soak the split peas according to the package directions (some must be soaked overnight). In a heavy, large kettle (preferably a Dutch oven) put the ham bone, the split peas, onion, carrots, celery, bay leaf and the cold water. Cover the kettle, bring to a boil, then lower the heat until the liquid is simmering. Cook for 2 or 3 hours, stirring once in a while to prevent sticking. When the peas are soft the soup is done. Remove the bay leaf, onion and ham bone but leave small pieces of edible ham which have come away from the bone. Put the soup through a sieve to puree. Correct seasonings. Refrigerate what you don't eat and save it.

OVEN-FRIED CHICKEN

1 broiler-fryer cut into serving pieces
Salt and pepper
Garlic salt
Paprika
1 teaspoon tarragon
½ cup melted butter or margarine
⅓ cup white wine (optional)

Preheat the oven to 350 degrees F.
Remove broiler pan from the range and take off the top grill. Grease the bottom of the pan lightly. Rinse chicken pieces under cool water and wipe dry with paper towels. Sprinkle meat side of each piece very lightly with salt, pepper and garlic salt. Place the chicken pieces in the pan, skin side up, far enough apart so they

253

don't touch. Sprinkle with salt, pepper and paprika. Add 1 teaspoon tarragon to the melted butter and drizzle or brush the mixture liberally over each chicken piece. Put the pan in the oven and bake for about 1¼ hours. Baste or brush the pan juices over the chicken several times while cooking so it doesn't dry out. To give added flavor baste the chicken with ⅓ cup white wine. If the chicken isn't crisp enough place it under the broiler flame for 5 minutes.

LIVER SAUTÉED

Have the butcher cut the liver slices as thin as possible. Remove the thin skin and heavy veins with the tip of a paring knife. Coat each slice lightly with flour that has been seasoned with salt, pepper and paprika. Melt 2 tablespoons butter in a heavy skillet over a medium heat; when the butter is bubbly sauté the liver slices quickly but gently. The meat will toughen if cooked too long at too high a heat. Serve immediately.

SHRIMP CURRY

1 tablespoon butter or margarine
2 tablespoons cooking oil
1 apple, peeled, cored and diced
½ green pepper, diced
2 stalks celery, diced
1 onion, diced
1 can cream of mushroom soup, condensed
1 cup milk
Curry powder to taste
1 lb. shrimp, cooked, shelled and deveined

In a heavy skillet put 4 tablespoons of butter or margarine and 2 tablespoons of oil. Sauté over medium heat the diced apple, green pepper, celery and onion until they are soft. Add the cream of mushroom soup, the milk and at least 2 tablespoons curry powder. Stir thoroughly and check if more curry is needed for your taste. Add shrimp and heat 5 minutes. Serve over boiled rice.

FRENCH TOAST

1 egg, slightly beaten
1 cup milk
½ teaspoon salt

Dash of pepper
½ teaspoon vanilla
1 tablespoon butter

6 to 8 slices white bread

In a bowl beat the egg, add milk, salt, pepper and vanilla. Heat 2 tablespoons of butter in a heavy skillet. Dip the bread slices in the egg mixture, one at a time, and brown on both sides in the skillet. More butter may be needed. Serve at once with syrup or a topping of cinnamon and sugar or jam.

OPEN-FACE CHEESE SANDWICHES

Toast white bread on one side under the broiler. Turn the slices over and grate a little bit of onion on the bread; cover with a piece of cheddar cheese on top of the bread slice. Return to the broiler to melt the cheese. Serve at once. Variations: crumble cooked bacon under the cheese or place a slice of tomato on top of the cheese so it grills while the cheese melts.

ROAST BEEF

Buy a 4- to 5-lb. boneless rolled roast (top sirloin, silver tip or eye round). Let the meat stand at room temperature for an hour before roasting. Preheat the oven to 450 degrees F. Rub 1 tablespoon of salt into the roast along with some pepper; cut a clove of garlic in two and rub the cut side on the meat surface, discarding the clove when through. Place the roast in a shallow roasting pan with a rack, fat side up. If the roast has little fat place two strips of bacon over the top to improve the flavor and help baste the meat. Insert the meat thermometer into thickest part of the meat. Roast for 20 minutes; turn down the oven to 350 degrees and continue to roast. Baste with the pan juices once in a while to make sure the meat doesn't dry out. A boneless roast can take from 15 to 25 minutes per pound, depending on how well done you like it. Check the meat thermometer for the desired internal temperature. When the meat is cooked, remove it from the roasting pan to the carving board. Skim the excess fat from the juices and serve as a natural gravy.

BROWNED POTATOES

Peel medium-sized white potatoes; cut large ones in two. Parboil them in salted water until they are partially cooked (about 7 minutes). Drain and let stand for a few minutes to dry. Place them

255

around the roasting beef so they will finish cooking with the meat and brown at the same time in the pan juices. Turn the potatoes several times to brown evenly. Serve with the roast beef.

SALAD DRESSING

½ cup oil	1 teaspoon dry mustard
½ cup vinegar	1 teaspoon dry parsley
½ cup catsup	1 teaspoon oregano
4 teaspoons salt	Paprika
1 teaspoon pepper	1 clove of garlic minced

Mix all ingredients in a glass jar; with the lid on shake thoroughly to combine. This dressing can be stored in the refrigerator for a week or more and is good for all green salads. Use only what is required to blend the salad greens. Never drench a salad with too much dressing.

SECOND WEEK OF MENUS

Sunday
Brunch:
Grapefruit
*Shirred or baked eggs
Sausage
Muffins   Jam
Coffee or milk

Dinner:
*Meat loaf
*Noodles Alfredo
Peas   Lettuce and tomato salad
Angel Food cake with raspberry sauce
Coffee

Monday
Breakfast.
Orange juice
Soft-boiled eggs   Toast
Coffee or milk

Lunch:
Roast beef sandwich (meat from Sat. night's roast)
Apple sauce   Cookies
Milk

Dinner:
*Macaroni casserole
Tossed green salad
Ice cream   Cookies
Coffee

Tuesday

Breakfast:
Grapefruit juice
Hot cereal with fruit
Toasted English muffins
Coffee or milk

Lunch:
*Omelette with fines herbes
Melba toast
Fruit gelatin   Milk

Dinner:
*Flank steak
Parsley potatoes
Carrots   Green salad
Custard   Cookies
Coffee

Wednesday

Breakfast.
Apple sauce
Poached eggs on whole wheat toast
Coffee or milk

Lunch:
Cream of mushroom soup (canned)
Sandwich made from leftover flank steak
Fresh fruit   Milk

Dinner:
*Spaghetti with meat sauce
Garlic bread
Tossed salad
Canned pears   Coffee

Thursday

Breakfast:
Orange juice
Scrambled eggs
Toast
Coffee or milk

Lunch:
Vegetable beef soup (canned)
Lettuce and tomato sandwich
Fruit   Milk

Dinner:
Pork chops   Apple sauce
*Skillet-browned potatoes
Green beans
*Brownies   Coffee

Friday

Breakfast:
Grapefruit juice
Cereal with fruit
Blueberry muffins
Coffee or milk

Lunch:
Tunafish salad sandwich
Pudding   Milk

Dinner:
*Beef stew
Rice
Tossed salad with tomatoes
Brownies topped with ice cream
Coffee

Saturday

Breakfast:
Grapefruit
Pancakes and syrup   Bacon
Coffee or milk

Lunch:
Tomato soup
Peanut butter and jelly sandwiches
Fresh fruit   Brownies
Milk

Dinner:
*Chicken breasts in sauce
*Rice pilaf
Crisp green salad with oil and vinegar dressing
Lemon ice   Cookies
Coffee

SHIRRED EGGS

Preheat the oven to 350 degrees F.
In heatproof individual ramekins or custard cups melt one teaspoon of butter per cup. Break one or two eggs in each, depending on the size of the cup. Top each with ½ teaspoon of cream. Bake until the eggs are set but still creamy (from 9 to 12 minutes). Serve with salt and pepper to be added.

MEAT LOAF

1½ lbs. chopped meat (round and chuck combined are good)
1 onion minced   1 tablespoon Worcestershire
1 teaspoon salt   sauce
½ teaspoon pepper   1 egg
1 tablespoon parsley   ½ cup catsup or chili sauce
1 strip of bacon

Preheat the oven to 350 degrees F.
Mix the meat, onion, salt, pepper, parsley, Worcestershire sauce and egg together lightly and form into a loaf; place it in a loaf pan. With a kitchen knife make several cuts down through the

259

meat. Pour catsup or chili sauce over the top of the meat, making sure some goes into the cuts in the meat. For added flavor lay a strip of bacon over the top. Bake uncovered in the oven for 1¼ hrs. Serve in thick slices.

NOODLES ALFREDO

Cook noodles in salted water. When they are done, drain into a sieve, run water over them briefly. Over a low heat melt 2 tablespoons of butter in the pan; return the noodles to the pan and toss with a fork so the butter coats them. Add ¼ cup cream and ¼ cup Parmesan cheese, toss and heat through. Be careful the cheese doesn't stick to the bottom of the pan.

MACARONI CASSEROLE

1½ cups macaroni	1 lb. chopped meat
1 clove of garlic	1 teaspoon salt, peper to taste
4 tablespoons cooking oil	1 can condensed cream of
½ green pepper diced	mushroom soup
1 onion diced	½ cup cheddar cheese grated
3 tablespoons Parmesan cheese	1 egg, slightly beaten

Preheat the oven to 350 degrees F.
Cook macaroni in salted water until done; drain.
Using a heavy skillet brown a minced clove of garlic in 4 table-spoons of cooking oil and discard the garlic. Add to the same oil the green pepper and onion; sauté until soft; sauté the chopped meat until it loses color, breaking the lumps up with a fork. Drain away any excess liquid and remove from heat. To the skillet add salt and pepper, cooked macaroni, undiluted can of soup, the slightly beaten egg and cheddar cheese. Toss to blend the ingredients and turn the mixture into a greased 2-quart casserole. Sprinkle the top with Parmesan cheese and bake uncovered for 45 min.

FLANK STEAK

Preheat the broiler. Trim away any excess fat from the flank steak. Rub the meat with a cut garlic clove and season with pepper. Dot the steak with butter and broil, 5 minutes on each side. Flank steak should not be overcooked. With a very sharp knife make thin slices on the diagonal against the grain of the meat. (See page 245 on carving.) Pour the pan juices from the broiler over the slices and serve.

OMELETTE WITH FINES HERBES

An omelette is best done in small quantities or individual servings. Beat two eggs, add a drop of Tabasco, ¼ teaspoon salt and minced fines herbes (the combination of parsley and chives or parsley, chives and chervil). Heat 1 teaspoon of butter in a small skillet; swirl so the butter coats the sides. When it is bubbly hot pour in the egg mixture and shake gently to prevent sticking but do not stir; let the bottom of the omelette set. Lift up one section slightly with a fork and tilt the skillet in that direction so the top liquid will run down; level the skillet. The omelette is done when the top is still runny. Fold into thirds over the center and slide onto a waiting plate.

SPAGHETTI WITH MEAT SAUCE

½ onion minced	½ teaspoon oregano
1 can tomato paste	1 teaspoon parsley
½ cup water	¼ teaspoon garlic salt
1 8-oz. can tomato sauce	½ lb. chopped meat
½ teaspoon basil	8 oz. spaghetti

In a heavy saucepan or skillet sauté the onion until it is soft. Add the tomato paste, water, tomato sauce, basil, oregano, parsley and garlic salt. Simmer for 1 hour. During the last 10 minutes of cooking time add the chopped meat, breaking it up with a fork. The meat cooks quickly but is still tender and juicy. Adjust the seasoning if salt is needed. Cook the spaghetti in salted water, drain, run clear water over it and serve with the meat sauce on top.

SKILLET-BROWNED POTATOES

Parboil white potatoes until they are almost done. Drain and let them stand for a few minutes to dry. In a heavy skillet melt 3 tablespoons of butter over medium heat. Brown the potatoes, turning occasionally.

BEEF STEW

1 clove of garlic diced	1 bay leaf
Cooking oil	2 tablespoons flour
2 lbs. beef chuck cubed for stewing	1 can beef bouillon (beef broth)
1 onion diced	½ cup red table wine
1½ teaspoons salt	2 large potatoes
½ teaspoon pepper	2 carrots
½ teaspoon marjoram	1 6-oz. can mushrooms
½ teaspoon thyme	Frozen peas (optional)

In a heavy kettle or Dutch oven, brown a clove of garlic in cooking oil. Sauté the onion until soft and add the cubed meat; brown on all sides. Turn down the heat before seasoning with salt, pepper, marjoram, thyme and bay leaf. Sprinkle the flour over the meat; pour in ¾ cup bouillon and the wine. Cover and simmer for 1 hour. If the liquid has been reduced, add more bouillon and red wine in the same proportions. Add to the stew 2 large potatoes, peeled and cut into 1-inch cubes, 2 carrots sliced and the can of mushrooms. Cover and simmer for another hour. Frozen peas may be combined with the stew 15 minutes before the cooking time has expired.

CHICKEN BREASTS

2 boned and skinned chicken breasts
   (4 fillets)
Flour for coating
Salt, pepper, paprika
½ teaspoon tarragon
Butter
½ cup chicken broth
¼ cup white wine
½ to ¾ cup sour cream

Coat the chicken breasts in flour seasoned with salt, pepper, paprika and tarragon. Sauté them in butter over low heat in a heavy skillet. When they are light brown on both sides turn down the heat, add chicken broth and white wine. Cover and simmer 15 min. or until the breasts are thoroughly cooked. Remove them to a heated serving dish and add the sour cream to the pan broth to thicken it to a gravy. Heat but do not boil. Pour the sauce over the chicken breasts and serve.

RICE PILAF

1 medium onion minced
¼ green pepper minced
3 tablespoons butter or margarine
1 cup rice uncooked
2¼ cups chicken broth
2 teaspoons salt
1 pimiento (optional)

Using a heavy saucepan sauté the onion and green pepper in the fat. When they are soft add the uncooked rice and stir so it is coated with butter and browns slightly but does not burn. Turn down the heat to simmer, pour in the chicken broth and salt over the mixture. Cover tightly and cook for 25 minutes or until all the moisture has been absorbed by the rice. Garnish with pimiento.

BROWNIES

4 squares of chocolate	1 teaspoon vanilla
2/3 cup soft shortening	1 cup flour
4 eggs	½ teaspoon baking powder
1¾ cups granulated sugar	½ teaspoon salt
1 cup brown sugar	½ cup walnut meats

Preheat the oven to 350 degrees F.
Melt the chocolate and shortening in a heavy saucepan or in a pan over boiling water. In a bowl beat eggs slightly, add the sugars, vanilla, flour, baking powder and salt. Combine the chocolate mixture with the ingredients in the bowl. Add nuts. Pour into a greased 13" x 7" x 2" baking pan and bake for 30 minutes or until the brownies spring back.

10

Be a Gracious Hostess

A SUCCESSFUL HOSTESS is one who makes her guests feel that
they are genuinely welcome in her home—if not just a little bit
special. It may seem that all of the trimmings are secondary to the
general atmosphere of hospitality. Look into the background,
however, and you'll see that sound planning and good coordina-
tion have gone into the party preparations. Your gracious host and
hostess may give the illusion of entertaining effortlessly, but there
is more to it than appears on the surface.

Entertaining is a very individual affair—young couples often
prefer to have guests on an informal basis rather than in the
traditional manner. Many first homes are apartments with limited
dining facilities and closet-sized kitchens. Space is not an instant
guarantee—one can have a twelve-room house and spend lots of
money on an elaborate party in which no one has a good time.
The answer is in you—how you project a welcoming ambience

264

and how you follow through to make guests feel that you really care about them and their comfort.

Plan with a purpose—know the limitations of your budget and facilities; decide how you want to entertain and whom to ask. Will it be a brunch, a luncheon, a cocktail party, a dinner, a dessert bridge, a buffet or just a night with old friends listening to favorite records and talking? Discuss all of these possibilities with your husband—he probably has some very definite ideas and suggestions about how he wants to entertain in his own home. Decide together how you want to give a party, then work together for the pure joy of providing hospitality.

Do not fall into the trap of "keeping up with the Joneses." Don't allow yourself to become entangled in a too-ambitious party merely to impress someone. Entertain in a relaxed manner in which you control the situation. In time, and with experience, you'll undoubtedly develop a specialty, a kind of party which comes naturally to you—brunch or cocktails, dinner or supper.

Naturally there are exceptions to every rule. Some of the greatest gatherings in your home may be completely spontaneous. But these occasions are usually made up of old friends or small groups taking potluck and enjoying the spur-of-the-moment camaraderie.

You will entertain different people in different ways. Your own friends may prefer the casualness of kicking off their shoes to dance or sitting cross-legged on the floor to talk. It's doubtful, though, that your mother-in-law would be as enthusiastic if she were expected to behave the same way. When you invite the boss and his wife to dinner you'll probably plan to seat everyone at the table in a more or less traditional style. A special occasion will call for a variation on your usual way of entertaining. However you choose to amuse your guests, make sure that you, as a couple, have fun, too. There is a great satisfaction in seeing others have a good time in the home that you have created together.

YOUR FACILITIES

Take stock of the space you have in the living room, dining room and kitchen. The room, plus the amount of furniture, will partially determine what kind of party you have and how many

people you can invite at one time. If the dining area is infinitesi-
mal, you have two options open—either have only a few guests for
a sit-down dinner or have more people for a buffet where sitting is
not so important.

Size up your kitchen. Four-course dinners can be turned out of
tiny kitchens with a maximum of organization, but are you capable
of doing this? Do you have ample counter space not only for
serving but also for clearing up afterward?

Take inventory of other party needs. Do you have enough
china, silverware and glassware to accommodate the number of
people you would like to invite? Now is the time to make good use
of the special wedding presents such as a chafing dish, a fondue
set, a hot tray, a big salad bowl, an electric grill, a lazy susan or
a cheese tray. Make your plans to include the use of any or all of
these valuable assets. If you are lacking many of these assets but
want to give a large party, look in the telephone book to see if your
community has a business which rents party equipment. Some
concerns rent everything from chairs to chafing dishes, and to rent
them is cheaper than to buy them.

YOUR GUESTS

Select your guests carefully and thoughtfully. Bringing together
the right combination of people is the requisite to any good party.
With people you know well it's fairly easy to determine who is
going to like whom and what combinations should be avoided at
all costs. Every gathering does need at least one effervescent spirit
who can be counted on to keep the conversation sparkling. No
hostess can always be right about mixing guests—sometimes, for
no apparent reason, there will be friction between two guests
which can cast a pall on the evening. Barring these unforeseen
mishaps, you can sidestep the obvious social disasters:

1. Don't invite guests who are all quiet and introverted to one
party. You'll end up frantically trying to keep conversation
going.
2. Don't invite people together who are known to loathe one
another.

266

3. Don't have a party in which all the guests are "obligations." Everyone has a list of people they feel must be invited— disperse the "must haves" among several gatherings.
4. Don't invite every fascinating, gregarious person you know to one party. They may compete for attention and ruin the evening.
5. Unless it is a small, intimate party, don't invite guests who are all strangers to one another and have nothing in common.
6. Don't attempt to give a large party until you have learned to handle small groups of people.

THE PREPARATION

Plan your entertainment when it is most convenient for you and when your home looks its best. For the working bride, probably the weekend is the best possible time to have guests, when there is time to prepare adequately without being rushed. Invite guests at least a week in advance unless yours is to be a small, impromptu gathering. Mailed invitations must be sent out at least two weeks before the event to give the invited guests a chance to receive them and reply. Be specific on the invitation—give the time you expect guests to arrive, the occasion (if it is a special one), where the party is to be held and where they can reach you to respond to the invitation.

A WEEK BEFORE the party decide what you are going to serve; make a shopping list of the supplies required. If you are serving a meal, plan the menu now with an eye to practicality and efficiency.

1. Make the menu simple enough so you can prepare and cook it easily.
2. Have at least one major dish which can be done a day or two in advance.
3. Plan dishes which can be held in case guests are late or the cocktail hour extends beyond your schedule.
4. If you haven't a maid, plan dishes that will be easy to serve and allow you to spend most of your time with the guests, not in the kitchen.

5. Plan dishes that require a minimum of last minute preparation and avoid an excessive need of pots and pans. Organize your kitchen so there will be space to facilitate serving and clearing.

Check to make sure that all equipment you intend to use is in good working order. If you are renting anything, make arrangements to have it delivered on the day of the party. Check your own clothes and table linen to see if anything has to be laundered or dry cleaned.

FOUR DAYS BEFORE, shine the crystal, polish the silver and any other metal.

THREE DAYS BEFORE, do the marketing. Order any special cut of meat, bread or pastry. Ask your husband to check the liquor supply and see what is needed in the way of mixers.

TWO DAYS BEFORE, prepare dishes which can be prepared, cooked and, if need be, stored in the refrigerator until party time. The clever hostess has included a casserole or a stew in the menu. Dishes of this nature often improve in flavor by being made ahead of time.

ONE DAY BEFORE, market for supplies either forgotten or unexpected. Buy flowers, leaves or whatever you are going to use for decorations or a centerpiece. Continue food preparation. Shine up the house. Move any furniture or lighting which may be better located for the party.

PARTY DAY, pick up the house. Arrange the centerpiece or other decorations and lay the table with linens, silverware and dishes. Set out trays, bowls and serving pieces. Set up the bar with glasses, utensils and garnishes. Be sure all ordered items are in the house at least two hours before the party. Two hours before serving time, set out cheese which is to be served at room temperature. Take an hour to relax, have a leisurely bath and don your party clothes. Except for the cooking that must be done just before serving, you are ready, composed and smiling to greet your guests.

THE PARTY

Welcome your guests warmly, introduce strangers and make them feel at ease. If you know all of your guests well, the conversation will flow very naturally. Draw everyone into a general conversation by inquiring about their interests and their life in general. Try not to let one person dominate the conversation. Be a good hostess and rescue the poor hapless guest who gets stuck listening to the party bore for too long.

If you are serving drinks before a dinner party don't let the cocktail hour extend too long. After all of the preparation you want the guests to taste the food. Here is where there is a need for teamwork between husband and wife. Let him know when you are about to serve so he will not offer anyone refills.

Arrange the kind of party that allows both of you to enjoy your guests and have only a pleasant minimum of duties to perform. It can hardly be fun for either of you to spend the whole party time serving, waiting on guests and then cleaning up. The good hostess quietly clears the table, empties ashtrays, stacks the dishes in the kitchen and returns to her guests.

After the last person has gone, sit down for a few minutes with your husband and bask in the afterglow of a wonderful evening. Then put on your apron and together, clean up.

THE KIND OF PARTY—WITH FOOD SUGGESTIONS

Brunch This can be a good, inexpensive and informal way to entertain on a weekend. With everyone dressed casually the mood is light and the preparation is not extensive. Serve sherry or Bloody Marys before the meal, or no drinks at all. Start with a fruit cup or ice cold fruit juice. For the main course here are some suggestions: scrambled eggs and sausage with stuffed mushrooms on the side; waffles topped with creamed tunafish; a mixed grill of baby lamb chops, chicken livers and bacon. With any of these courses, serve hot breads with jam or preserves and plenty of coffee.

Luncheon A midday meal can be informal or formal. Either you can seat guests around the table or you can have them serve themselves, buffet style. On warm, sunny days serve alfresco on

269

the balcony, patio or garden. Start with a light drink, if you are serving liquor. For the main course here are some suggestions: whole tomato stuffed with chicken or shrimp salad; cold chicken with tomato aspic; a cheese soufflé. Serve rolls or a hot bread with the lunch. For dessert have something light such as a fruit gelatin mold, fresh fruit, ice cream, an Italian ice or cheese and crackers. End the meal with coffee or tea.

Dinner A dinner party, even for only four, requires more than a little bit of planning unless you are an old experienced hand. Choose the menu by evaluating exactly what you are capable of doing well in the culinary field. Many women develop one special dish which they have perfected and come to rely on when having guests. Sometimes it's not always what you serve but the way in which you present it which makes the best, most lasting impression on guests. One of the best ways to lick the serving problem is to incorporate the first course with the hors d'oeuvre. This can be done by serving shrimp to be dipped in a tomato or mild mustard sauce or by having a pâté on melba toast. If you are unsure of yourself, and your timing, select a foolproof casserole, a good salad and dessert. As you gain confidence, choose a more complicated dish, perhaps with a salad, rolls and dessert. Never make the meal so involved that you need to spend a great deal of time in the kitchen. Plan dessert to be special. If the meal is heavy, counteract it with a light dessert. After a light dinner pull out all the stops and have a great confection.

Buffet Entertaining this way is perhaps the most fun. You can schedule one or more casseroles to be made well ahead of time or you can bake a ham or roast beef and slice it hot or cold. While there may be more food and more dishes involved, there is less serving to do since everyone helps himself. A good buffet for a party should have one meat, perhaps a casserole, a vegetable, either a salad or relishes, and bread. Unless you have a hot tray or some kind of buffet heating unit do not plan to keep everything piping hot as you would at a seated dinner. After the main course is over, clear the buffet table and set out dessert and coffee. As in the main course you can offer several selections: fresh fruit, individual pastries or dessert cheeses.

Cocktail party How much you and your friends drink will govern the cost of this type of party. Individual drinks, made to order, can be served, or you may prefer to have only one type of liquor for all—punch, sherry or champagne. Aside from the liquor, you will need a tasty array of nibbles which can be peanuts, cheese spreads, potato chips and any number of packaged snacks. Have an assortment of hot delectable bits from the oven as well. Secure bacon around a water chestnut with a toothpick and broil to crispness or make cheese wafers. There are so many canapés which can be served. The problem is not so much what to serve but rather how much to offer. If you want to extend the party fare into a partial meal, serve a cold ham with very thinly sliced rye bread and mustard. A cocktail party can be as simple or as complex as you feel like making it.

The late supper Entertaining in this way is usually done after the party has been to the theater, a concert or even a skating party. In the summer you can have a cold salad; in the winter a hearty casserole or a fondue plus a salad and dessert. Accompany the meal with an appropriate wine and end it with coffee.

Dessert bridge Bridge players, the serious ones, usually like to get on with the game as soon as possible. Everyone is seated at a bridge table which is covered with a luncheon cloth and served where he or she will start to play. What you need is a memorable dessert such as cherries jubilee, an excellent cake or a nesselrode pie and coffee. After the dessert, remove the linen and let the game begin.

Barbecue The time can be midday, midafternoon or evening. You don't need a garden or a patio to barbecue—a balcony or a wood-burning fireplace can serve as a place to put the charcoal grill. If you do burn charcoal indoors, be sure there is plenty of ventilation. The true flavor of charcoal is so wonderful that it really doesn't matter what the menu is—you can have frankfurters, hamburgers, steaks or a roast. Plan the meal to take full advantage of the fire; wrap well-scrubbed potatoes and peeled onions individually in aluminum foil and nestle them among the coals to cook. Turn them occasionally with a fork so they cook evenly. Make a salad for the side, have plenty of beer or wine to cheer on the cook and it's a great feast. Finish with a light dessert and coffee.

271

Picnics Not all entertainment has to be done in your home. On a mild spring day, a great beach day or a tangy autumn day, ask a few friends to join you in having a picnic. Make it cooperative or designate yourselves as the official host and hostess. You can turn it into a barbecue by bringing along a little portable hibachi stove with charcoal to cook on the spot, or you can make a cold meal with delectable sandwiches, deviled eggs, cole slaw, potato chips and brownies. Bring along a thermos of hot coffee or cold lemonade. The open air is sure to stimulate appetites and help you give a great party. Be sure to pack any perishable food in an insulated container with ice if the day is warm so there will be no danger of spoilage.

PARTY RECIPES
Here are a few suggested recipes to help you plan menus for all sorts of parties. Included are casseroles, main dishes, salads and desserts.

CHICKEN IN RED WINE SAUCE (4 servings)

Buy one broiler-fryer cut into serving pieces. Dredge each piece in flour which has been seasoned with salt, pepper and paprika. Brown in a heavy skillet, using salad oil. Lower the heat. Combine a can of cream of mushroom soup, ½ cup milk and ½ cup of red wine, pour over the chicken and cover to simmer for about 45 minutes until the chicken is tender.

BEEF BURGUNDY (4 servings)

10 small onions or 5 large ones
Salad oil
2½ lbs. beef chuck cut for stewing
1½ tablespoons flour
½ teaspoon rosemary, crushed
½ teaspoon marjoram
½ teaspoon thyme
Pepper and 1 teaspoon salt
Beef bouillon (canned beef broth)
1 cup dry red wine
½ lb. fresh mushrooms

Sauté the sliced onions in a Dutch oven using salad oil, cooking very slowly until they are soft. Remove from the skillet. Brown the meat. Sprinkle over it the flour, rosemary, marjoram, thyme, salt and pepper. Add ½ cup bouillon and 1 cup of red wine. Simmer for 1½ hrs. Add more liquid if necessary. Add the mushrooms which have been sliced and the sautéed onions. Cover and simmer for another 45 minutes.

272

VEAL CHASSEUR   (6 servings)

1 large onion chopped	Bay leaf
1 clove garlic minced	½ teaspoon thyme
Salad oil	1 teaspoon parsley
3 lbs. veal, cut in one-inch cubes for stew	2 teaspoons salt
	½ teaspoon pepper
1 can brown gravy	½ cup white wine
2 cups chicken broth	½ lb. fresh mushrooms
2 tablespoons tomato paste	2 tablespoons dry sherry

In a Dutch oven sauté chopped onion and minced garlic clove in salad oil until soft. Remove from the pan and set aside. Sauté the veal, browning on all sides; drain away the excess grease; return onions to the pot. Add the can of brown gravy, chicken broth, tomato paste, bay leaf, thyme, parsley, salt, pepper and white wine. Lower the heat, cover and let simmer for 45 minutes. Add the sliced mushrooms, cook another 45 minutes until the veal is tender. Transfer the meat and mushrooms to another pot with a slotted mixing spoon. Reduce the cooking fluid in the Dutch oven by one-quarter by boiling it rapidly. This will take 5 or 10 minutes. Return the meat to the reduced liquid, add a dash of white wine and the sherry. Serve.

SHRIMP-HAM CASSEROLE (4 servings)

1 8-oz. package spaghetti	½ cup dry sherry
5 tablespoons butter	1½ lbs. ham steak cut into ½-inch cubes
5 tablespoons flour	
4 cups of milk	1 lb. fresh shrimp cooked, shelled, deveined
Salt and pepper to taste	
Swiss cheese slices	

Preheat the oven to 350 degrees F.
Boil the spaghetti in salted water, drain in a sieve and run clear water over it. Meanwhile make the sauce: melt the butter in a pan, take it off the stove, add the flour to make a paste, add the milk and return to the stove to cook, stirring as it thickens. Boil for 5 minutes, turn off the heat and add salt, pepper and the sherry. In a greased casserole, place the spaghetti, ham and

273

shrimp; pour the sauce over and top with Swiss cheese slices. Bake uncovered for 40 minutes.

BASIC TOMATO ASPIC (6 servings)

Soften 2 envelopes of unflavored gelatin in ¾ cup tomato juice. Heat 2 cups tomato juice and 1 cup chicken broth to just under boiling. Add 3 tablespoons grated onion, 3 teaspoons salt, 1 tablespoon Worcestershire sauce and 1 tablespoon lemon juice. Removing it from the heat, add the softened gelatin. Cool and place in a large mold or individual molds. Chill.

RATATOUILLE (6 servings)

2 onions sliced	2 green peppers, seeded and sliced to thin strips
2 cloves of garlic, minced	
6 tablespoons salad oil	4 tablespoons parsley
3 medium zucchini, scrubbed and sliced thin	1 bay leaf
	1 teaspoon basil
1 medium eggplant, unpeeled and cut into 1-inch cubes	5 med. tomatoes peeled or 1 lb.-can stewed tomatoes
Flour for coating	Salt and pepper to taste

In a heavy skillet or Dutch oven sauté the onion slices and garlic in oil until they are soft. Coat the zucchini slices and eggplant cubes in flour, add to the pot with the green pepper, parsley, bay leaf and basil. Cover and simmer for ½ hour over a very low heat. Stir occasionally until the vegetables start to give up their liquid so they won't stick. Add the tomatoes, salt and pepper, cook uncovered over a low heat until thick (about another ½ hr.). Serve hot or cold.

COLE SLAW (6 servings)

1 head cabbage shredded	1 teaspoon seasoned salt
1 red onion chopped fine	Pepper to taste
1 green pepper chopped	2 teaspoons capers
1 carrot grated	1 teaspoon dill weed
2 teaspoons India relish	¼ cup wine vinegar
1 teaspoon celery salt	Enough mayonnaise
2 teaspoons celery seed	to moisten well
2 teaspoons parsley	

Combine in a large mixing bowl the cabbage, onion, green pepper, carrot, India relish, celery seed and salt, parsley, salt, pepper, capers, and dill weed. Pour over it the wine vinegar and let stand for a few minutes. Add enough mayonnaise to bind the salad but not to drench it (1/3 to ½ cup). Toss well and refrigerate, covered. This salad is better made the day before so the flavors have a chance to blend.

ZUPPA INGLESE (10 servings)

4 layers of sponge cake or angel cake	3 tablespoons sugar
1 package vanilla pudding mix	1 teaspoon vanilla
1 teaspoon grated lemon peel	½ cup dark rum
1 cup heavy cream for whipping	1 cup raspberry or strawberry jam with whole fruit

Bake the cake according to directions. (Two layers can be split into 4 when cool.) Prepare the vanilla pudding mix using only 1½ cups of milk. Add the lemon peel and cool with plastic wrap placed directly on top of the surface. Whip the cream, adding the sugar and vanilla when it is stiff. Fold in 1 cup of the whipped cream into the pudding. Chill. Place one layer of cake on the serving plate cut side up, sprinkle with 2 tablespoons of rum; spread 2 tablespoons of jam and ⅓ of the pudding mixture. Repeat with the other two layers. Place the top layer, cut side down, and sprinkle with rum. Spread the last of the jam over it. Frost the sides with the remaining whipped cream and refrigerate. Keep chilled until it is served.

II
You as an Individual

THE MANY FACETS of your new career in homemaking are all important to set a solid foundation for a happy, lasting marriage. But in your zeal to create a home, see to your husband's comfort, adjust to this new life and do everything first-rate, don't overlook your own self as a person. Just as you budget time and money for food, clothing and household necessities, so must you budget time and resources for your own personal requirements and satisfactions. To be happy with a husband you must be happy with yourself and show it in the way you look and feel. You need time for plenty of exercise, for grooming and for sufficient rest. You need private time to pursue personal challenges whether they take the form of a full-time career, further education, community service or hobbies. To live in harmony and to be a vibrant and interesting person you have to recognize that you are an individual as well as a loving wife and companion.

276

TO KEEP YOUR BEAUTY

GROOMING

High on your personal priority list of beauty care is good grooming. Retain the look of freshness and radiance so appealing to a husband by following simple beauty routines daily and weekly. With this kind of attention to your body, skin and hair, the natural endowments you have will come forth and shine. Your clothes require attention, too; keep them groomed by mending and cleaning when necessary. The combined efforts will produce a total look of you as a glowing, attractive woman, confident that she looks her best.

The stores are full of cosmetics, bath accessories, sprays, soaps and creams to aid and abet you. The trick is to find which ones will suit you best. Manufacturers are constantly developing new products which they say will do more for you. A certain amount of experimentation is needed to see if a new preparation is better than your old familiar "tried and true" product. Of course, there are always the fads in makeup which everyone likes to try for the pure fun of being up-to-date. But buy in moderation—don't clutter your dressing table with a lot of costly mistakes. Once you've found a basic preparation which seems best for you, don't give it up easily for another. Several manufacturers of cosmetics specialize in hypo-allergenic makeup, hair sprays and creams for you who have an allergic condition. There are also medicated products which bring some therapeutic benefits to your skin.

Budget your time daily and weekly to include a beauty routine. It needn't take long, but the results will keep you looking healthy, lovely and desirable. Start the day with a neat, clean look and try to stay that way from breakfast to bedtime. Eat good, nutritious food to maintain a healthy complexion and a slim figure. Munching on candy bars and eating too many fried foods drenched in cooking fat are not going to improve the appearance of your skin or your figure. Get plenty of exercise and rest daily. Lack of sufficient sleep can bring out unwanted fatigue lines and shadows in your face. After a hard day at the office come home and take a brief nap or languish in a hot bath to relax before going to a big evening party. If your feet are down at the arches from exhaustion, soak them in a solution of warm water and Epsom salts for five minutes. Allot a definite time of the week (two to three hours) for the sole purpose of doing your hair and nails and giving yourself a real beauty treatment. Check your clothes and repair sagging hems, broken zippers, opened seams and hanging buttons.

Daily Organize your schedule so grooming requirements are second nature, especially in the early morning rush. First thing up, during your stint in the bathroom, rinse your face with cold water to wake up, brush your teeth to get rid of any early morning fuzz and brush your hair to free it from snarls and tangles. If it suits you, tie your hair with a ribbon. Put on an attractive housecoat and start preparing breakfast. Your husband can't help but appreciate your tidy appearance, and it can help both of you start the day in a better mood. Bathe, shower or tub daily, either morning or night according to your preference. It's wiser, for you who have dry skin, to bathe only every other day in the dry winter months, so say skin specialists. Use a deodorant, choosing a brand which doesn't irritate your skin or stain clothes. Apply makeup with care, using shades suitable for daytime wear.

Before leaving the house for work or marketing, survey yourself in a long mirror to see that your total appearance passes inspection. Unless it is absolutely necessary, never go out with your hair up in pins or curlers. If you must, cover them with a scarf or a cloche-like cap. At home wear one of the frilly coverings made especially to cover curlers. There is hardly anything less romantic to a man than seeing his beloved in curlers. Sometime during the day, preferably in the morning, limber up by doing some basic exercises. Daily check your fingernails for signs of dirt and chipped nail polish. File a rough or snagged nail immediately with an emery board before it becomes a painful tear. When washing dishes or using strong cleaning detergents wear rubber gloves for hand protection. Apply lotion to hands several times a day after washing them, especially in the wintertime. Do not apply fresh makeup over old. If you are going out in the evening remove all remnants of your day makeup and start from scratch with new shades appropriate for evening. Remove all makeup at night before retiring with a cream and/or soap and water. Do not go to bed with a heavy cream slathered on your face—take pity on your husband and use one of the moisturizing creams which is absorbed into your skin but does the same work.

Weekly Shampoo and set your hair or have it done in a beauty shop. For those of you who have very oily hair, limit washings to no more than three a week. Too frequent shampooing makes an oily scalp oilier. Between washings clean hair strands (not the scalp) with cotton pads soaked with witch hazel or alcohol. Before shampooing brush your hair thoroughly to stimulate the scalp and brush out flaky remnants of hair spray. Don't use too stiff a brush. There are shampoos that condition and setting lotions that give body. Be sure to rinse your hair well so all the soap is removed; set and dry it. The new home dryers are marvelously efficient. While drying your hair, relax and read or give yourself a good manicure.

Take a long, leisurely, relaxing bath with bath oil or salts added to the water. Use a pumice stone on heels to smooth them and remove dead, calloused skin. Push back the toenail cuticle after bathing while the skin is still soft. If your toenails need cutting, trim them round but not deep into the corners. After bathing, apply a dipilatory or use a razor to remove underarm and leg hair.

To start your manicure remove all of the old nail polish to let the nails breathe. File your nails with an emery board to smooth them into oval shapes. Don't file too far down into the corners because it will weaken the nail. Gently push back the cuticle with an orange stick and apply a fresh coat of polish. Let it set before putting on an overcoat. If you are having trouble with peeling, weak nails leave the polish off for several weeks.

Give yourself a good facial. Every woman's skin has its own peculiarities; for one woman soap and water is the right way to cleanse the face and combat an oily skin condition; another woman must rely on moistuizing creams only. Determine the best way to cleanse your skin. Afterward smooth on an emollient cream and massage your throat and face gently but firmly with upward strokes. Pat lightly but swiftly under your chin. There are packaged preparations in tubes which form facial masks when applied. After you remove the mask your face feels tingly and glowing. Tweeze any stray eyebrow hairs which are out of line or between the brows. Be careful where you tweeze because not all hairs grow back.

EXERCISING

The right kind of exercise keeps you supple, flexible, firm, healthy and feeling on top of the world. It helps firm up flab and shape the body into more pleasing contours. Doctors tell you it is necessary for physical fitness in general.

The ideal way to exercise is to swim or play a fast game of tennis. While you are enjoying yourself you are also increasing blood circulation and stretching muscles which might not be used otherwise. But it isn't always possible to find a swimming pool or a tennis court so you must look to other means of keeping fit. Many people have taken up jogging and have worked up endurance so they can trot for miles; others have learned to ski, a great sport but an expensive one and, at best, a weekend treat. If you can afford it, there are private health clubs and if you are short on cash, there are the facilities at the local "Y". A great trimmer of legs is bicycle riding—why not buy one with a basket and use it for light shopping?

There are some good gadgets you can purchase for home use. Probably the least expensive and the best for vigorous exercise is a jump rope (if the people downstairs don't complain). Many at-home exercise machines can be purchased and are effective. There are several bicycle types which can be set up in an unused corner of your home. Depending upon the model some have speedometers to show how fast you are cycling, some have a triple action with the seat, handlebars and pedals moving to give you an energetic ride. There are slant boards, some to simply relieve tension by removing pressure from the legs and feet while others are more elaborately designed with controls which allow you to cycle or row. And then there is the popular exercise wheel—a small single or double rubber-tired wheel with handles on both sides which you push while on hands and knees to firm up abdominal muscles. An indoor jogging machine offers a treading platform so you can jog in all kinds of weather, indoors.

There are also exercises without gadgets—the shaping-up kind which help tone up little-used muscles, increase blood circulation and combat fatigue and nervous tension. A daily routine should be established to allow half an hour a day for calisthenics. If you find it difficult to keep up a satisfactory regimen at home by yourself, investigate the "Y" and see what classes it offers—modern dance,

1.

2. a   b

3. a   b

c   d

yoga or calisthenics. The idea is to keep the shape you have or trim down to the one you want, and it may take the discipline of a class to get you started.

For serious exercising here are some suggestions before you start:

1. Do not practice strenuous exercises on a full stomach. The best time is at least two hours after a regular meal. The morning hours are excellent for this reason.
2. Do not wear restrictive clothes or shirts that flap to get in your way. The most satisfactory outfit is a leotard and tights or stretch slacks and a jersey top.
3. Push back the furniture so you will have plenty of room.
4. If you can, exercise in front of a full-length mirror on a carpeted floor or on an exercise mat.
5. Take it easy at first. No matter how young you are, don't risk pulling a muscle by being too ambitious in the beginning. Start with a 10-minute session and gradually increase to the half-hour daily routine.

RECOMMENDED EXERCISES

1. To limber up: stand tall with feet slightly apart, lean forward from the waist with head dropped, arms down, knees straight, and bounce gently, each time getting closer to the floor with your hands until you touch the floor. Repeat 12 times.
2. For posture: stand tall, feet together, buttocks pressed together so you are "tucked in" and the spine is straight, arms at the sides. Bend the knees and assume a deep-knee bend, crouching with arms extended straight out in back (like a skier's crouch). Straighten to standing position and raise the arms straight overhead, stretching as high as you can. Lower the arms to extend straight out from the shoulders and, not bending them, rotate in small circles, using only the shoulder joints for movement (like a windmill). Start with small circles and increase the diameter to roughly 2 feet. Repeat several times.
3. For posture and waist-suppleness: hunch your back and bring up the bent right knee to the chest, lower your head and

extend the arms straight out. Then arch backward, stretching
the head back, the arms following the head and the right leg
extended straight back as far as it will go. Return to standing
position; stand tall with hands over the head, feet slightly apart,
knees straight, and bend to the right side over the right hip with
the left hand curving over the head, following the body movement and the right hand extending well down along the right
leg. Stretch as far as you can in this position. Return to the
standing position and slowly bend forward from the waist,
dropping the head and arms until your hands touch the floor.
Shake out your arms and legs and repeat the exercise using the
left arm and leg.

4. For back flexibility and general suppleness: sit on the floor
with legs spread far apart. Bend forward from the waist and try

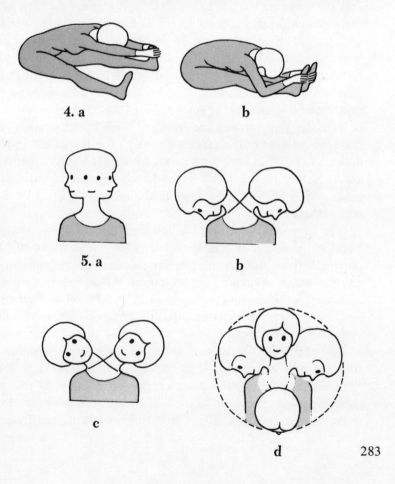

4. a   b

5. a   b

c

d   283

to grasp the left foot with your hands, then the right foot. If you can grasp an ankle you will do well the first few times. Put your legs together and try to grasp your hands around your feet with elbows on the floor on either side of your knees and your head as near your knees as possible. In time, and with practice, your elbows should touch the floor and your head touch your knees.

5. For the neck and facial muscles: sitting cross-legged on the floor with your spine straight, hands resting on the knees, turn your head as far to the right as you can, looking over the shoulder and keeping the shoulders perfectly straight; turn your head to the left the same way. Repeat 3 times. Do the same, but this time try to touch your chin to your shoulder without raising the shoulder. Repeat on both sides 3 times. Looking straight ahead lower the top of your head to the right as though you are touching the ear to the shoulder. Repeat on both sides 3 times. Looking straight ahead try to touch the tip of your nose with the tip of your tongue. Shake the head vigorously; closing your eyes drop your head in front and gently let it roll up to the right around to the left and drop down in front. Repeat 3 times, once starting on the right, then on the left. Massage the back muscles at the base of the neck to relax any taut muscles.

6. For the bust: sitting cross-legged with spine straight, raise the arms to bust height, elbows bent so the hands are in front; make a fist of one hand and cup it in the other hand. Move the arms slightly to the right, press hands together hard and release, move to the center, then to the left, performing the same press-release motion.

7. For the hips: sitting, balance yourself back on your buttocks, using your hands and legs for balance but not support, roll from side to side, as far to one side as you can and still maintain balance. Don't bounce. After rolling five times each way, walk on your hips—with the slight aid of your upper legs, inch along using your hips for progress across the floor, your arms for balance.

8. For abdominal muscles: lie flat on your back, arms at the sides; slowly raise both legs (straight) to where they are at right angles with your torso, keeping the small of the back pressed against the floor so the abdominal muscles must do the work. Lower the legs slowly to within a few inches from the

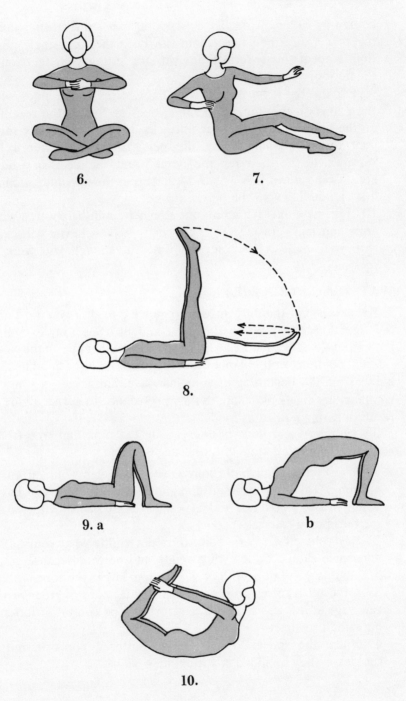

6.

7.

8.

9. a

b

10.

floor; open them wide like a scissors, and slowly bring them together again; then raise them slowly to the right-angle position. Repeat this several times without letting your feet touch the floor or your knees bend.

9. For the back: lie flat on your back, arms at the sides with the palms on the floor. Bend the knees and place the feet flat on the floor as close to your buttocks as you can. Slowly raise your torso, beginning with the pelvis and lift, vertebra by vertebra, to the shoulder until your whole middle is in a high arch. Come down just as slowly, lowering the shoulder section first and ending with the pelvis.

10. For the spine: lying on your stomach, arch backwards with arms and legs; grasp your ankles or feet (whichever you can) with your hands. Rock several times as though you were a rocking horse.

WATCHING YOUR DIET

Exercise is not the only answer to glowing health; you must eat the right kinds of food to stay trim and fit. (See four essential food groups, pages 210–212.) By keeping a weather eye on the calories and planning well-balanced meals you are building good health habits from the beginning of your marriage. Shiny hair, a smooth complexion, strong nails, and built-in resistance to germs all are a result of eating nutritious foods.

To keep you and your bridegroom in the pink and free from weight problems try some of these suggestions:

1. Invest in a good bathroom scale and weigh yourself each morning. Take into account a slight gain just before you have your period. But if the extra pounds don't vanish afterward, start dropping calories.

2. Buy yourself a calorie counter to determine what your daily allowance should be for your weight and height. Because your husband is going to need more, serve him larger portions.

3. Serve salads often with an interesting mixture of greens and raw vegetables. Use herbs to add zest and be careful of fattening salad dressings.

4. Watch the snacks. Potato chips, buttered popcorn, nuts, cookies— they're all laden with hidden calories.

5. Serve lots of vegetables but keep rich sauces and butter to a minimum. Flavor them with chives, dill weed, parsley or basil.
6. The so-called hearty breakfast of hot cereal is more fattening than the more nutritious eggs, toast and fruit.
7. For the cocktail hour replace high-calorie chips and dips with fresh vegetables—carrots and celery (in matchsticks), bits of cauliflower and radishes. Shake seasoning salt over them for flavor.
8. Take a combination vitamin pill daily if you feel you're not getting a balanced diet.
9. When frying, use vegetable oils which are absorbed less into food.
10. Buy some dietetic foods and see if you like them. Use skim milk for cooking and drinking.
11. Occasionally bring a lunch from home (hard-boiled egg, carrot sticks and cottage cheese) and add black coffee if business lunches are adding unwanted calories.
12. Buy whole wheat, protein or diet bread instead of white bread.
13. Cut down on salt in cooking—it only helps to hold unwanted water in body tissues.
14. For desserts, serve fruits or low calorie ice cream instead of rich cake and pastry.
15. Splurge a little. One day a week break away and eat what you want. Forget your calorie counter on special anniversaries. But the day after, return to watching calories again.

TO FOLLOW CHALLENGES

Your career Statistics show that a high percentage of today's brides are employed, at least for a while after marriage. They hold jobs for a variety of reasons: for extra income, for support of a husband who is finishing his education, for professional satisfaction, for prestige or for escape from boredom. Many of you have worked before you were married and prefer to continue, at least unless you become pregnant. There are some of you who have a very promising career in a profession and will pursue it indefinitely. Whatever your reasons, there are major factors involved in

287

being a working wife and they depend on the situation at hand and the temperaments of both you and your husband.

It is a fact that most working wives account for about one-third of the weekly family income. On the surface it would seem that the average young couple could save, buy furniture, live better and travel more. Look deeper and you will see some of the drawbacks— the added income puts you into a higher income tax bracket (unless you are the only breadwinner) so a bigger bite is taken from your check for taxes. Figure also on increased expenses for office clothes, carfare, lunch money, grooming and the extra expense of running your household—convenience foods, outside laundry, more dry-cleaning bills and possibly household cleaning help. Sometimes there is little left to contribute toward the so-called nest egg. But if you like your work, you derive satisfaction from it and it makes you a more interesting companion to your husband, it's worth it. Many brides work because they feel that there would not be enough to keep them busy at home, at least until they have a baby, so—why not bring in the extra cash?

According to authorities, the troubles come when the double paycheck lures a newly married couple into a higher standard of living. When, for reasons of pregnancy or job loss, the wife stops working, the couple finds it difficult adjusting to a lower income. Resentments develop from such situations unless common sense takes over and you adapt your mode of living to your present income.

To manage two careers successfully, here are some of the pitfalls to be aware of and try to sidestep:

1. You have the difficult task of adjusting to two lives. If your job is a time-consuming, interesting challenge, you must work extra hard to function as a homemaker.
2. Keep your own career in perspective and avoid competing with your husband. You may not realize it is happening, but in your enthusiasm to tell about your successful day you may not even hear about his equally important triumphs.
3. Think of your extra income as "ours" not "mine." Money matters can arouse some pretty violent passions unless you have a clearly defined agreement in the very beginning on how you

are going to handle a joint income. You are in partnership now—some couples prefer to have the money in a joint account, some like to have separate accounts but with an agreement that certain bills are to be met by a specified portion of the income, and others prefer to bank the wife's check as savings for future wants.

4. How will you run your household? Do you have the right to expect your husband to assume his fair share? This is a difficult area because every couple has its own approach. In this working world the roles of man and woman have become very flexible, but even with this relaxed standard, the responsibility of running the house still falls on the wife. A working wife should expect some consideration and cooperation from her husband such as wiping the dishes, picking up the laundry, keeping his clothes picked up, taking out the garbage, making an occasional pot of coffee and helping with the supermarket shopping.

5. Although you are working and used to making all sorts of decisions every day without consulting your superiors, take the time to consult your husband about decisions in your own home. He wants to be included in building a home, so weigh his opinion on whether you can afford to buy a new piece of furniture or if the cleaning woman should come twice a month or more. There is a delicate balance of power in marriage, particularly in the beginning, and you cannot issue orders like the office captain in your own home to your husband. Shift mental attitudes when you reach your own doorstep and try to change back into the loving bride he married.

6. Avoid telling him all the trivial or petty complaints about your day at work. If it isn't interesting or amusing, forget it!

7. Don't neglect your social life. This is unfair to both you and your husband. There are many nights when neither of you will feel like going out or having company. Then have a quiet evening at home and unwind together. But sometimes relaxation comes from doing something different rather than doing nothing. On these occasions come home and rest for a short while, get your second wind and have a lovely time on the town. Plan major entertainment, however, on the weekends when you have the time and energy to devote to preparations.

8. If the strain of working and running a home at the same time is turning you into a tense, nervous wreck, something has to give and it could very well be your marriage. Perhaps you just don't have the temperament to handle both careers. In this case, maybe part-time employment is the answer for you.

Success in managing your two careers hangs on how carefully you work out an efficient routine for running the household. Don't allow yourself to build up a smoldering resentment of being nothing but a drudge. You need a feeling of fulfillment along with leisure time to enjoy your husband. Here are some ways to achieve these goals:

1. Send sheets and your husband's dress shirts to the laundry rather than spending precious weekend time laundering them.

2. Hire a weekly cleaning woman if you can possibly afford it. The extra money you spend in this manner is well worth the price. It frees your weekend and saves you trying to draft a reluctant husband to help.

3. Organize your household so there is a place for everything and everything is in its place, more or less. Don't spend extra time in trying to track down an elusive item when there is no need for it. If you adhere to this practice, even your husband, with a little education, can function efficiently when you are late getting home or when some emergency arises.

4. Make morning and nightly pickups a habit so that the house doesn't have a chance of getting cluttered.

5. Plan menus which call for simple foods during the week. Leave the complicated recipes, with lengthy preparation, for the weekend when you have much more time. If you have a fair-sized freezer, on weekends make a main-dish casserole in double amount and freeze half of it for use later in the week. Take advantage of short-cut recipes; buy a certain amount of good convenience foods and mixes. The extra cost is worth the time you save.

6. Be efficient about errands. Make lists—don't rely upon your memory alone. Stop on your way home from work to run errands instead of leaving them all for the weekend.

7. Plan all of your shopping efficiently. If you work in an area

which permits, plan to do part of your clothes' shopping during a lunch hour. For expeditions that require more time, buy several items at once, coordinating everything with the wardrobe you have. Try to make only one major trip to the supermarket per week with your husband.

8. Once you are home from the office, relax! Sit down for a few minutes before you do anything—put your feet up and shed your office self. To make the transition to the role of homemaker and wife, many women find it easier to actually change clothes. By removing office attire for more comfortable clothes you may mentally shift gears. Get yourself some soft, feminine at-home outfits—it'll be good for a change of pace.

Your pursuits Every well-rounded person should have an individual interest, other than working and homemaking, regardless of how small it is or how often it is exercised. In the first months of marriage you may be so occupied in assembling the home and learning to run it efficiently that you have little time for other involvement. After the initial period of adjustment to marriage and housekeeping, broaden your interests with some form of outside activity, either alone or with your husband. If you have moved to a new community with few friends this is an excellent way to meet new people.

The non-working wife can contribute several hours of her time daily or weekly to community service. Volunteers are needed to perform many useful and worthwhile tasks in hospitals, libraries, churches and schools. Various charities will welcome with open arms your help with clerical and other duties. There are many service clubs which, through activities, contribute a great deal to the community. You may be interested in belonging to one of them.

Working or not, you can join the League of Women Voters and become a well-informed citizen. Many chapters meet at night to accommodate the career girl. And, if you are motivated in the direction of partisan politics, begin active work in the political party of your choice. Find out something about the people you elect and how they are functioning in office.

Any number of hobbies can be interesting and give great personal satisfaction. Even if you've never tried, think of joining a drawing or painting class. Maybe there's a latent talent you never realized you had. Craft classes of all sorts will help you to polish a skill and show you the right materials and instruments to use. You can learn about needlepoint, fine embroidery, woodcraft, even fine leather work. Collecting a specific item can be very gratifying and as expensive as you choose it to be.

Perhaps a sport is the activity for you. Many wives get involved in a particular one so they can play along with their husbands. Investigate what your community or private club offers.

For some of you, the goal may be education—returning to complete an interrupted course of study, taking an advanced degree or taking special courses because they interest you. If you are going to school on a full-time basis you'll need to handle your household routine very much in the way a career woman does. There is one difference, however; the working wife has her evenings free to enjoy with her husband while you may have to study for a course at home or at the library. Some brides who are still in school find it easier to cope with the situation when their husbands are also students because both interests lie in the same direction. If you are taking a course just because it appeals to you be sure it doesn't conflict with the leisure time you would normally spend with your husband.

ON BEING A WIFE

Besides the exquisite joy of being a "Mrs." there are certain functions, social duties and customs which go with the title. You may have been a breathless, forgetful, charmingly mad fianceé but it's a fair bet that your husband isn't going to find those traits so appealing when you fail to answer an important invitation for no valid reason. Certain social amenities have to be followed, sometimes for business, sometimes for pleasure.

1. After receiving a gift, a "thank you" note should be written to acknowledge that you received it and that you were pleased. Try to be sincere in writing—don't write a "thank you for the lovely gift" type of letter.

2. When kindnesses are extended to you in the way of parties or introductions, especially if you are new in a community,

respond with prompt appreciation. Older people, in particular, like this courtesy.

3. If you are living in a new community establish yourself as a couple by exploring the ways you can get acquainted. You may meet new people through common interests or through organizations which you join. The wife is usually the leader in establishing social contact.

4. Plan your first major entertainment very carefully. This is your first test as a hostess and it can be rather grim unless you marshal all of your forces, prepare to the best of your ability and then relax. Don't be disheartened if the party doesn't live up to your expectations—be a warm, gracious hostess and your guests will appreciate your efforts.

5. When you are invited out, respond to the invitation, be prompt and perhaps bring a small hostess gift as a thoughtful gesture.

6. Call or write a note to your hostess after a dinner party to thank her, a courtesy which cannot help but please her.

7. Your husband probably cares a great deal for his family but, consciously or unconsciously, he is going to expect you to communicate with them the most. If they live close by, telephone them regularly; otherwise, write to them.

8. You may think you know your husband very well; you may also find that his family observes certain holidays in a completely different manner than you are used to or that they follow customs totally unfamiliar to you. The only way to handle this situation is to be diplomatic and compromise. Spend one holiday with his family and the next with yours.

Pleasing your husband is not so difficult when you give it some serious thought. The trick is to keep the magic of romance alive long after the wedding bells have sounded. You may be an old hand at practicing many of the suggestions listed here.

1. Respect your husband's privacy as you expect him to honor yours.

2. Surprise him occasionally. In the middle of the week stage a romantic dinner for two, complete with candlelight, just for the fun of it.

3. Praise him. A few compliments can do wonders for anyone's ego.

4. Let him know that you really care for him. There is nothing silly about expressing yourself in loving words when you feel like it.

5. Let him do-it-himself. Many men like to putter around the house fixing things.

6. Try to please him with food. Everyone has definite likes and dislikes. Give him what he likes two nights out of three—and on the third night introduce a new food. Maybe he has never tasted it prepared as well as you do it.

7. Give his favorite hobbies a fair trial. More than one wife has become an ardent sports fan by tagging along after her husband. If you really don't care for his pleasures, stay home the next time.

8. Make a fuss over him; when he's sick, offer tender loving care. Most men do love to be pampered, especially when they have nothing worse than a bad cold.

9. Ask his advice on what you should wear, what you should serve, how you should solve a knotty problem. If you don't really agree with him, discuss it and listen to his views. If he likes you in a certain color, wear it once in a while though you may think it looks terrible with your coloring. Very often a man does know what looks the best on his wife.

10. Give him a present for no reason at all. It doesn't have to be much—a new tie or a silly present from the dime store. He'll like the thought.

11. Try to correct any small habits you have that annoy him.

12. Invite his friends to dinner. You'll probably like the majority of them.

13. Don't let him see all of your beauty tricks; practice some of them behind the closed bathroom door.

14. Be a loving wife. Greet him with a kiss; make the first romantic move later in the evening by putting on your most seductive negligee.

15. Watch his weight as well as your own.

16. Temper any criticism you may have; and don't get into the habit of nagging.

17. Remember anniversaries, not the big ones but the little ones, such as the day you first met.

18. When you choose furniture be sure there is one comfortable chair he can call his own. Let him surround himself with favorite belongings.

19. Whatever you do, don't make the bedroom you share with your husband so frilly he might feel uncomfortable in it.

20. Don't use his things without asking his permission. There are certain possessions which are inviolate—his razor, his toothbrush and maybe his favorite carpenter's tools.

21. Make a genuine effort to get along with your in-laws and speak kindly of them. You can fall into the habit of criticizing them all too easily.

22. Keep a record of birthdays and anniversaries in his family which should be acknowledged with a gift, a card or a telephone call. Most men are notoriously bad about remembering such dates.

23. Try to keep a balanced checkbook. If you can't do that at least record the checks you write accurately so he can justify the checkbook at the end of the month.

24. Establish an atmosphere in which you can communicate with each other. When you can detect a tone of anguish or frustration just below the surface of an otherwise normal conversation, you have begun to listen with a third ear and to hear what he really is trying to say. That's communication!

There are many ways to approach the role of homemaking but the best way is the philosophy and system that work best for you. It takes a bit of experimenting, testing and mellowing before the right mixture is found. Upon discovering it you will find yourself on the path to being a happy and complete person. Marriage can be the greatest experience of your lifetime.

INDEX

Index

Index

Index

terms applicable to, 60–63
see also housing, building; housing,
    buying; housing, renting
housing, building, 52–57
    see also housing; mortgages
housing, buying, 43–52
    financing, 57–60
    see also housing; mortgages
housing, renting, 38–43
    apartments, 40, 46–47
    see also housing

ice cream stains, removal of, 195
income, *see* budgeting; money management
ink stains, removal of, 194, 195
in-laws, 6–7
insurance
    companies, as mortgage sources, 39
    health, 28–30
    homeowners', 60
    liability, 60
    life, 24–27
    policies, name change on, 3, 4
    Social Security, 28
    title, 62
interest, 22–24, 62
investments, 30–35
ironing, 189–193
    scorch stains, removal of, 196
ironing boards, 191. *See also* ironing
irons, 189–190. *See also* ironing

jalousie windows, definition of, 92
jersey, description of, 156
joints, of wood furniture, 76
julienne, definition of, 234

kitchens, 198–200
    cleaning, 111–112, 113
    stocking, 208–210
    storage facilities, 117
    see also appliances; cookware;
        cutlery
knead, definition of, 234
knives, *see* cutlery

lace, description of, 156
lamb, 218
    carving, 245–247
lamé, description of, 156
lard (cooking term), definition of, 234
lard (fat), 226
latex paint, 87
laundry
    bleaches, 184–185, 193
    borax, 185
    detergents, 184
    dryers, 181, 183, 188–189
    fabric softeners, 185
    hand, 188
    ironing, 189–193
    preparation for, 186–187
    soaps, 184
    sorting, 186–187
    starches, 185

washing machines, 179–182, 187–188
washing soda, 185
water conditioners, 185
see also stain removal
lawn (fabric), description of, 156
lawyers, aid in house-building, 56–57
leases, 41–43, 46, 61
leather furniture, care of, 120–121
lemons, 222
lettuce, 221
    storing, 227
liability insurance, 60
lien, definition of, 63
life insurance, 24–27
    and mortgage insurance, 27, 60
lighting, home, 69–70
linen, 147
linens, storage of, 116–117. *See also*
        blankets; pillowcases; sheets;
        table linens; towels
linoleum floors, 82
    care of, 132
lipstick stains, removal of, 196
liver, 217–218
    sautéed (recipe), 253
load (for mutual funds), definition
    of, 34
loans, 24–26. *See also* mortgages
lobsters, 219
louvered shades and shutters, 92
luncheon parties, 269–270

macaroni casserole (recipe), 260
mace, 240
madras, description of, 156
magazine subscriptions, name change
    on, 5
mahogany furniture, 72
makeup stains, removal of, 196
maple furniture, 72
maple syrup, 225
marble
    floors, 83, 132
    -topped furniture, care of, 121
margarine, 226
margin (for securities), definition
    of, 33
marinate, definition of, 235
marjoram, 240
market value
    of property, definition of, 63
    of securities, definition of, 33
marriage adjustment, *see* adjustment
    to marriage
masonry floors, 83
    care of, 132
matelassé, description of, 156
material, *see* fabrics
mattresses, 80–81
    care of, 142
meal planning, 213–214. *See also*
        cooking; menu planning
measures, equivalent food, 231
meat juice stains, removal of, 196

302

Index

Index